Bonds of Enterprise

Bonds of Enterprise

John Murray Forbes and
Western Development in
America's Railway Age

AN EXPANDED EDITION

John Lauritz Larson

University of Iowa Press　Ψ　Iowa City

University of Iowa Press, Iowa City 52242
Copyright © 2001 by the University of Iowa Press
All rights reserved   *Cau*
Printed in the United States of America

http://www.uiowa.edu/~uipress

The publication of this book was generously supported by
the University of Iowa Foundation.

Printed on acid-free paper

Library of Congress Cataloging-in-Publication Data
Larson, John Lauritz, 1950–
Bonds of enterprise: John Murray Forbes and western
development in America's railway age / by John Lauritz
Larson
p.   cm.
Originally published: Boston, Mass.: Division of Research,
Graduate School of Business Administration, Harvard
University. 1984.
Includes bibliographical references and index.
ISBN 0-87745-764-6 (pbk.)

1. Forbes, John Murray, 1813–1898.   2. Railroads—United
States—Biography.   3. Businesspeople—United States—
Biography.   4. Railroads—United States—History.   I.
Title.
HE2754.F7L37   2001   00-054519
385'.092—dc21
[B]

01 02 03 04 05 P 5 4 3 2 1

*Frontispiece photograph of John Murray Forbes from the collection
of the Manuscripts and Archives Department, Baker Library,
Harvard Business School.*

For Obert and Mary Lou

Contents

Introduction to the
Expanded Edition

THE "RAILROAD QUESTION" was a central preoccupation in American life at the end of the nineteenth century—especially in rural, agricultural communities, especially in the West and Midwest. In the space of a single generation, steam railroads virtually nullified the economic impact of time and space by pegging the price of transportation, not to distance or cost, but to arbitrary maps and tables based on railroad competition, the value of goods, and the whims (or so it seemed) of railway executives. As a practical consequence, certain merchants and farmers—sometimes whole towns—withered under discriminatory railroad rates, while others no more deserving grew fat. People who considered themselves self-governing found it impossible to prevent or punish such wrongdoing without suffering retaliation from the railroads on which they now depended absolutely for economic survival.

What made the railroad question intractable for the post–Civil War generation was its many disguises. To railroad managers it appeared as an aberrant form of competition that threatened to destroy their expensive, far-flung properties with reckless discounts, demanded by their customers, that set off vicious bouts of cutthroat rate reduction. To retail and wholesale merchants, especially along the older roads and waterways, the same discounts appeared as price discriminations that favored competing over noncompeting centers, long hauls over short, and large-scale shippers over small fry who could not order by the carload or demand special discounts on volume purchases. To farmers, the railroads appeared to wield arbitrary power over services and prices such as no player in competitive markets ever had before. To local legislators, judges, and governors the railroad question seemed to threaten sovereignty itself, as corporations laughed off state police powers that in the past had brought *all* enterprise to heel beside political authority. Each group caught up in the tangle cursed the ignorance or wickedness of those who did not (could not?) see it from their own point of view. At stake was nothing less than the rights of property, freedom of enterprise, popular democracy, the rule of law, the sovereignty of states, and the dignity of honest labor.

In 1893 retired Iowa Governor William Larrabee wrote a book called *The Railroad Question*. Even then shelves were beginning to sag with the burden of similar treatises, and soon enough the literature on railway economics itself could qualify for carload rates. For a century and more, analysts have struggled to understand and regulate relations between a free people and their giant corporate instruments of trade and transportation; still, that literature bears in almost every case a partial, even partisan aspect. Rarely have readers been invited to stay within the history of the problem instead of seeking an escape in theoretical claims, models, constructs, scoldings, or pontifications that find their ultimate justification in outcomes that are really the *consequences* of the problem, not its causes. *Bonds of Enterprise* was first conceived as an effort to explore peoples' struggle with this railroad question in an explicitly narrative, historical framework that would cut across the boundaries of scholarship that tended to privilege one viewpoint or another.

It was my concern in 1984, when *Bonds of Enterprise* first appeared, that most analytical studies were designed, by definition, to stabilize a multitude of variables in order to expose the behavior of one or two. Such strategies necessarily fail to comprehend the experience of coming to terms with the multiplicity of new conditions in the railway age. The railroad question created a complex struggle among many different groups of farmers and merchants, competing carriers, and local and state politicians. Which perspective should we adopt? Were these railroads truly "soulless" corporations or benevolently innovative enterprises? Were farmers "ignorant," "extortionate," "pathetic," or merely confused? Were local politicians venal stooges in the pay of corporations? Heroic reformers battling for peoples' rights? Some of each? And were these market forces "natural" and ineradicable, or were they rules dictated by the powerful few to take advantage of the bewildered masses? Inherently historical, utterly dependent on particular realities of time and place and personal character, these questions were too often addressed by assumption or postulation. Existing literature seemed incapable of appreciating all the different perspectives.

The integrated narrative I sought in *Bonds of Enterprise* promised to address these particularities, but it could not be approached on the scale of national market development, interregional railroad systems, or even regional economies. Far too many actors stirred up hundreds of variables, reproducing precisely the chaos of choices that baffled contemporary victims of the railroad question. What I did instead was identify a leading player and get to know his ways and his playing field, allowing the instruments of his enterprise to draw for me the boundaries of the system and to name the other players whose actions complicated the choices for all involved. Because of his pioneering role I selected John Murray Forbes of Boston—head of a major capitalist investment group—followed him to China for early life influences, then back to an America booming with westward expansion and railroad development that drew his interest toward Chicago, across the prairies of Iowa, the plains of Nebraska, and finally to Denver and the mountain West. A long, narrow, regional community emerged—the Chicago, Burlington & Quincy Railroad and the territory it served—comprising specific corporate officers, their agents, rivals, and customers, and the politicians who claimed to govern those people in their home states and across the Union. *Bonds of Enterprise* is a study of the railroad question as experienced in that very real historical community.

I had hoped when the book came out that it would model in a small way the kind of integrated history that might reconcile claims about the impact of the railroads, the plight of farmers, the intentions of political reformers, and the efficacy of government regulation—all issues about which historians, economists, geographers, and rural sociologists had argued bitterly for many decades. Alas, the literature since 1984 continues to fall into several different threads of isolated conversation. Most railroad histories, for example, still mirror the boundaries and interests of the firm or an integrated system of cooperating lines. H. Roger Grant's studies of the Chicago Great Western and the Chicago & North Western, and Maury Klein's new volumes on the Union Pacific—to name just two skillful practitioners of a thriving genre—illustrate the impact of a subject railroad across a century of operations, seen primarily from corporate headquarters. Individual titans from this colorful era still generate biographical studies—the best example being Klein, again, with his new portrait of Jay Gould. Albro Martin recently tried to address the impact of railroads on America from start to finish; but the task is daunting, and his *Railroads Triumphant* does not replace John Stover's older *Life and Decline of American Railroads*.

Economists and policy analysts continue to revisit railroad regulation in their efforts to discover how the "laws of trade" (if such there are) really work in a modern, global, capitalist system. Legal historians, judges, and constitutional theorists probe court decisions past and present for patterns and ruling precedents. Recent works by Gerald Berk and Frank Dobbin explore, respectively, the underlying ideology and the absence of industrial policy in America's business system. Social scientists, led by Stephen Skowronek and Theda Skocpol, have re-introduced historians to the role of the state as an institutional force, a player with characteristics and a history of its own. So-called new institutionalist economic historian Colleen Dunlavy pursued similar questions in comparative perspective, but always with a social-science eye to structured behavior, patterns, and predictable forces. Paul J. Miranti's work on statistical records and the rise of professional accounting has shed important light on arguments first advanced in 1977 in Alfred D. Chandler's *The Visible Hand.* Shelton Stromquist's study of workers in Iowa railroad section towns suggests the excellent labor history that can be written from the bureaucratic sources so lovingly compiled by labor's nemesis, the giant corporation.

Histories of the once-popular agrarian revolt have not kept up with either railroad or regulation studies. Jeffrey Ostler's careful study of the Farmers' Alliance in Kansas, Nebraska, and Iowa clearly replaces John D. Hicks's much-overused 1931 tome, *The Populist Revolt.* Ostler sifted through much of the same documentary evidence I used and re-tells the story of William Larrabee's battle with the railroads, but he oddly takes no notice of the nonpolitical dimensions I found at work in the same story. Thomas A. Woods has written a fine new biography of Grange founder Oliver Hudson Kelley, lifting up (perhaps too ardently) the rhetoric of American republicanism that so informed that popular movement. Disappointingly, neither of these historians took advantage of *Bonds of Enterprise,* and very little other work has come out on the cultural politics of the farmers' age on the Middle Border.

Historical geographers contributed much to my original understanding of the problems faced by midwesterners during the railway age. A new study of midwestern river towns by Timothy Mahoney employs many of the same useful concepts, especially central place theory, to illuminate the development of systems of commercial (and unavoidably human) interaction. Donald Parkerson's work on New York state at midcentury exploits technically sophisticated tools of mobility analysis to explore the transformation of agricultural communities. Mark W. Summers has written extensively on political corruption as a feature of southern railroad promotion and control, and James A. Ward produced an intriguing book-length essay, *Railroads and the Character of America.* But these contributions appear almost randomly without reference to each other or a community of interpretation. The 1990 call for a synthetic new approach to regional development so neatly articulated in Andrew R. L. Cayton and Peter S. Onuf, *The Midwest and the Nation: Rethinking the History of an American Region,* has yet to be answered, except perhaps in cultural historian Jon Gjerde's wonderful new book on "ethnocultural evolution in the rural Middle West" (although the railroad question scarcely ripples the surface of Gjerde's material).

Two works have come close to the kind of analysis I envisioned in *Bonds of Enterprise*, although neither builds intentionally on that platform. Carol Sheriff, in *The Artificial River: The Erie Canal and the Paradox of Progress*, exposes the ambivalence and the transformational dilemmas experienced by all parties when confronted with a major transportation "improvement." More significantly, William Cronon exploits the advantages of allowing railroad systems to define the field of interaction (and therefore analysis) in *Nature's Metropolis: Chicago and the Great West*. Taken together, along with the Cayton-Onuf volume, these works begin to suggest the possibilities for research strategies and regional developmental stories that approach the level of integration and particularity I naively pursued nearly twenty years ago.

I do not believe scholars have intentionally rejected the integrated model that I set out to explore with the story of Forbes, the Burlington, and the Iowans. Not many appear to have seen it. More likely, historians are still not reading across the old disciplinary boundaries and have not recognized that *Bonds of Enterprise* addresses their questions within the framework of historical narrative. A series of misfortunes affected the circulation of the original edition, and for this reason I am especially pleased that the University of Iowa Press now offers it a second lease on life. Iowa readers never had much chance to discover a work that at one level *is* state history. At the same time, students interested in the old railroad question, the disappearance of traditional rural communities, the newly fashionable market revolution, the strange career of entrepreneurial capitalism in the American countryside, or the role of government and private enterprise during America's developmental adolescence will find in *Bonds of Enterprise* an example of the use of particularity to understand general problems and past experience. That is, in the end, what I believe historians do best.

The bibliography at the end of this introduction identifies newer works I would have learned from had I written the book today, along with a few omissions including (oddly enough)—*The Railroad Question* by William Larrabee—that failed to make it into the original list of sources. Not meant to be truly exhaustive, such a list will put the serious researcher in touch with references that should, in turn, lead him or her in all appropriate directions. In addition to reiterating my indebtedness as expressed in the original acknowledgments, I want to thank Holly Carver for encouraging this new edition and Drew Cayton for urging me years ago to seek another publisher. Whatever remains wrong with the book I will cheerfully shoulder once more.

UPDATED BIBLIOGRAPHY

Bain, David Haward. *Empire Express: Building the First Transcontinental Railroad.* New York: Viking Press, 1999.
Berk, Gerald. "Adversaries by Design: Railroads and the American State, 1887–1916," *Journal of Policy History* 5 (1993): 335–354.
———. *Alternative Tracks: The Constitution of American Industrial Order, 1865–1917.* Baltimore: Johns Hopkins University Press, 1994.
———. "Constituting Corporations and Markets: Railroads in Gilded Age Politics," *Studies in American Political Development* 4 (1990): 130–168.
Binder, John J. "The Sherman Antitrust Act and the Railroad Cartels," *Journal of Law and Economics* 31 (1988): 443–468.
Cayton, Andrew R. L., and Peter S. Onuf. *The Midwest and the Nation: Rethinking the History of an American Region.* Bloomington: Indiana University Press, 1990.
Cronon, William. *Nature's Metropolis: Chicago and the Great West.* New York: W. W. Norton, 1991.
Dilts, James D. *The Great Road: The Building of the Baltimore & Ohio, the Nation's First Railroad, 1828–1853.* Stanford: Stanford University Press, 1993.
Dobbin, Frank. *Forging Industrial Policy: The United States, Britain, and France in the Railway Age.* New York: Cambridge University Press, 1994.
Donovan, Frank P., Jr. *Iowa Railroads: The Essays of Frank P. Dovovan, Jr.,* ed. H. Roger Grant. Iowa City: University of Iowa Press, 2000.
Dunlavy, Colleen A. "Organizing Railroad Interests: The Creation of National Railroad Associations in the United States and Prussia," *Business and Economic History,* 2nd ser., 19 (1990): 133–142.
———. *Politics and Industrialization: Early Railroads in the United States and Prussia.* Princeton: Princeton University Press, 1994.
Eagle, John A. *The Canadian Pacific Railway and the Development of Western Canada, 1896–1914.* Kingston, Ontario: McGill-Queens University Press, 1989.
Ely, James W., Jr. "The Railroad Question Revisited: *Chicago, Milwaukee & St. Paul Railway* v. *Minnesota* and Constitutional Limits on State Regulations," *Great Plains Quarterly* 12 (1992): 121–134.
Evans, Peter B., Dietrich Rueschemeyer, and Theda Skocpol, eds. *Bringing the State Back In.* New York: Cambridge University Press, 1985.

Ferleger, Lou, ed. *Agriculture and National Development: Views on the Nineteenth Century.* Ames: Iowa State University Press, 1990.

Gjerde, Jon. *The Minds of the West: Ethnocultural Evolution in the Rural Middle West, 1830–1917.* Chapel Hill: University of North Carolina Press, 1997.

Goldin, Claudia, and Gary D. Libecap, eds. *The Regulated Economy: A Historical Approach to Political Economy.* Chicago: University of Chicago Press, 1994.

Grant, H. Roger. "A. B. Stickney Builds a Railroad: The Saga of the Minnesota & Northwestern," *Midwest Review* 6 (1984): 13–26.

———. *The Corn Belt Route: A History of the Chicago Great Western Railroad Company.* DeKalb: Northern Illinois University Press, 1984.

———. "Midwestern Railroad Leader: Marvin Hughitt of the Chicago & North Western," *Hayes Historical Journal* 8 (1988): 5–16.

———. *The North Western: A History of the Chicago & North Western Railway System.* DeKalb: Northern Illinois University Press, 1996.

———. "Railroaders and Reformers: The Chicago & North Western Encounters Grangers and Progressives," *Annals of Iowa* 50 (1990–1991): 772–786.

Gray, Susan. *The Yankee West: Community Life on the Michigan Frontier.* Chapel Hill: University of North Carolina Press, 1996.

Hicks, John D. *The Populist Revolt: A History of the Farmers' Alliance and the People's Party.* Minneapolis: University of Minnesota Press, 1931.

Huneke, William Frederick. "The Heavy Hand: The Government and the Union Pacific, 1862–1898," Ph.D. diss., University of Virginia, 1983.

Klein, Maury. "Competition and Regulation: The Railroad Model," *Business History Review* 64 (1990): 311–325.

———. *The Life and Legend of Jay Gould.* Baltimore: Johns Hopkins University Press, 1986.

———. *Unfinished Business: The Railroad in American Life.* Hanover, New Hampshire: University Press of New England, 1994.

———. *Union Pacific.* 2 vols., Garden City, New York: Doubleday, 1987.

Larabee, William. *The Railroad Question: A Historical and Practical Treatise on Railroads, and Remedies for their Abuses.* Chicago: Schulte Publishing Company, 1893.

Mahoney, Timothy R. *River Towns in the Great West: The Structure of Provincial Urbanization in the American Midwest, 1820–1870.* New York: Cambridge University Press, 1990.

Martin, Albro. "Light at the End of a Very Long Tunnel: The Railroads and the Historians," *Railroad History* 155 (1986): 15–33.

———. *Railroads Triumphant: The Growth , Rejection, and Rebirth of a Vital American Force.* New York: Oxford University Press, 1992.

Mercer, Lloyd J. *E. H. Harriman: Master Railroader.* Boston: Twayne Publishers, 1985.

————. *Railroads and Land Grant Policy: A Study in Government Intervention.* New York: Academic Press, 1982.

Mickelson, Sig. *The Northern Pacific Railroad and the Selling of the West: A Nineteenth-Century Public Relations Venture.* Sioux Falls, South Dakota: Center for Western Studies, 1993.

Miranti, Paul J., Jr. "The Mind's Eye of Reform: The ICC's Bureau of Statistics and Accounts and a Vision of Regulation, 1887–1940," *Business History Review* 63 (1989): 469–509.

Noe, Kenneth W. *Southwestern Virginia's Railroad: Modernization and the Sectional Crisis.* Urbana: University of Illinois Press, 1994.

Ostler, Jeffrey. *Prairie Populism: The Fate of Agrarian Radicalism in Kansas, Nebraska, and Iowa, 1880–1892.* Lawrence: University Press of Kansas, 1993.

Parkerson, Donald H. *The Agricultural Transition in New York State: Markets and Migration in Mid-Nineteenth-Century America.* Ames: Iowa State University Press, 1995.

Piott, Steven L. *The Anti-Monopoly Persuasion: Popular Resistance to the Rise of Big Business in the Midwest.* Westport, Conn.: Greenwood Press, 1985.

Robertson, Donald B. *Encyclopedia of Western Railroad History.* 3 vols., Caldwell, Idaho: Caxton Printers, 1986–1995.

Salamon, Sonya. *Prairie Patrimony: Family, Farming, and Community in the Midwest.* Chapel Hill: University of North Carolina Press, 1992.

Scharnau, Ralph. "The Knights of Labor in Iowa," *Annals of Iowa* 50 (1990–1991): 861–891.

Schlesinger, Keith Robert. "In Search of the Power that Governs: The Growth of Judicial Influence over Public Policy in Illinois, with Special Reference to Railroad Regulation, 1840–1890," Ph.D. diss., Northwestern University, 1985.

Schulp, Leonard. "Republican Loyalist: James F. Wilson and Party Politics, 1855–1895," *Annals of Iowa* 52 (1993): 123–149.

Sheriff, Carol. *The Artificial River: The Erie Canal and the Paradox of Progress, 1817–1862.* New York: Hill & Wang, 1996.

Silag, William. "The Conquest of the Hinterland: Railroads and Capitalists in Northwest Iowa after the Civil War," *Annals of Iowa* 50 (1990–1991): 475–506.

Skocpol, Theda. See Evans, Peter B.

Skowronek, Stephen. *Building a New American State: The Expansion of National Administrative Capacities, 1877–1920.* New York: Cambridge University Press, 1982.

————. "National Railroad Regulation and the Problem of State-Building: Interests and Institutions in Late Nineteenth-Century America," *Politics & Society* 10 (1981): 225–250.

Stone, Richard D. *The Interstate Commerce Commission and the Railroad Industry: A History of Regulatory Policy.* New York: Praeger, 1991.

Stover, John F. *The Life and Decline of the American Railroad.* New York: Oxford University Press, 1970.

Stromquist, Shelton. *A Generation of Boomers: The Pattern of Railroad Labor Conflict in Nineteenth-Century America.* Urbana: University of Illinois Press, 1987.

Summers, Mark W. *Era of Good Stealings.* New York: Oxford University Press, 1993.

———. *Railroads, Reconstruction, and the Gospel of Prosperity: Aid under the Radical Republicans, 1865–1877.* Princeton: Princeton University Press, 1984.

Summers, Mary. "Putting Populism Back In: Rethinking Agricultural Politics and Policy," *Agricultural History* 70 (1996): 395–414.

Ulen, Thomas S. "Cartels and Regulation: Late Nineteenth-Century Railroad Collusion and the Creation of the Interstate Commerce Commission," Ph.D. diss., Stanford University, 1979.

Ward, James A. "Early Railroad Empire Builders, 1850–1873," *Railroad History* 160 (1989): 5–21.

———. *Railroads and the Character of America, 1820–1887.* Knoxville: University of Tennessee Press, 1986.

White, W. Thomas. "A Gilded Age Businessman in Politics: James J. Hill, the Northwest, and the American Presidency, 1884–1912," *Pacific Historical Review* 57 (1988): 439–456.

Williams-Searle, John. "Courting Risk: Disability, Masculinity, and Liability on Iowa's Railroads, 1868–1900," *Annals of Iowa* 58 (1999): 27–77.

Woods, Thomas A. *Knights of the Plow: Oliver H. Kelley and the Origins of the Grange in Republican Ideology.* Ames: Iowa State University Press, 1991.

Acknowledgments

IN WRITING THIS BOOK I have contracted financial and intellectual obligations that it is finally my pleasure to acknowledge. My
wife, Suzanne, supported me for several years' reading and research.
The Newberry Library awarded me a summer stipend to work in the
Burlington Archives. The John E. Rovensky Fellowship, awarded by
the Lincoln Educational Foundation, permitted me to write uninter-
rupted for one year. Finally, my parents, Obert and Mary Lou Larson, have financially supported my scholarly ambitions with unflag-
ging confidence.

I have had the pleasure of working in several fine libraries
whose services must be recognized. The Newberry Library is a de-
lightful place to study because of its excellent and courteous staff,
and I am especially indebted to John Aubrey for access to the Burlington Archives. Robert Lovett of the Manuscripts Division, Baker
Library, Harvard University (now retired), gave generously of his
time and knowledge during my research there. The librarians of the
State Historical Society of Iowa, Iowa City, responded cheerfully to
my impatient needs during two hurried visits to their collections. The
staffs of the Rockefeller Library and John Hay Library, Brown University, were constant aides during my long residence in Providence.
Several persons not connected with libraries also assisted my research
efforts. Frank Carpenter, then of the Museum of the American China
Trade in Milton, Massachusetts; David C. Forbes and Forbes Perkins, both of J.M. Forbes & Co., Boston; and Allan Forbes of Cambridge, Massachusetts, all gave advice and interviews.

Many persons contribute to a book by providing the intellectual
society in which one is written. I am indebted in various ways to Earl
J. Leland, James C. Hippen, A.G. Roeber, Patricia Stutzman Roeber, John and Lynne Eckhart, Walter Conser, Leslie C. (Skip) Aber-
nathy, Richard Kazarian, Robert McCauley, and Robert D. Ron-
sheim for advice and counsel. A. Hunter Dupree, Albro Martin,
Richard C. Overton, James T. Patterson, and Mary A. Yeager each
read the manuscript at different stages, and their comments im-

proved the work at every step. John L. Thomas gave this book special attention without which it might never have reached its present state.

A final special note of thanks is due my wife and children, who share with me the joys and difficulties of academic life.

Introduction to the
1984 Edition

BONDS OF ENTERPRISE is a study of one Boston capitalist's career as a western developer and railroad builder, and of the transformation of America from a rural agrarian republic into a continental industrial nation. In the first case this is a story of almost unbroken progress; in the second it is a tale of steady dislocation and loss of traditional bearings. The "bonds" of trade and commercial development that forged a national American market also destroyed the dreams of many local entrepreneurs and the integrity of their communities across the country.

In this study the bonds of enterprise are railroads running between the American heartland and the commercial East—lines of transportation and trade that brought unlimited opportunities to inland communities and exacted as their price the subjugation of local advantages and prejudices to the national network. Yet these bonds implied partnership as well as subjugation. That the parties entered into "bondage" freely, often eagerly, illustrates the complexity of their motives. The local farmers and businessmen and the outside capitalists who built their railroads were not really contestants with different objectives. They were all free enterprise capitalists, all believers in progress and economic growth; but they saw their interests at different levels of the system, and they struggled to improve their standing within the economy as the new order unfolded. In the process of building something entirely new, untold changes were incurred, conflicts encountered, hardships endured, and benefits enjoyed.

The real consequences of their purposeful action was perhaps beyond the vision of those contemporary men and women. Through the story of John Murray Forbes and his railroad developments in the upper Midwest, I have tried to illustrate the process of change in business and society and the detailed interactions of ideas, individuals, and events that made up the larger history. This narrative represents facets of that larger picture: It includes some things and omits others that might seem germane from another perspective. This book is biographical, but it is not a proper biography of John Murray Forbes. I have included long accounts of his China experience and his activities during the Civil War because these bore directly on his understanding of railroad development. Other aspects of his personal career, especially his interest in politics and other railroads after the Civil War, had to be left aside.

Not all of Forbes's railroads are treated equally either. The Michigan Central figures prominently in Forbes's initiation into western railroading, then slips from view. The Chicago, Burlington & Quincy, the firm with which Forbes was closely identified for over half a century, stands as an instrument of change throughout the book, but the railroad company is not the subject of the story. (For a balanced history of the CB&Q the reader must turn to the works of Richard C. Overton.) Finally, in order to achieve a sufficiently detailed look at unfolding events, I have narrowed the focus to the Iowa lines of the CB&Q. Something like the same story might be told for Illinois, Nebraska, and points farther west, or for that matter, for a number of entrepreneurs, their railroad companies, and their local constituencies.

This is not to say that historical situations are universal or that case studies are substitutes for broader treatments. In writing this book I used a method of investigation that promised to highlight the complex connections that are set aside in other forms of inquiry. I examined the maze of influences that accompanied the enormous changes the railroad engendered by walking through the period with articulate individuals who expressed themselves on paper. John Murray Forbes proved an ideal companion, and his associates and opponents provided a full cast of characters. My conceptual framework was confirmed by the language of Forbes and his contemporaries: They were at once aware of the importance of their work and incapable of fully recognizing the consequences of their actions.

The narrative of railroad development begins with general background material and moves toward specific cases concerning Forbes. Forbes, the steam railroad, and the people of Iowa are introduced separately and brought together in their proper time. The focus narrows as the complexity of developments requires a smaller field of scrutiny. At the same time the analysis of the railroad as a revolutionary force in nineteenth-century American life expands to embrace the many levels of influence attending this new technology. Originally an engineering problem alone, the steam railroad quickly became a business organization and a network of trade that profoundly affected the enterprise of other people. Questions of economic and social policy arose, and these soon found expression in politics at all levels. Fundamental assumptions about government and the economy were ultimately adjusted to suit the railway age. As the railroad accumulated real and symbolic influence, it changed the fabric of American society. By the end of the century the steam railroad was deeply embedded in American culture.

Bonds of Enterprise

1

The Liberal Merchant

THE OPENING DECADE of the nineteenth century was charged with conflict and opportunity. The nations of Western Europe had been at war almost continuously for a generation. Democratic revolutions in America and France had shattered the foundations of divine right monarchy and traditional social hierarchy. At the same time commercial men had outgrown the boundaries of crown empires and mercantilist economies, launching a revolution in trade and industry. By 1800 the interests of free trade and republicanism, empire and monarchy, were being reflected imperfectly in the Napoleonic wars. No member of the Atlantic community could escape the seaborne struggle between England and France—two great eighteenth-century powers fighting for control of the new age ahead. Technically neutral but inevitably partisan, Americans were bitterly divided in their support for the French or British cause.

Into this war-torn sea, in January 1811 a young Boston woman set sail with two small boys aboard a schooner full of cod, bound for France and reunion with her merchant husband. Besides enduring the hardship and fear that accompanied a transatlantic passage before the age of iron and steam, Margaret Perkins Forbes traversed a battlefield. Intercepted in March by a British warship, the schooner was finally landed several weeks later on a small barren island off the coast of France. From there Margaret Forbes was delivered to Ralph Bennet Forbes; they continued in Europe on business. Late in 1812 the family took up housekeeping in Bordeaux and there, on February 23, 1813, the exiled Margaret gave birth to her third son, John Murray Forbes. The unfortunate child was barely three months old when he endured his own first crossing of the violent Atlantic and was deposited in Boston nearly dead from hardship and the laudanum employed to quiet him. It was an inauspicious beginning.[1]

1

John Murray Forbes was destined to see eighty-five years of the tumultuous century he had entered; he would play an active role in the century of "progress" for seven decades. Throughout his long life he wrestled with the contradictions that marked Napoleon's France at his birth. He perpetuated until his death an eighteenth-century style of business, emphasizing family connection, personal responsibility, and the traditional conservative views of the Boston mercantile clan into which he was born. At the same time he indulged with enthusiasm a dynamic urge toward innovation, pressing onto the frontiers of America's industrial development, breaking down the barriers of time, space, and tradition that were the containers of the older "community" he loved. Forbes came to revere the democratic republic as the only type of government to which a virtuous citizen owed allegiance, yet he remained by temperament an aristocrat, impatient with the tendency of the mcb to challenge its natural leaders. Above all he was an entrepreneur, a title eminently suited to men of the nineteenth century. He was a leader among those in Europe and America who transformed the operations of the shopkeeper and the merchant prince into a system of world capitalism that would one day rival civil government as the organizing principle of society. John Murray Forbes was one of those American entrepreneurs who engineered the cultural transformation of the nation from that of Thomas Jefferson to that of J. Pierpont Morgan. He loved progress even as he mourned its corrupting influence on individuals and society.

A MERCANTILE YOUTH

John Murray Forbes was born into a close community of Boston merchants whose wealth and influence had been established in the decades surrounding the American Revolution. The Forbes line descended from a Scottish clergyman named John Forbes who had settled in the home of his bride, Dorothy Murray of Milton, Massachusetts, in 1773. John Murray Forbes's mother was Margaret Perkins, younger sister of the wealthy importer, Colonel Thomas Handasyd Perkins. The marriage of Ralph Forbes and Margaret Perkins was the foundation of the Boston Forbeses and the crucial link with an expansive and prosperous trading family. Of the eight children born to Ralph and Margaret Forbes, all three sons—Thomas Tunno,

Robert Bennet, and John Murray—served their apprenticeship in the Perkins countinghouse and entered the China trade. The boys' father had never joined the Perkins firm, but instead sought his fortune in independent ventures. Plagued in early life with recurrent gout (some said from too much drink), he was never a good provider. The proud and industrious Margaret managed a frugal household with the help of her sons and such aid from the Colonel as her pride would allow. As a child, John Murray knew his father only as an invalid who failed to provide while his mother and brothers struggled for a living. Ralph Bennet Forbes died in 1824, leaving eleven-year-old John with an ambivalent grief for the man who never secured the independence his mother craved.[2]

As a consequence of their father's ill fortune, the Forbes boys were early put to work. After five years' training in the Boston store, eighteen-year-old Thomas was stationed in China for Perkins & Co. Bennet, a year younger than Tom, went before the mast at the age of thirteen and took over his first command at twenty. Their contributions to the family purse allowed young John a more formal education before taking up his working life. He was enrolled, at brother Tom's expense, in the experimental Round Hill School that had been recently opened in Northampton, Massachusetts.[3]

Round Hill was a middle school for boys that combined a classical curriculum with heavy emphasis on sport, games, and nature study. Its founders, George Bancroft and J. G. Cogswell, envisioned the school as a liberating alternative to the restraints of Harvard College and the Cambridge intellectual community. They settled on a pastoral estate outside Northampton where they hoped to fuse the timeless moral virtues of the classics with the democratic promise of American country life. From their retreat would come young gentlemen of integrity and mental refinement without the pretensions of the class-ridden city system. John Murray Forbes was among the first scholars at Round Hill in October 1823.[4]

Forbes was a precocious boy. Although he loved sport, he was generally serious-minded and too eager to grow up. He had been introduced to the role of merchant at the age of eight when his brother sent him small shipments of Chinese trinkets, which he dutifully reported sold "very well" in Milton village. While at Round Hill he declined his mother's offers of cake and sweetmeats in favor of "manly things." He read all his brothers' letters home, so that he might keep up with family affairs. When his brothers were both abroad, the ten-year-old boy assumed an attitude of grave family responsibility, offering copious advice to his mother and sisters as the male voice in the fatherless household.[5]

For young Forbes, the Round Hill experience produced more character than intellectual attainment. Throughout his life he extolled the virtues of gymnastic and field sports, and he treasured the personal models of Cogswell and his tutors. No doubt the greatest advantage of the school for Forbes lay in the few years of freedom it gave him before sinking into the routine of trade—time to be a boy growing. Here he internalized the virtues of duty and fair play. He drew from that environment both a sincere devotion to moral right and a practical energy more suited to the world of men. In later years Forbes freely blended the "eternal truths" that had inspired his tutors with the shrewd calculations of a practical man of business; the combination often resulted in a double standard, but it never produced a crisis of confidence.[6]

Duty seemed uppermost in the mind of the youth as he contemplated his future career. As a poor boy dependent on family connections, his calling was never really open to question. At the end of Forbes's five years at Round Hill, Headmaster Cogswell recommended him for the mercantile life, and the youth seemed instinctively to understand his destiny. He had known for years that his fortune lay, if anywhere, in trade. Now in 1828 he admitted that "whether I went into the Perkins's store in Boston or not, I must end by going to Canton." Plagued by the image of his father's failures and already indebted to his brother, the young man felt an urge toward independent wealth which he tried to explain to Thomas:

> It is true that it must be painful to me to leave all our friends here, but I feel that it is better to make any sacrifice than to be a useless member of our family. . . . I almost envy you the pleasure of being able to render one so dear [his sister Emma] to us all independent, and hope most sincerely that, if fortune is favorable to me, it may be my first pleasure, as it is yours, to share it with those I love.

It was decided in October of 1828 that John, then fifteen, would leave what he called the "aristocratical and free-thinking government of Round Hill" and enter the house of J.&T.H. Perkins to learn something about the more regulated world of business. Within a year he was bored with sweeping the store and wearing out shoes "for the service of P. & Co." He was chafing to get aboard a Canton packet.[7]

While biding his time in the Perkins store, Forbes studied his own personal development with clarity and detachment. To his brother Tom in August 1829, he wrote with growing impatience of his immaturity and unsettled prospects. He despaired of his constantly shifting "tastes and views," which seemed to alter with every change of place and habits, and which had been sharply jolted since his introduction to trade. Philosophically he assumed that a trip to China would bring yet another shock. The depressed conditions of trade just then, and the business failure of certain friends of the family, had momentarily dimmed his natural optimism. In fact, he thought there was a "poor chance for the coming generation," which he supposed must be content to "work hard and get little." Recoiling from the gloom, he looked for as good a chance for happiness in "passing our lives this way as in any other if we are only willing to do so." Certainly there was a better opportunity in Canton of learning the "principles and practice of trade and of becoming a merchant in a liberal sense of the word." On the other hand, would the connections formed in Canton serve him as well in later life as those he would give up in Boston?[8]

The whole burden of young Forbes's uncertainty was thrown on his brother. While he waited the winter months of 1829 for advice and guidance, he could not have known that his letters were never read. A typhoon had carried off brother Thomas, and the news of his death would throw a green and impressionable John Murray Forbes directly into the exotic bustle of the Canton factories.

OPIUM: THE CHINA CONNECTION

By the time Forbes sailed for Canton in 1830, the China trade had accumulated a long and troubled history. It was inherently one-sided: Europeans and Americans wanted Chinese teas and silks, but these Western "barbarians" had little of value to offer the Celestial Empire. Early Western traders depended on cash transactions or tried to force their wares on the Chinese market. By the early years of the nineteenth century the systematic development of the opium trade had corrected this structural imbalance and prevented a serious specie drain to the Orient.[9] At the same time, Western commercial economies were beginning to realize the possibilities of an expanding world commerce in which the *circulation* of goods and the *flow* of wealth became the sources of profit. In this emerging worldwide commercial network, the China connection took on even greater importance as a point of exchange and a generator of capital for the industrialization of the West.

The Chinese concept of trade derived from tribute rather than exchange; the imperial court misunderstood Western commerce, and the mercantile class was despised by the official bureaucracy. Foreign trade in China was carried on through the Hong merchants who made up the monopolistic Cohong. The Cohong system was devised to insulate the empire from contamination by limiting contact with the barbarian outside world. By 1745 the Hong merchants were responsible for their own commercial conduct *and* the behavior of foreign traders. After 1760 European trade was restricted to the port of Canton and handled exclusively by the merchants of the Cohong.[10]

As they evolved their dual role in government and private trade, the Hong merchants became the primary intermediaries between the imperial court and foreign entrepreneurs. They set prices, sold goods, provided and leased the factories (warehouses), managed banking and exchange—in short, they governed all commercial aspects of the trade. Yet the Hong merchants acquired their lucrative monopoly at a great cost in personal liability. They were expected to restrain foreigners in China, to act as interpreters, guarantee duties and control smuggling, support local militia and schools, and "make all manner of presents and contributions to the authorities far and near." (The "squeeze" or graft required by the bureaucrats frequently bankrupted the Hongs.) While official court policy denied the importance of foreign trade, by the late eighteenth century it had become a necessary source of wealth for officialdom at every level. The merchants of the Cohong served uneasily as both a channel and a barrier for commerce with Western nations.[11]

In the foreign quarter outside the city wall, three major interests maintained their own uneasy harmony. The Honourable East India Company was the entrenched British monopoly in the Far East, maintaining the official trading concession at Canton as well as full government control in much of India. Outside the East India Company, and increasingly important to its revenues, were the "country traders"—private British and Indian merchants who operated within the Asian circuit but were prohibited from the main arterial trade with London. Finally the Americans, largely dominated by the Boston house of Perkins & Co., ran ventures through the gaps and outside the boundaries of this British colonial system with growing success. Forced into cooperation by the sometimes baffling attentions of

Chinese officialdom, by the 1820s each of these competing elements had developed a unique role in the Asian network that rendered it indispensable to the others.

The British monopoly provided the original foundation for the system. The East India Company had maintained the only agency in Canton until the last years of the eighteenth century, by which time it exported almost nothing but tea to Great Britain. The company had been forcing British woolens and other goods on the Chinese market, always at a loss, to pay for a fraction of its tea investment. The balance came from specie. In the last decades of the century the East India Company discovered that the produce of India—raw cotton and opium—commanded a steady market in China. By 1804 the Indian connection was reversing the flow of treasure to the Orient.

The East India Company tried several times to engage in this Indian "country trade" itself but eventually gave it up to licensed merchants living in India. Like the Canton business, the country trade was in chronic imbalance, leaving large funds in Canton to be remitted to India. A triangle was formed when the East India Company began selling its bills on London or Bengal for the cash receipts of these private merchants at Canton: The cash was used to purchase teas for London and the bills conveniently remitted private funds back to India or home to England.[12]

This arrangement suited the East India Company but it barred private merchants from engaging in the full spectrum of profitable ventures in China. It fell to private British and American shippers to begin forcing open the business. First working under the cover of foreign diplomacy, a number of Scottish traders established agents in residence at Canton and offered banking and commission services (though not direct trade) in competition with the monopoly. After 1813 direct trade with India was thrown open, and the Lancashire exporters discovered the same profitable triangle through the private agencies in Canton. In a similar manner, Americans established a foothold in Canton in the first years of the new century and, along with commercial services and a fair quantity of specie, they brought American bills on London which provided a competing financial instrument.[13]

John Murray Forbes's uncle, Thomas Handasyd Perkins, was a major figure in the American link. Perkins had entered the China market with furs and exotic goods from the Pacific Islands. By 1805 this market was saturated and, barred from the Indian opium trade, Perkins turned to Turkish opium. He quickly discovered that the

East India Company's restrictions could be used as a shield for an American monopoly in the Turkish drug. Idled at Canton by the British blockade after 1812, Perkins's nephew John P. Cushing worked out a tidy mechanism for regularized smuggling once the war was over. The system removed Perkins & Co. from direct involvement with the drug, in deference to Howqua, the influential Hong merchant whose confidence Cushing enjoyed. The business was further sanitized, after an imperial crackdown in 1821, by the adoption of the storeship or "Lintin" system, which shifted actual smuggling entirely to Chinese hands.[14]

Together, the country traders and the Americans gradually undermined the East India Company's monopoly at Canton while providing indispensable services to that firm's Eastern operations. Because of its official and diplomatic status the East India Company steadily dissociated itself from the drug traffic upon which its solvency depended. This policy simply strengthened the private agencies in China, while each concession to freer trade engendered more pressure to drop the barriers. After 1820 the Perkins house exercised its advantages to consolidate the American branch of the opium trade, drawing together the major trading families of Boston—Sturgis, Cabot, Bryant, Higginson, Cushing, and others—into a worldwide network of kinship and commercial enterprise.[15]

Ultimately what displaced the old British monopoly in China was not competition alone, but the evolution of a new business system—the system in which John Murray Forbes would learn his trade. Between the old structures of the charter monopoly and the private ship's venture (where the *voyage* was the enterprise), these innovators in China erected the agency or commission house. In contrast to the "supercargo" who sailed with the ship, the agent remained behind to perform essential services for others. These agency houses established the skeleton of commercial capitalism on the fringes of a reluctant society. The resident commission merchants became bankers, bill brokers, insurers, freighters, shipowners, buyers, and sellers for merchants from all over the world.

Such agencies were soon able to manipulate the market, holding off sales or stockpiling teas out of season, sifting fragments of information about markets, and smoothing the curves of supply and demand. By charging commissions on each service, men of small capital grew rich sharing the profits of their clients' investments. The agents then loaned their own earnings at interest or invested in ships and cargoes that brought new revenues to their houses. Because everyone's profit in these arrangements depended on the judgment and ability of the agent, success tended to consolidate the trade in the hands of close-knit groups, often blood relatives, whose worldwide connections gave them the best credit and freshest information.[16]

In this lively new system a cumbersome monopoly like the East India Company was at a positive disadvantage because it discouraged volume. The new merchants, like John P. Cushing, tried to corner the market for information and services while drumming the volume of trade constantly higher. By the middle of the 1820s Cushing was the preeminent American in Canton and the practical master of the Turkish opium market. Besides heading the Perkins house, Cushing was a partner in James P. Sturgis & Co., which handled the Turkish trade; he also supported Russell & Co., which specialized in Indian opium and the old country trade. After twenty-five years of pioneering in this market Cushing finally pronounced the system secure. In 1828 he set sail for home, leaving the China business in the hands of Thomas T. Forbes.[17]

CANTON APPRENTICESHIP

Thomas Forbes was lost at sea in August 1829, but the news of his death did not reach Boston until the following February. John Cushing had left Tom to command the firm in Canton without so much as an apprentice training. Tom had also been the financial mainstay of his family, keeping his mother comfortable and paying his father's old debts. In time both roles would fall to John Murray Forbes, but for the moment he was still a boy, and temporary arrangements had to be made. Russell & Co. took up the Perkins business after Tom's death, and Cushing sailed directly from Europe the following spring to prepare a place for the younger Forbes. John was to leave from Boston that summer with Augustine Heard, a junior partner in Russell & Co. Seventeen years old, eager to shoulder the burden but deeply saddened over the loss of a brother who was perhaps more of a father to him, Forbes set sail for China on July 7, 1830.[18]

Forbes had not resolved his own uncertainties about going to China, and he considered this first trip a temporary expedient. Cushing had secretly arranged for him to receive a partner's share in Russell & Co. at the beginning of the new term; but upon his arrival, Forbes was installed as a clerk. His only advantage over a simple apprentice was his introduction to Howqua, the wealthy head of the Cohong. Cushing and Thomas Forbes had been personal agents for the old Hong merchant, conducting his large overseas business for a handsome fee. Howqua accepted John as their replacement, and by his own account Forbes was soon chartering ships and sending off thousands of dollars in trade goods, carried in his own name, for the account of Howqua. He took to the business quickly, receiving and dispatching shipments and writing in triplicate the innumerable letters that were the primary instrument of business. His youth was partly masked, as he put it later, by "the appearance of being much older" (he was balding already), and he was soon "playing a man's part."[19]

For just over two years the young clerk remained at Canton mastering the routine operations of a commission house until he became ill in 1833, and he was sent home to recover. Among his several anxieties during this period was the want of a wife, a situation he rectified with remarkable haste eight months after landing in Boston. He was quietly married in February 1834 to Sarah Hathaway, one of twin daughters of a solid Quaker family in New Bedford. It was a lucky and permanent match, one that lasted sixty-four years, but it was rudely interrupted in the first month by Forbes's sudden return to China. Marriage had only increased his need for a career. Convinced that his China training was "entirely different from anything wanted for business in this country," Forbes seized an opening in another China voyage. The house of Bryant & Sturgis had offered him the position of supercargo on the ships *Logan* and *Tartar,* in turn. He sailed on March 7, 1834, still ignorant of his share in Russell & Co. and planning to return to Boston with the *Tartar* and perhaps take a place in the Perkins firm.[20]

Forbes's absence, however, was not to be a short one. Others had made a place for him in Canton that he could not refuse, and his mercantile career was firmly established during his second stay in China. Howqua had urged his return because, he said, Forbes understood him better than any other foreigner. The old gentleman assured John's brother Bennet that John would accumulate "all that he will require in a reasonable time & return to his family and friends before he is many years older." When John arrived in Canton the second time, Howqua offered him a 10 percent share in all his ventures handled in Forbes's name. Furthermore, Forbes discovered his partnership in Russell & Co., which already amounted to $14,000. Profits as supercargo seemed far less promising, and finally, Augustine Heard became ill and threatened to die in harness unless John stayed to help manage Russell & Co. Faced with these surprisingly good offers, Forbes informed the captain of his ship that he was "half tempted to do a wise thing and stay."[21]

Unable to wait the long months for advice from home, Forbes weighed his options carefully and finally accepted the offer of Russell & Co. He informed his personal connections in October 1834 that their business should be addressed to the house. Howqua brought his large trade to the firm at a flat 2 percent commission, although it was still done in Forbes's name because the real owner of the property required secrecy for his trading abroad. With the decision made, Forbes agonized over his choice and put off for months the delicate task of explaining to Sarah why he was not coming home. When he finally sat down to write, it was status, not wealth, that governed his thoughts. "You must recollect," he explained, "that though I had the entire confidence of my friends before, yet to others I was only known as a clerk and a very young man." He thought supercargoes were "dog cheap," and without more responsibility on his shoulders he could not gain confidence in himself. Having become a partner in the most respectable American house at Canton, however, he had "acquired a confidence that would enable me to undertake any business in any part of the world."[22] The multitude of personal hardships notwithstanding, Forbes had chosen to stay in China because at last he was becoming a "merchant in a liberal sense of the word."

These personal sacrifices were not made lightly, for John Forbes did not enjoy life in Canton. The isolation in a hot, wet, unhealthy climate, surrounded by the squalid poverty of the Chinese and the condescending attitudes of the Mandarins, left him cynical and depressed. Western merchants—"foreign devils"—were crowded into their compound on the banks of the river with little to amuse themselves besides schoolboy games and sailing. Forbes complained frequently of boredom and feared for his physical and mental health. He grumbled fiercely over trifles regarding servants and petty thieves and feared he was "constitutionally irritable," having developed a "morbid desire to be let alone." Business secrecy circumscribed all society outside the house, and since the Chinese, with certain loyal exceptions, were assumed to be vicious scoundrels, the mental strain of loneliness was severe. Forbes longed for home and the society of friends and loved ones. By the summer of 1836 he complained of a "*tomb*-like feeling about Canton."[23]

Canton must have seemed a crucible of mankind's vices to a

proper Bostonian. The flagrant graft and the whims of the arrogant Mandarins offended Forbes deeply. The plague of beggars outside the compound wall outraged and sickened him, but the exercise of charity toward one of them produced a violent scramble that frustrated even that Christian response. Nor did he find solace in the European community. Captains and supercargoes were a coarse lot, but they were no more distastefull than the English nabobs and their American imitators. With ingratitude and pretension abounding, moral rectitude apparently wanting, and charity proving actually dangerous, there was little in Canton to curb Forbes's cynicism or reinforce the pastoral ideals of a boy from Round Hill School. His fragile grasp of religion failed him, and he confessed to his wife that "theres [sic] not much hope of my reforming—for I am sure there is misanthropy and hard heartedness in the very atmosphere of this place." Physical decay haunted Forbes, and the slow death of his dear friend and kinsman, Handasyd Cabot, left him broken with fear and depression. Yet even while innocence and virtue were struck down in this world, Forbes maintained a strong face and hospitable temper. In the midst of his own trials he instructed his wife to be polite to all who claimed to know him at Canton, as it was "only a forcible example of the near connection between duty and self-interest."[24]

Despairing of enjoyment of either the climate or society in the foreign quarter, Forbes turned to business for his hope and his reward. Fortunately there was usually much to occupy him. With the uncertainties of communication and the high risks of transportation halfway around the world, as well as delicate relations with the imperial authorities to contend with, a successful China merchant had to be shrewd and decisive. If the commission house provided more rational and flexible business structures than the old East India Company, the system still rested on the good name of the resident partners. Caught between the old kinship methods of trade and truly modern bureaucratic commerce, the resident merchant in the early 1830s had to adopt more efficient, standardized methods while maintaining the tangle of personal alliances at the core of the house business. A merchant's reputation in the free trade system depended on fair and equitable service to all his customers, while his reputation as a gentleman required "doing the right thing" for his friends.

Forbes took up the role of resident partner in Russell & Co. just months after the British Parliament had repealed the East India Company's monopoly. Suddenly thrown open to free trade, Canton was swarming with British interlopers and profiteers who pressed the established American houses much the way Perkins & Co. had previously threatened the East India Company. As early as February 1834, Howqua was begging Forbes (still in Boston) and Cushing (in London) to ship only silver because "we shall be overwhelmed with British goods of every description on the opening of trade." By the time Forbes arrived in Canton that autumn, matters had taken just such a turn. There were too many vessels in China. British goods were a drug on the market, and the newcomers had bid the price of teas out of reach. Forbes reported to Cushing, "I believe that we must make up our minds that the China Trade is not subject to the rules of commerce elsewhere & that no calculation can be made in it; people seem to be launching into it almost as freely as ever." Even the old seasonal regularity that followed the monsoons was lost in the new competition: By 1836 "the good old times" were gone and American ships were loading all through the summer.[25]

With business in chaos, only some careful reforms could save Russell & Co. Even before the flood of new competition the house had suffered from informality and poor organization. Partners and clerks shared menial tasks indiscriminately, and their correspondence mixed business information with personal family matters. These habits had suited an aggressive new firm breaking into the market, but now the increased volume of trade exhausted everyone and resulted in numerous errors and lost business. John C. Green, a New York merchant who became a lifelong supporter of Forbes's enterprises, was sent out to reorganize the house at the new term in 1834. Green's arrival brought in new clients, while the rapid promotion of young Forbes helped stop the drift of Boston business to other American houses in the Far East.[26] As the onslaught of free trade overwhelmed the Canton factories, the new partners bent with a will to the task of reforming Russell & Co.'s operations and securing its position in the American China trade.

REFORM AND COMPETITION

One of the inherent difficulties of the China trade had been communications, and now more than ever improvements were needed. Letters were commonly five or six months out-of-date when they arrived in China. Even then, the captain or supercargo often withheld the ship's letterbag until the cargo was sold and a return was secured. This sometimes meant another three months' delay, a particular hardship on the resident merchants because family news was sequestered along with business. The severe demand for fresh information naturally gave rise to all kinds of skulduggery. Ships' officers enhanced their purses by selling early deliveries, sometimes jeopardizing their employer's interest.[27]

Forbes's first response to this villainous system was to exploit its weakness in his own favor. He explained the system to Baring Brothers of London; they should send duplicates of their letters with *their own* captains, "with orders to dispatch them to Canton by the first Boat that boards," and to await further orders before delivering the regular mail sacks. This arrangement didn't solve the problem, however, because native scoundrels on a Chinese boat might sell the letters—and Europeans almost surely would. A year later Forbes was still complaining about captains and couriers who served the highest bidder.[28]

The first positive alternative to holding back the news was the advent, in 1835, of the London overland mail. This was still largely a water route, but it crossed overland at Suez rather than sailing the long way around the Horn. Forbes was intrigued with the prospect of faster, more regular communication with London and Boston and urged his brother Bennet to experiment with the new route:

> I call your attention to this mode of sending letters as one which may often bring us late accounts from you, and I wish you to write me a *business letter* quoting prices prospects ships coming & all other matters that may be interesting to the House by the 8th packet of every month except April June & July when ships are coming direct[;] it will then reach London by the 1st & come on overland[;] postage must be paid in London about $3 for single letters (I believe[)] Send a duplicate of your letter with your next overland despatch and a triplicate to be sent by ship from England in this way if you pursue the plan systematically the experiment may be fairly tried in a year.[29]

While the overland system did quicken the pace slightly, especially in the off-season for American vessels, it could not fully remove the news delay, and China merchants continued to rely on their gambler's instinct. So deeply was the communications problem ingrained in the business that when, in the 1860s, the electric telegraph finally broke the time barrier with near-instant information, the old-fashioned China merchant ceased to exist.[30]

Because they frequently operated in the dark, men like Forbes relied on a network of commission merchants around the world whose integrity they trusted. The character of these brokers was of primary importance. Each must be trusted to accept a consignment of goods, often without warning, and then sell them, hold them, or reship them elsewhere, depending on *his* judgment of the local markets. The proceeds, less commissions and charges, had to be remitted in cash or goods of sufficient value in the consignor's home market. Significant losses resulted even from selecting the wrong form of money for a cash remittance! Young Forbes filled copybooks with letters to agents in Europe, throughout Asia and in America, either announcing the impending arrival of fifty or one hundred thousand dollars worth of goods to their care, or asking them to buy a like amount and bill him for it. The web of credit and tangle of bills that accompanied the merchandise worked as long as endorsements were honored; a good name in this business was essential.[31]

When Forbes took up his partnership in 1834 he sent his business connections a specimen of his "Russell & Co." signature and outlined the principles on which he identified with the house. Russell & Co. had a long record of paying "*promptly* & in cash." Its agents had "acquired a standing with the Chinese" that would "generally enable them to have the choice of the Teas in Market," and they were now staffed adequately to handle the volume of business at low and *fixed* rates of commission. It was becoming a point of honor with Forbes that Russell & Co. should not speculate in ventures on the house account. The company's whole capital was employed in carrying out the business of its clients; no conflict of interest should arise. Forbes condemned speculations in short-term investments with a client's unclaimed funds. The practice not only risked the unnecessary loss of other people's money, it was generally carried on by rate-cutting houses who did the commission business "for nothing for the sake of getting large funds to pass through their hands." Forbes thought Russell & Co. should be judged on economy, efficiency, and quality of service as a conservative, dependable agency. He was not prepared to answer for the occasional windfalls of reckless gamblers.[32]

Facing the ruinous pressures of cutthroat competition in the mid-1830s, Forbes and John C. Green advertised their new policy of uniform charges and tried to implement protective rate agreements among the other established houses. Explaining this policy to John Cushing, Forbes wrote: "We wish to have our charges uniform & consider it only fair to treat all alike; we have made a bargain with

Wetmore [a New York-based China house] never in future to do business for less than our usual rates & I believe no other houses here charge less or so little."[33]

Not everyone shared Forbes's enthusiasm for this new kind of equality. The new agreements meant *raising* the commissions of those who had financed Forbes's return to China on the ship *Logan*. Cushing apparently let the matter pass, but William Sturgis exploded. He accused Forbes of profiteering on old family connections and transferred his business to the Wetmore house, which promptly took him in at the old rate. The encounter left Forbes hurt, angry, and in serious trouble with family and friends in Boston. Because of the six-month delay as letters traveled around the globe, it took until August of 1836 for Forbes and Sturgis to reach an understanding. Collusive rate agreements broke down quickly in Canton, but Forbes stuck doggedly to the principle of equal charges and gradually won back the confidence of his friends.[34]

As ruthless competition cut margins to the bone, merchants like Forbes relied increasingly on discretionary judgments to rescue their clients' ventures. This method carried its own risk. Because a commission merchant did not share in the outcome of his transactions, as had the old supercargo, he was supposed to be a neutral agent. Still, imperfect knowledge on the part of the principals forced them to grant broad discretionary powers to their hired agents. This meant the agent had to make entrepreneurial decisions while the owner remained free to quarrel if things turned out badly. Forbes was usually given price limits by his clients, but he was expected to violate orders as his immediate knowledge of the market dictated. When he did so and failed, his client was disgruntled. Yet when he followed instructions and failed, his client was furious! The dilemma bothered Forbes most during his first year back in China. He was still only twenty-one years old, and he frequently wrote to the older partners at Bryant, Sturgis & Co. for approval and more specific instructions. As he acquired experience and confidence, however, his discomfort disappeared. A "merchant in a liberal sense" learned to ignore the abuse and to stand on his actions boldly.[35]

Forbes was making a great deal of money and learning valuable lessons in Canton, yet by 1836 he was personally troubled once more. He asked his brother Bennet to withdraw his homebound funds from trade and to close out any joint ventures that might be pending. By March 1836, he feared that his connections in Canton were becoming so uncertain that he asked Samuel Cabot in Boston for a job at home, even though he had assured Cushing just a week earlier that prospects for Russell & Co. were very good indeed.[36]

At the root of Forbes's new personal crisis was the question that his brother Tom had not lived to answer: Should he seek his fortune in China or at home? He wrote darkly now of a "path of duty," trying once again to explain his decision to stay in Canton. Nothing but a "*positive* obligation" prevented him from sailing at once, but he never made clear whether his debt was to Cushing, Tom Forbes and the past, or his wife and mother and their future "independence." Money alone could not hold him: "It would go hard," he confessed, "if I could not make a living at home and perhaps it was my mistake in not seeing this plainly two years since." He admitted that in staying he had acted "upon a theory regarding 'happiness'," and now he mourned the "loss of friends[,] the years of youth & probably of happiness which I threw away in Exchange for a doubtful good money." Nevertheless, he proposed to stay until the end of the season, when he could arrange to leave "with perfect confidence" and also be assured of "some occupation at home."[37]

In fact, Forbes was completing a plan whereby he could end his exile in China and still keep Russell & Co. as the focus of his future career. The immediate concern was for John C. Green to anchor Russell & Co. by staying in China until a suitable person could be groomed to fill his place. Forbes was convinced that the China trade was best tended by men of like mind and *like family*, gentlemen brought up to trade and bound by a close mercantile community back home. He hoped to combine the values of that old mercantile system with more modern ideas of long-run interest and managerial oversight. Properly guided from a distance, Russell & Co. might continue to provide him with a moderate income for administrative services. It could offer a perfect opportunity for Forbes to place picked men whose fortunes and allegiance he might continue to command, and it would keep him in close touch with the great commercial capitalists of the world. Houses like Russell & Co. were originally outposts of the home firm. By reversing that relationship, Forbes was determined to make himself the Boston agent of the Canton firm, "to be on the spot with the last and best information on all subjects connected with China."[38]

Why was the young man who hated China determined to build his fortune around it? The answer lies in the one positive image he found in Canton—the great Hong merchant Howqua. Thin, frail, marked in his visage by a wisp of beard and that exquisite pride of

Oriental leisure, Howqua impressed the athletic American with his delicate strength. Like most Westerners, Forbes never understood the Confucian doctrines of collective responsibility and right conduct that governed Chinese lives. What he did see was the immense fortune and power that Howqua possessed and the code of honor that governed the use of both. He found something captivating in a man who had "certain control over foreign trade," who could "lord it over the other 10 Hongs," while remaining humble and generous and maintaining "all the members of his family, including near and far cousins, in a certain style," according to Chinese custom.[39] Forbes's own preoccupation was not with wealth itself, but with the prospect of independence and a surplus to share with those he loved. A single fortune was easily lost; what he needed was a structured system for making money, the fruits of which he could direct into the hands of deserving friends and relatives. To Forbes's eye, jaded by the surrounding images of greed and poverty, Howqua appeared as a model entrepreneur—driven by duty, not avarice, and enjoying great power closely checked by an equal and intimate sense of responsibility. Forbes knew that Russell & Co. was no place to spend his life, but perhaps it was the foundation on which to build this larger dream.

HOME TO A CRISIS

Forbes sailed from China in December 1836 with a modest fortune ("perhaps $100,000") and the confidence that he could relax at home before taking up any new business. When he landed in New York in March 1837, his hope for domestic peace was shattered by a major financial panic that was sweeping the commercial world. He fell to work immediately, covering his debts and trying to salvage Russell & Co. The great danger to merchants in this kind of monetary crisis resulted from the fact that no one in the regular course of business kept specie on hand to cover a company's total paper debt. Bills and credits flowed more quickly than merchandise, and the goods usually sold well enough to make up the balance in time. At the first sign of trouble, however, prices fell and creditors demanded specie, which sent everyone scrambling for cash to cover the bills. Half a million dollars in Russell & Co. bills were refused payment by bankrupt houses in London, and Forbes's only hope was that Baring Brothers would cover the debts. He warned the China house, however, not to make a formal request, since that would obligate them to reimburse Barings on demand. Patience and a cool temper were crucial now, and he advised the residents to stay clear of loans to the Hongs, extend no credits whatever, and begin assembling what cash they could. At home, Forbes beat a path between New York and Boston, dunning those whose bills had been protested and arranging a large shipment of ginseng to get funds in Canton while specie was suspended in America. The Barings did cover Russell & Co.'s outstanding bills throughout the spring, and by July all that remained for the house to do was to ship money to Barings as quickly as possible.[40]

Russell & Co. survived the panic of 1837 because of its solid reputation and the timely exertions of all the partners. The panic was an intense personal crisis for Forbes and the others involved because commerce was not yet covered by limited liability. In such a personal system of business, creditors holding bad bills pursued each endorser until they found one who could pay. Even at Canton Forbes had worried about credits, and now with a wider view from Boston, he could see the full extent of the abuses. After investigating the causes of the widespread failures, he decided that "the immense credit which has been obtained on little or no capital" lay behind "all the late stoppages." The reckless behavior he had managed to restrain in Canton had run totally out of control in the larger world, and the storm of retribution struck down the innocent with the guilty.[41]

When the emergency had passed, Forbes realized that the United States was gradually slipping out of the mainstream of the China trade. He found that he was no longer in the best position to direct that commerce or to influence the workings of Russell & Co. Forbes's new role in Boston was not yet clear, and his judgments were frequently challenged by the Canton residents. Moreover, his news from Boston was not as fresh as that out of London because he unaccountably failed to use the overland mail route he had introduced to the house. He was rebuked for giving Bennet Forbes authority to use the house signature and was severely reprimanded for charging commissions on house business while collecting a partner's share as well.[42]

A serious strain in relations among the partners came in the summer of 1838, when a young man named Joseph Coolidge, working with Baring's agent Joshua Bates in London, purchased a large shipment of British goods for Howqua in direct violation of the Hong merchant's orders. Coolidge claimed his authority through Forbes and Cushing. Forbes denied any part in the purchase and branded

Coolidge a scoundrel. The house threatened to hold Bates and Coolidge personally liable, while Howqua relieved Forbes of all authority to trade in his name. By the following summer Forbes had succeeded in mollifying Howqua, but Coolidge intensified his attack on Forbes, charging him with misappropriating £50,000. This personal quarrel was exacerbated by the diplomatic crisis in China over the opium traffic.

Russell & Co. stood firm until February 1839, when it officially abandoned the drug traffic. Business was at a turning point. War was threatening in China. The term of partnership was due to expire at the first of the next year. Forbes saw this as the time to capture Russell & Co. for his own family interests and then reduce his personal involvement in trade to a minimum. Although not unresisted, Forbes's reorganization was carried through, and in 1840 Robert Bennet Forbes was sent to Canton for the start of the new three-year term.[43]

It was now clear to John Murray Forbes that the China trade was an on-the-spot business. More than ever he viewed Russell & Co. as a place for deserving young men or embarrassed older ones to make a quick fortune and get out. His interest in controlling the house was in the power to name succeeding partners and to dip into that well himself should he ever face bankruptcy. Though safe at home now, he felt strangely vulnerable. His own fortune was scattered, much of it floating in outstanding personal loans and accommodation paper for friends or still tied up in foreign trade. He began collecting his resources and he adopted a very conservative policy toward trade: Ship only if the chance of gain is "very great but above all the chance of *loss very small*"; risk in trade at sea no more than you can afford to lose in that season.[44] John Murray Forbes appeared to be following the path of many older China hands who had salted down their fortunes in order to clip coupons at home by the fire. In fact he was discovering a richer and more exciting field for investment on land than he had found in the South Seas.

It is hardly surprising that a young man who had spent most of his few adult years in China and had missed the first stirrings of the Industrial Revolution in America came home in the late 1830s skeptical of the new spirit of enterprise that preoccupied the nation. In his last years at Canton, Forbes had demanded that Bennet invest his homebound funds, not in railways and manufactures, but in safe bank stocks and insurance firms. Once settled at home, however, he relaxed these restrictions. He began buying land, creating a large estate in Milton for his own future use. He cautiously built up a portfolio of land mortgages and interest-bearing securities of local transportation and manufacturing companies, whose principal owners he knew and trusted. He became the trustee for a number of family members and friends, and Howqua sent him nearly half a million in surplus capital to invest in American enterprises. Forbes slipped comfortably into the conservative role of investment manager for a much larger capital than his own fortune. He quickly extended his holdings into several sectors of the fast-moving American economy.[45]

Forbes's investments in the 1840s were clustered in four major areas of opportunity which lay at the core of American industrial development: land, iron, steam, and railroads. Both at home and in the developing West, Forbes indulged what he thought was a natural Scottish impulse to buy land. Except for local real estate and land mortgages, his extensive property holdings corresponded with his other major investments in iron and, later, in transportation. He intensely disapproved of the "dirty" practice of land speculation and usually justified his own involvement as being ancillary to his other developmental investments.[46]

Bennet Forbes's bankrupt Farrandsville Coal and Iron Company introduced John Murray to the iron business. John assumed the management of this Pennsylvania nail works after its accounts were lost in the panic of 1837. For two years he tried to nurse the company back to health, but its poor transportation facilities, incompetent technical staff, and voracious appetite for Forbes's capital finally forced him to cut his losses and sell the property. Undaunted he took an interest in the Mount Savage Ironworks. When this concern too ran into trouble, Forbes and Erastus Corning of Albany bought the property at auction, hoping to add "$200,000 in money" and make it "the great Iron Co. of this Country." Despite the firm's steady calls for capital and consistent failure to show much profit, Forbes stuck doggedly to Mount Savage until the late 1850s, when he renounced the iron business altogether. "Its [sic] a big business," he wrote to cousin Paul Forbes in 1859, "& ought not to be lightly touched by Amateurs like you & me."[47]

Steamships were a natural interest for a merchant with iron investments. Robert Bennet Forbes had dedicated his life to the sea, and he designed most of the ships in which John took an interest. Bennet's technological pioneering was no more successful financially than his other enterprises, and John's enthusiasm for ships cooled perceptibly by the late 1850s. Still, he allowed himself to be dragged into building "one last steamer" after another, which he hoped to sell in China or to the government in case of war. Inevitably, this line of business didn't pay well.[48]

Iron and steam, land and trade eventually converged on railroads, but Forbes entered that field more cautiously than he did others. While still in China in the middle 1830s, Forbes had concluded that American railways would fail "after the first few years; the wear and tear proves ruinous." Railroads were capital intensive and very risky; Forbes's lessons from trade had taught him to spread his risks even on the best of goods. However, when he returned from China and found that many of his old mentors like John Bryant and William Sturgis were involved in Boston's major railroads, his attitude softened. At first he took bonds in local roads, but within a few years he was buying stocks and bonds in New England companies for such conservative ends as his sister's dowry. Although he was still a passive investor with no role in railroad management, by 1843 he was routinely buying railroad securities for his trust accounts as well as himself. As the market picked up in the next two years, and as railroads proved their capacity to earn, Forbes's holdings spread into Maine, Connecticut, New York, and Pennsylvania, and his railroad enthusiasm expanded apace.[49]

When John W. Brooks approached Forbes in 1846 with a proposal to buy the Central Railroad from the state of Michigan, Forbes was not surprised. In the course of seven or eight years, he had made the difficult adjustment to a new career at home. He was becoming an ambitious capitalist, actively reaching out from Boston for the investment opportunities constantly thrown up by the rapid development of the West and a growing industrial economy. The focus of Forbes's career was shifting away from Russell & Co. by 1845, and he was already recognized as a major broker of funds for domestic enterprise. John Murray Forbes was not forced out of trade by its dwindling prospects; he was drawn by the positive attractions of the new domestic economy:

> I am rather inclined to Sell out my shipping, & turn my
> attention to Stocks and other things which I can manage myself.
> I am now making arrangements to buy some coal and Iron lands
> in Pennsylvania which I think very promising—then there's the
> Michigan RR. In fact every day there are openings for investment here which I think better than Trade & far less troublesome.[50]

As his business career was taking shape, Forbes also set his personal life in order. He divided his estate in Milton into spacious lots and tried to settle all his family and friends in a pastoral community there. Those he could not persuade to settle in Milton, he insisted on helping in business. He introduced young men to his business connections. He endorsed their notes and placed several of them for a term in the house of Russell & Co. He rescued his cousin Paul Forbes from bankruptcy in South America and sent him to Canton in 1842, where Paul stayed on as American Consul for many years. In return for his benevolence, Forbes assumed the right to advise and instruct these quasidependents—a task that he often performed with excessive zeal! This personal ambition might have been offensive had he not carried it off with such style and grace that most individuals found it comfortable to submit to his ministry.[51]

The exception was Bennet Forbes. John adopted a custodial generosity toward his brother that was nothing short of patronizing, and the offense was not lost on the older man. Since 1839, when Bennet's finances failed, John had pressed him to give up his thriftless habits. Failing that, he begged Bennet to retire altogether in 1843 and live off a trust fund administered by John. Reminding Bennet that his own fortune was great enough for both their expenses but not for both their losses, John finally snapped: "I shall never feel that I am rich & independent till I see you in the only true track—vis a rigid restriction of all your expenses clearly within your income." Independence was an obsession with Forbes, and he saw in Bennet that strain of "ill luck which dogged our Fathers actions."[52]

In his own affairs John Murray Forbes seemed to thrive on tension. His high brow, deep eyes, and long elegant nose, wreathed in the classical style by the remnant of his hair, lent a deceiving calm to his bearing that only partly concealed the nervous energy emanating from his mouth and hands. His mind would not rest. When he was not forging ahead with some bold new venture, he was frantically retrenching and clearing out his accounts. He searched constantly for system and order on the grandest scale, yet he could bring none to his own activity. He worked himself to exhaustion writing letters and making arrangements. "I wonder he don't go mad," wrote Bennet, "with his hurried and disorderly habits." John recognized his weaknesses and always commanded his correspondents to *"Do as I say & not as I do."* In the early 1840s he began a lifelong habit of "retiring." For the next forty years he periodically withdrew to Milton or Naushon Island for a retirement from which he soon emerged, each time returning to even bigger business. On his Milton estate he adopted the style of a country gentleman, a "farmer" as he insisted. "Squire" Forbes rode into Boston for the two hours at midday when merchants gathered at the exchange; but this was a pose, for the squire of leisure regularly sat at his desk at home all day without lunch or half the night by a taper writing the endless stream of letters that governed his business.[53]

In time Forbes's intensely personal style would become a liability as businessmen turned to the cooler bureaucratic methods of corporate management. But midcentury was a time of heroic entrepreneurs. Forbes coupled an almost tribal paternalism with the American ideals of republican virtue and liberal capitalism, pouring the whole into a new corporate mold. He recognized no clear division between his public and private life. His personal relationships and sense of duty flowed outward from his wife and children to relatives and friends, corporate stockholders, and political allies, blending into a general patriotic feeling for the nation as a whole. He began employing the limited liability corporation in business, but he perceived it as an extension of the family firm and the well-tempered commission merchant. Through the corporate device he could see himself performing a great public good, making a fortune building railways, and remaining in essence a merchant "in a liberal sense of the word."

John Murray Forbes was entering a period of global change more rapid and thoroughgoing than anyone had ever seen. By the 1840s the application of iron and steam and human ingenuity to systems of industry and transportation were causing almost daily changes in the commercial marketplace. Opportunities for gain (or loss) were multiplied as the revolution in transportation opened markets that had been closed to competition by geographic barriers. The productivity of labor was not only increased but revolutionized by the new methods of manufacturing, and agriculture in the United States was extended beyond the limits of imagination a generation before. Historically such extraordinary changes had been resisted by people who found their security in organic continuity and order, but in Forbes's generation the excitement of the possibilities overwhelmed the fear of disorder and a spirit of progress was born. The railroad became the symbol of a new world coming, and as Forbes embraced the future his vision soared: "I should like to build the first Rail Road in China!" More prosaically, he wanted to "join Boston to the Mississippi River!" With almost delirious confidence, men like Forbes began to redirect the flow of trade and annihilate the boundaries of space and time.[54]

2
An Assault on Space and Time

JOHN MURRAY FORBES'S years in China coincided with the pioneer decade of railway building in the United States. The late 1820s and early 1830s saw the first railroads constructed near seaboard cities and witnessed the emergence of a new spatial vision among commercial men. In the ten years before 1837, critical experiments in railroad technology were carried out. Engineers quarreled over the technical details of railway construction, while the public joined in a lively debate over the relative merits of railroads and canals. Forbes's absence from the American scene during this experimental decade left him ignorant of many details, but it also spared him the embarrassment and bitterness that many innovators felt when the panic of 1837 swept away the fruits of their labors. By the time the nation's economy had righted itself in the early 1840s, Forbes was in a position to see, with the clarity of a novice, that the structure of commerce in the American interior would be raised on footings of parallel iron rails.

By the middle 1840s, real evidence of the success of railroad technology was combined with a new excitement over industrial progress to produce the first American railway mania. Intense debates over the merits of railroads and canals, locomotives and horses, ensued. These stemmed from qualitatively different attitudes toward opposing systems of technology and culture. One was slow paced and and required only modest energy inputs; the other was vigorous and energy consuming. The two technologies offered as marked a contrast in styles as the popular images of a fire-breathing locomotive and a languid mule on a towpath. The men of Forbes's generation who embraced the new transportation system could scarcely predict its consequences, but the view from the foreground was benevolent and marvelous.

INVENTION BY INCREMENT

No such radical change in cultural values as the railroad engendered could be made by a single decision, and the key to the influence of railroad technology was its incremental development. The
railroad emerged from longstanding efforts in England and America
to improve the conditions of overland transport. In the United States
the railroad was born of a popular campaign for internal improvements that began after the Revolution. Interregional trade in the new
republic was frequently more expensive, uncertain, and time consuming than communication with London and the ports of Europe.
In fact, in 1790 the free navigation of sailing ships set the standard of
excellence in transportation: Canals, turnpike roads, river improvements, and the earliest railroads were all designed to bring inland
routes up to the level of efficiency of overseas travel.

The first improvements followed established routes, eliminating
sandbars, swamps, muddy roads, or short necks of land that blocked
obvious lines of travel and trade. Seaboard cities also turned their
attention inland to extend their market radius with turnpike roads,
canals, or river improvements. New York City set the competitive
pace, first with steamboats that offset the downstream flow of the
Hudson River, then with a revolutionary canal along the unique
water-level route to Lake Erie in the West. For American port cities
the race was on even before 1825, when the Erie Canal was completed. American engineers and entrepreneurs explored every means
of improvement with uncommon energy. The lure of the continental
interior was irresistible; the transportation revolution was at hand.[1]

Forbes was still a schoolboy at Round Hill when the first contest
to open the West began. By 1825 Boston, Philadelphia, Baltimore,
and cities down the coast had reached into their immediate hinter-
lands with turnpikes and canals. But the opening that year of an
interregional waterway from the Great Lakes to New York City
posed a serious threat to the future expansion of these marketing
centers. To compete for the inland trade, these cities must create
routes where none existed. In 1826 Pennsylvania launched its massive ill-fated effort to cut a canal through the rugged mountains in
the center of the state. Virginia interests set to work on a similar
canal through the Cumberland Mountains to connect the Ohio Valley with Washington City. Charleston, Baltimore, and Boston, with
less geographical encouragement than the Pennsylvania and Cumberland regions, pinned their hopes on railroad projects, which be-

fore 1830 were even bigger technological gambles than canals through the mountains.[2]

The concept of the modern steam railroad combined contemporary ideas about turnpikes and canals, the old hardware of the colliery tramway, and tenuous new experiments in steam locomotion. Like the canals a generation before, railroads were first considered special feeders to the established channels of trade and only gradually were recognized as general purpose thoroughfares in their own right. The British experience, which was contemporary with the American efforts, offered only the slightest precedent. Although the Stockton & Darlington Railway opened in England in 1825, steam power was not perfected until 1830, when the Liverpool & Manchester placed a locomotive in general service. Americans were seldom more than a few months behind the British in their experiments, and Boston men were among the first to study the question even if they were slow to build their first railroad.[3]

Responding to an appeal from Governor Levi Lincoln in 1826, the Massachusetts Board of Internal Improvements spent three years surveying ground and studying technical reports on the state of the railway art. The commissioners had been asked to prepare specific plans for two railroads to be built by the state—one from Boston to Providence, Rhode Island, and one from Boston to Albany, New York. Because they could see the whole road as a unit, the commissioners were satisfied with the Boston–Providence plan by 1828. They proposed, in effect, a limited access turnpike with iron-strapped stone rails mounted on parallel beds of masonry. Elaborate technical calculations of friction and elevations, energy and cost benefits, and materials and methods filled the pages of their report. Because tests had shown that horses endured short heavy exertions better than long continuous ones, an undulating road was thought to be cheaper to build and operate. The railroad would be single track, and carriages would run at fixed times in caravans, meeting at passing tracks according to schedule. Anticipating objections from the traveling public, the commissioners insisted that fixed schedules and rates of speed were simply a *successful* application of the principles of regular stagecoach lines. Finally they calculated the field of impact for the forty-four mile road. They estimated that a diamond-shaped area of "210 square miles," measuring ten miles wide at the midpoint of the road and tapering to a point at each terminal city, would be affected by the railroad. Within this field trade would increase and flow more quickly and cheaply to either of the terminal markets. The

Boston–Providence project was conceived as a relatively closed system whose costs and economic impact could be projected with some certainty.[4]

This impressive display of science and systematizing was wholly wanting in the Boston–Albany proposal. The commissioners were overwhelmed by the vast distance, the wildly rugged terrain, and the variables involved in operating such a road. At first, horse power seemed the only way to facilitate "that endless variety of loading, which a dense and industrious population requires," and the commissioners favored the "most simple system . . . which in practice will be found to comport with the common habits and opinions of the people." Further study suggested that steam traction might be needed "to move large loads . . . at a rapid speed," but such service was deemed inappropriate in western Massachusetts. In 1829 the commissioners finally recommended a double-track horse railway which, like a canal, would provide an improved route but not integrated transportation services. Dismissing the possibility of all-weather service, the commissioners simply assumed that the line would be closed by snow in the winter but reopened in the spring before canals or the common roads were passable.[5]

These Massachusetts reports were not convincing enough to persuade the government to undertake any railways at public expense. While private capital did take hold of the Boston–Providence line, the western project lay dormant for two more years. Experience alone would distinguish the proper method of railroad building, and Boston's wealthy entrepreneurs were in no hurry to invest in the unknown. Where construction was under way, as on the Baltimore & Ohio (B&O) Railroad, each section of track showed the benefits of experience from the previous section. The B&O quickly recognized this technical evolution and established its own engineering department in 1830 to conduct experiments and analyze the data collected along its own line. Proposals for roadbeds, rail patterns, materials, and weights were disputed and tested. Carriage, wheel, and locomotive designs were refined. The adoption of the steam locomotive after 1830 forced the major lines to use heavier rails, more substantial but flexible roadbeds, and long gradual curves and grades. Strap iron was replaced with rails of a T or H pattern weighing sixty pounds or more to the yard; rigid stone was replaced with more flexible wooden timbers for ties and undersills. As reported in Canton, these experimental railroads impressed John Murray Forbes as being imperfect and too risky for his purposes. Many of the railroads whose securities

he might have taken did suffer from rapid deterioration that con-
sumed their profits in constant rebuilding. Toward the end of the
1830s the basic technological components of the modern steam railroad were taking shape, but the experiments had often been costly.[6]

Technological hardware was only a small part of a functional
railroad system. The business organization of railroad companies in
the pioneer period underwent changes similar in many ways to the
reforms with which Forbes experimented in China. Although railroad companies were chartered corporations rather than partner-
ships like Russell & Co., the primary concern of both businesses was
the well-regulated flow of goods and information. Unlike the commission house, however, the railroad's large capital was literally fixed
on the ground.

Early American railroad charters were modeled on turnpike
companies, which had received limited rights and privileges in return
for a service of general public utility. Railroads not directly owned by
state governments were often granted limited liability, eminent domain, the right to collect tolls, and freedom from competing lines. In
return the railroads were declared "public highways" and subjected
to regulation of their rates and profits. The turnpike analogy soon
proved inadequate; the very nature of the railroad implied an operating monopoly as well. On a railroad the "public highway" and the
"common carrier" were one and the same. Rates of toll for use of the
road could not be distinguished from rates of fare or freight for transportation services. Individuals frequently raised legal challenges to
run competing trains on the same railroad line, but the railroad
companies successfully defended their monopoly status. Between
1834 and 1837 the states of Pennsylvania, New York, Massachusetts,
and Rhode Island clearly rejected the highway analogy as leading to
dangerous confusion on the railroads, threatening loss of life and
property, and impeding the very progress that railroads were designed to ensure.[7]

The establishment of operating monopolies was an important
victory for the railroad interests. Another system would have left the
owners of the road powerless against rate-cutting carriers who neither
maintained the roadway nor paid interest on the investment. Furthermore, as the traffic increased and technical improvements multiplied, companies found it essential to control both the equipment and
the operating procedures over their entire line. By the early 1830s a
few farseeing men, like D. K. Minor of the new *American Rail Road
Journal,* were already calling for a uniform track gauge and standard-

ized operations across the entire network, but most railroad men at the time were content to keep ahead of their own immediate problems. The experience of the first decade was neatly summed up in 1837 by William C. Young, superintendent of the Utica & Schenectady Railroad: "A Rail-Road and its fixtures, together with motive power, and persons operating the same, is but a single machine, and must be operated by one governing hand; more will destroy the harmony of its movements." Finance, construction, equipment, maintenance, scheduling, and train operations—all were so thoroughly interconnected that they must follow some central plan. As another superintendent put it succinctly, "This system must embrace the whole business."[8]

This body of technical experience provided the foundation for the idea of a communications revolution that would capture the imagination of John Murray Forbes in the coming decade. As early as 1832 the directors of the B&O Railroad claimed that a railway network could so bind the "most remote sections" of the country as to perfect and preserve the Union:

> The system, if advantageously applied and sufficiently extended, will give to the people . . . an identity of feeling, a harmony of interests, and a facility of social intercourse, which must . . . secure to our country all the advantages resulting from the productiveness of a mighty continent, with the conveniences of communication incident to a small island.[9]

Such enthusiasm for the promise of railroads spread rapidly in the middle 1830s and quickly outpaced the canal movement, then at its height. The image of speed and economy seen in these primitive railroad lines suggested limitless possibilities for an American technology "still advancing towards perfection." The railroad idea seemed to fit perfectly with Jacksonian America's restless drive to get ahead, and it was not long before its spokesmen were able to portray the new transport system as a symbol of prosperity and freedom. Conservative merchants like Forbes were drawn to the portrait of a "mighty" continental market, unified by the "harmony of interests" and free from the aggravating barriers they encountered in foreign trade. Once viewed as a possible intrusion on the "common habits" of the people, steam transportation by 1840 could be hailed by some as a "great moral agent" which would "increase the influence of men, and their virtue."[10]

When John Murray Forbes returned to Boston in 1837, he found that wealthy and influential men had taken hold of the railroad business. The panic of 1837 and the ensuing depression brought many railroads down and curbed the earnings of others, but the railroad idea survived unscathed. By 1840 there had developed a respectable American literature on railroads, and trade journals like Hunt's *Merchant's Magazine* carried features on the new industry. Books and articles offered a historical pespective, pointing out the follies of the early years and confidently predicting the perfection of the art. The question for Forbes and others in the early 1840s was no longer the technological viability of railroads but their profitability. Few of the lines built in the 1830s had returned the expected profits. Critics often cited government promotions of premature and unwarranted improvements as a cause. Private enterprise, they assumed, could satisfy the legitimate demands for transportation without saturating the market. No one doubted that, properly built and soundly managed, railroads would become a large and successful industry. Eastern commentators looked forward to the day when the numerous short lines could be forged into "continuous chains" of communication throughout the established regions of the nation and extending westward into the heartland of the continent. Intrigued by the prospects of a western market and convinced that railroads flourished best in the hands of private capitalists, John Murray Forbes saw a broad field for his personal talents in the development of the West.[11]

THE MICHIGAN SYSTEM

Pioneer conditions west of the Alleghenies gave rise to a dominant public role in railroad building in that region during the 1830s. The peculiar dilemma of western people stemmed from their tremendous need for transportation improvements and their great shortage of capital. Eastern lines were easily promoted between established market centers where private investment met demand relatively well. In the West, however, ambitious towns faced the difficult choice of taking hold of mammoth projects or trusting their fate to outside interests. Public enterprise became the popular solution to the West's transportation problems, and it resulted in a distinctly western view of the railroad itself. As early as 1832 an Ohio editor was denouncing the elaborate and expensive character of the Pennsylvania, the Baltimore, and the Massachusetts railroads. What the West required was a cheap, simple railroad, substantial enough to last twenty years "or long enough to pay for itself." The ground was flat; labor and materials were abundant. Horse power seemed clearly adequate for immediate needs. The important point was that the West needed a plain railroad now, not a "splendid" one at some future date.[12]

Unwilling to wait for the eastern lines to reach them and fearful of depending on outside corporations, in the 1830s the states of the Old Northwest launched ambitious systems of public works funded and built by the "people's governments." These projects were not necessarily ill conceived, but they were entirely financed with state debt and were barely under way when the panic of 1837 deflated their paper assets. Within a few years these state systems were bankrupt or nearly so, and their property was put up for sale. Sensing that the time was right for private enterprise to open this western region, in 1846 John Murray Forbes stepped in to rescue one of these faltering lines—the Michigan Central—and began his lifelong career in western development.

The Michigan Central Railroad, although primitive and unfinished, was the centerpiece of the Michigan internal improvements system. Agitation for improvements on the Michigan peninsula began as early as 1827 and intensified throughout the territorial period. By the early 1830s nearly everyone had agreed that a railroad would be both cheaper and more profitable than a canal across Michigan's level terrain. When a federal government survey in 1834 declared the "central route," running west from Detroit to Lake Michigan, superior from an engineering standpoint, the businessmen of that city organized their railroad company. Within a year the people of Michigan had convened their constitutional convention; and in the process of drafting their charter, they bound the new government to promote works of internal improvement in an "equal, systematic and economical fashion." In January 1837, a committee of the new state legislature adopted a plan for building state-owned trunk lines, leaving branches and feeders to local entrepreneurs. Conceived as an investment in the future, Michigan's internal improvements system was expected to yield an ample profit and "materially" reduce the public burden.[13]

The committee bill was designed to protect the general public from the predatory interests of private speculators and reserve any dividends for the taxpayers' benefit. In the Michigan legislature, however, it was quickly set upon by special interests and local partisans with their own particular claims. The final product was a cumbersome package including plans for three railroads and two canals across the state. Enabling legislation required equal expenditures on each of the projects, overriding any economic or engineering advantages that might be gained from a concentration of effort. Some legislators even tried to prorate liability for state debt according to actual expenditures in each county. Because its route had already been surveyed and partly improved, the Michigan Central Railroad progressed more quickly than the other projects. The result was increased jealously elsewhere in the state: When the depression stopped work on most of the system in 1839, partisans of another state railroad refused to give up their iron rails to the Michigan Central, where the trains at least were running. The antimonopoly sentiments of the people that had originally motivated the state-owned system were now turned against the government itself. "The interests of no one section of the State," proclaimed the angry citizens of Monroe, "should be sacrificed to the interests of a great Central Monopoly, or any other."[14]

Thus hampered by disgruntled democracy, the state Board of Internal Improvements could not even capitalize on its only successful project, the Michigan Central Railroad. Although the first thirty-mile section of the Michigan Central had opened in January 1838, the lack of funds slowed construction the following year. By the end of 1841 price competition from stagecoaches kept revenues on the Michigan Central at the level of costs. The commissioners assumed that a longer and more ambitious railroad might achieve the economies expected from the new technology, but financial failures of the Bank of Michigan and the Bank of the United States in 1839 left the board few assets with which to continue the work. Furthermore, experience had proved that the line was too lightly built to sustain the volume of traffic needed to make a profit.

The improvement of traffic and revenue on the Michigan Central Railroad in 1844–45 simply compounded the maintenance problems on the older portions of the line. In their report for 1845 the Michigan commissioners explained their quandary. The Central had shown that it could do a heavy business in freight at good rates, but now the road had to be completely rebuilt in the "most substantial manner" and laid with heavy T rail. Without immediate and extensive reinvestment the value of the work already done would be lost. Yet with the state's credit ruined and its other projects abandoned, it was both financially and politically impossible to spend more on the Central line. Accordingly, the board recommended the conditional sale of the property to private capitalists as the only feasible way to save the railroad.[15]

The proposal to sell the Michigan Central revealed a serious contradiction in western thinking. The people of Michigan preferred the system of free enterprise in an open market and feared that a *private* railroad corporation would control their market. At the same time, the simple, cheap railroad afforded by their primitive economy was quickly found to be inadequate to their needs. The growth and savings they demanded required a more "splendid" railroad than the state could provide. It seemed that Michigan wanted something it could neither afford nor do without. Stymied by the larger question, supporters of the sale focused on the inability of legislators to make the entrepreneurial decisions required in the railroad business, while their opponents charged that special interests in Detroit were conspiring to erect a private monopoly.

Such standard Jacksonian rhetoric concealed an important variation on the idea of a railroad that would increasingly distinguish western promoters from eastern developers like John Murray Forbes in the decades ahead. Many westerners already suspected that the concentrations of capital behind first-class railroad systems might somehow be used to reorient trade and determine the course of local development. Their initial defense was to improve local networks and encourage the free and rapid development of indigenous trade and industry. But their system was not working, and John Murray Forbes and his associates could provide both the entrepreneurial skills and the badly needed funds to build a proper railroad across Michigan. The proposed corporate system would free the railroad from legislative meddling and petty local interests, which the politically sensitive commissioners were bound to respect. Still, this corporate freedom might cost the local democracy its legitimate voice in determining economic growth. The people of Michigan had failed to make the railroad their public servant; now they wondered if Forbes would make it their master.

BOSTON'S INVESTORS

Two young men—John Woods Brooks and James Frederick Joy—who became Forbes's most trusted lieutenants over the next thirty years were directly responsible for bringing the Michigan Central to his attention in 1846. Brooks was a civil engineer. Born in

Stow, Massachusetts, in 1819, he was trained in his field by Laommi Baldwin in the middle 1830s. Brooks was chief engineer on the Boston & Maine Railroad in 1839 and worked in the lumbering business for four years before returning to railroads, in 1843, as superintendent of the Auburn & Rochester in upstate New York. He was interested in securing western connections for this New York line when he heard of the Michigan Central's possible sale. In the summer of 1845 Brooks paid a visit to Detroit to investigate the property as a possible investment for Erastus Corning of Albany and John E. Thayer of Boston.[16]

In Detroit, Brooks met with James Frederick Joy, a New Hampshire native who had acquired a keen interest in the railroad development of his adopted state. Joy was born in 1810 and was educated at Dartmouth College and the Harvard Law School. In 1836, after two years as a teacher, Joy took up his legal profession in Detroit and soon formed a partnership with George F. Porter, who was one of the Michigan commissioners of internal improvements. Both men were convinced that the state would never finish the Michigan Central Railroad, and Joy wrote several letters in Detroit newspapers agitating for the sale of the road. Joy and Porter were impressed with Brooks's connections in Boston, then the major center for railroad capital, and they agreed to support an offer from Brooks's friends. For his part, Brooks found the property sufficiently appealing to recommend it to his patrons in the East. While he prepared a lengthy report on the road for general publication, Corning and Thayer drew up a bill encompassing the terms of their offer, to present to the Michigan legislature in December 1845.[17]

The proposed charter for the Michigan Central Railroad Company listed several leading Boston capitalists among the incorporators, including Josiah Quincy, Jr., John Bryant, William Sturgis, John P. Cushing, Thomas Handasyd Perkins, and John Murray Forbes. When Joy presented the proposition to the Michigan legislature, however, he was met with a loud outcry against this band of "Yankee speculators." The initial hostility was gradually overcome, in part at least, because of the patient efforts of Michigan Governor Alpheus Felch. The governor encouraged the sale, emphasizing the importance of liquidating the state's debt. He admonished the legislators to reserve for the state such regulatory powers as they deemed prudent, being careful "to protect as fully as possible the public weal on the one hand, and not to defeat the possibility of a sale, by unusual restrictions and impractical requirements on the other." Within these boundaries an agreement was finally reached on March 28, 1846.[18]

The act of incorporation gave the new company protection against parallel railroads within five miles of its line. The location of the western terminus was left open, and the corporation was empowered to combine with steamers on the lakes. The sale price was $2 million in cash or securities of indebtedness of the State of Michigan, $500,000 due in six months, the balance with interest twelve months later. The acceptance of Michigan paper at par was an important advantage for the buyers because Michigan bonds in the market were selling at 75 or less. On balance, however, this was not a one-sided bargain. The state specifically reserved the power to regulate rates and to repurchase the road in twenty years at its market value plus 10 percent. The act set forth strict schedules for rebuilding the old sections and completing the new, all with sixty-pound T rail. Finally, the state fixed a tax on the capital stock and required that $300,000 of the shares be held in Michigan by at least 300 individuals.[19] The bargain was struck: If $500,000 was paid into the Michigan treasury by September 28, 1846, the company could take possession of its railroad.

In Boston, most of the leading mercantile figures who had chartered the Michigan Central withdrew before the capital campaign was under way. John E. Thayer, the Boston banker who had sponsored Brooks's original investigation, turned his attention to a more adventurous man like John Murray Forbes and asked him to head up a consortium of capitalists. Yet Forbes was initially cool toward the Michigan project and refused to lead until others had shown the way. Using Brooks as his technical advisor, Thayer set about gathering the pledges that would bring Forbes around.[20]

Despite his initial hesitancy, Forbes was a strong candidate on which to focus the Michigan Central campaign. He was well respected among the old moneyed elites in Boston and New York but still a young man of wealth and ambition who was not too heavily engaged in any one enterprise. His "retirement" from trade had dissolved into a multiude of commercial and industrial investments which by 1846 were turning out profitably. His business had grown larger than his personal fortune because of his access to credit and what he called "exaggerated ideas, outside of my means," deriving from his management of Howqua's money. Although his advice to the commission merchants at Russell & Co. remained strictly conservative, his domestic investments were becoming more daring. He was speculating in real estate as far away as Buffalo and in coal and iron lands at even greater distances. His railroad holdings were wider and now included more stocks as well as bonds. He admitted he was trying to "mix up some speculation with tolerable security" in his railroad investments.[21]

The general recovery of the economy since 1844 had also improved the western picture in the minds of prudent men like Forbes. He had lost nothing in the economic wreckage after 1837 and could view the future of the West with an open mind. The credibility of railroad enterprises was given an added boost in 1845 when the conservative analyst Freeman Hunt of the *Merchant's Magazine* endorsed them as good business investments—better than banks! Hunt further singled out a Michigan route as one western project worthy of immediate attention from men in the East.[22] In such a climate of chastened optimism men like John Murray Forbes, while unwilling to plunge, were open to persuasion.

John W. Brooks's *Report on the Merits of the Michigan Central Railroad* was a masterpiece of persuasion and a remarkable explanation of an integrated railroad system. Where the Michigan legislature had perceived a discrete trunk road, Brooks envisioned an entire system of transportation enterprise. Brooks examined the condition of the roadbed, superstructure, and permanent fixtures, noting their serious deficiencies and estimating the costs of improvement. He considered depots and warehouses an integral part of the transport system and found them wholly wanting on the Michigan Central. The topography of the route, he noted, was nearly flat, having its "steepest grades . . . descending eastward, which is favorable to the heavier freighting business of the line." Abundant hardwood forests offered ready supplies of fuel and timber, while the character of the soil made grading easy and would encourage the rapid expansion of agriculture along the line. Stepping back to view the part within the whole, Brooks considered the function of the Michigan Central in a combined route of railroads and steamboats from Buffalo to the West. He recommended swinging the Lake Michigan end of the line several miles south of St. Joseph to New Buffalo because, while St. Joseph was closer to Chicago by water, it was twenty-eight miles farther by stagecoach in winter.[23]

Despite the deterioration of the road itself and the inadequacies of its facilities, Brooks developed estimates of costs that compared favorably with his conservative projections of traffic and earnings. In fact the Michigan Central, in spite of its condition, was returning a

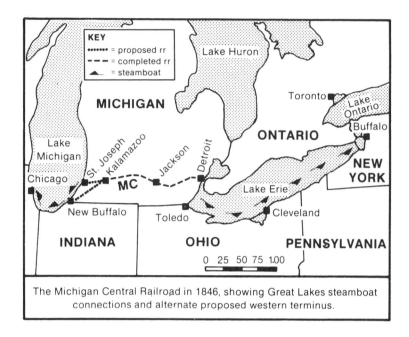

The Michigan Central Railroad in 1846, showing Great Lakes steamboat connections and alternate proposed western terminus.

profit even though it could handle only a fraction of the business brought to it. If the line were suitably constructed, properly equipped, and operated as an integrated enterprise, Brooks concluded, its potential for earnings as the country developed must exceed all his estimates.[24]

If Brooks's systematic treatise contained little that was new to men like Erastus Corning, who were already experienced in the railroad field, it provided a critical education for merchants like Forbes, whose ignorance of the technical details of railways made them hesitant to invest outside their circle of trusted friends. Forbes was confident that Brooks knew his business well, and on the assumption that the young engineer would actually carry out the work, Forbes determined to take hold of the Michigan Central without getting enmeshed in the details himself. Although he was deeply involved in business by 1846, Forbes still enjoyed his image as a squire of leisure. Excusing himself from the close attention and orderly business habits he expected in others, Forbes insisted he was a "farmer, a Tree Planter & a Hunter & now Prest. of the Michigan R. Road!!!" For no one except Brooks was the Michigan Central a major career focus at this time. Forbes and the other eastern men were finally induced to invest by the promise of profits of nearly 10 percent. Several individuals who took large shares were already holders of Michigan state securities that were unmarketable except in payment for the Michigan Central Railroad. The eastern directors wanted full control of the business in order to manage it as an investment for the recovery of their capital. Even Forbes saw the Michigan Central as a single money-making unit instead of part of a regional transportation plan. Already he considered himself "so deep in R. Roads & steam" that he ought to retrench, and he told his cousin Paul that he only accepted the presidency to "get the thing going & keep it warm" for brother Bennet.[25]

While he posed as a dabbler, Forbes nearly failed to "get the thing going" at all. As late as August 1846 the new owners had done nothing toward securing the down payment for the Michigan Central. The interested parties hung back, waiting for someone else to make the first move. Finally on August 18 the New Yorkers acted: Erastus Corning, D. D. Williamson, George Griswold, and Forbes's old China partner John C. Green each subscribed large blocks of shares. Presented at last with real pledges, Forbes and Thayer rallied the Boston men, and the Michigan Central Railroad Company was officially organized on the last day of the month. The payment was due in 28 days—too little time to raise cash from subscriptions. Forbes went straight to work gathering funds. He wanted Michigan securities and offered stock, bonds, or company notes to get them. D. D. Williamson accepted the railroad company's 7 percent bonds for the Michigan state paper held by the Farmers Loan & Trust Co. of New York; but Corning demanded notes at 60 and 120 days for his Michigan iron bonds.

The campaign was faltering by September 7. Brooks had "grown poor with anxiety & exertion." Forbes canvassed his friends in Boston, New Bedford, and New York, squeezing out all the cash and credits he could. With Michigan securities selling at $70 and accepted at par by the state, $350,000 would raise the necessary $500,000, but by mid-September Forbes was still $17,000 short. The first call on the stock was due September 15, and expecting that money shortly, Forbes made up the balance with his personal draft. The payment was made September 23, just five days ahead of the deadline. The Michigan Central was sold.[26]

If John Murray Forbes stepped lightly into railroad management in 1846, he quickly "stayed to pray." Brooks had detailed the improvements needed to upgrade the Michigan Central to its full potential, but it required more time, effort, and money than Forbes and the directors anticipated to bring these plans to fruition. Some of the lessons in management, organization, and local public relations Forbes had learned in China were applicable to the railroad business, but the scope and complexity of a railroad manager's duties were as yet far from clear. It was the experience of running the Michigan Central in the 1840s and 1850s that transformed the "liberal" young merchant into a railroad builder and western developer.

DISCOVERING A STRATEGY

The Boston directors' intention to exercise "the whole control and management" of the business conflicted with the technical necessity of placing engineer Brooks in charge of contracts and materials. Brooks was given his freedom on matters of construction on the basis of his own expertise, but he was soundly rebuffed a few months later when he interfered with Forbes's plans for an issue of 8 percent convertible bonds. Forbes gradually learned that railroad managers faced both technical and business problems which required different talents. He concluded that a close partnership between "business men" and "railroad men" was essential to the enterprise. The distinction blurred, however, in the field of operations, where technology governed costs, and the laws of commerce influenced rates and revenues. Here was the common ground on which the two men gradually found accommodation. As their first year in the Michigan Central drew to a close, Forbes and Brooks achieved a communion in theory and practice that would cement their trust and reliance in joint railroad endeavors for thirty years.[27]

Characteristically, Forbes's initial view of a railroad emphasized "trim" over grandeur. He enlarged this view slowly according to experience, but he was never enthralled by the sprawling systems later envisioned by James F. Joy or more famous "Empire Builders." Forbes wanted the scale of the railroad to fit the natural growth of the territory and not run too far ahead of local demand. His sense of natural pace was greatly reinforced in 1847 by his first trip to the Michigan country and Chicago. He was overwhelmed by the "*size of the* Country" but also its incredible rudeness. He did not doubt that the region had a great future, but he saw no need for haste. It would take years of hard work to transform such a wilderness into civilization. After touring the soggy streets of frontier Chicago, Forbes agreed it would some day be their logical terminus; but his immediate goal was to rebuild the first section of the line where traffic was already heavy. Economic growth would naturally spread westward in the region if it were properly fed from the eastern edge. The western shore of Michigan and the territory beyond, however, must have time to grow into its future importance.[28]

To best implement this developmental strategy of repair and extension, Forbes and Brooks reformed the entire operating system of the Michigan Central with an eye to economy and the encouragement of business. Forbes considered it the "true policy of the Company to simplify their business to the utmost" by performing only those services that were the "usual business of rail road transportation." He was soon forced, however, to build steamers to protect the railroad's business from an "organized steamboat combination on the lakes." Since his experience in China, Forbes had detested cutthroat competition; now he rejected price warfare as a means of breaking the steamers, trusting instead that "regularity in fares, speed and comfortable arrangements" would capture the traveling public soon enough. In the freight end of the business, Brooks recommended large, slow trains as most economical. Looking toward the future, he urged local farmers to diversify into coarse grains like corn as insurance against wheat failures, and he established a new schedule of rates that discriminated in favor of these cheap, bulky commodities. Of course, each improvement that streamlined operations injured certain local interests dependent on breaks in the flow of transportation. Although Forbes recognized the plight of the forwarding merchants, he felt they must not be allowed to impede the general progress of the territory. "Where we hurt one of these Gentlemen we shall help and conciliate a dozen farmers."[29]

The complaint of the Michigan forwarding merchants was only the first example of local hostility to developmental railroad builders. Instead of spreading that "identity of feeling" and "harmony of interests" that Forbes liked to expect, major railroad lines disrupted the whole structure of market relations that had traditionally served wagon and water transportation. The conflict was endemic to the change in transportation systems, yet the parties involved continued through the next several decades to personalize the injury, and local interests conveniently blamed outsiders for their displacement. From the beginning Brooks and Forbes were in perfect agreement about the importance of developing local business. The economic growth of the railroad's territory was the foundation of value in the enterprise. Forbes could never comprehend local opposition to their efficient services and rational reforms; he had forgotten what the Massachusetts commissioners had recognized in 1828: that the modern steam railroad might not "comport with the common habits and opinions of the people."[30] In a raw frontier society like Michigan in the late 1840s, even such obvious reforms as faster passenger trains and heavier, more frequent freight trains precipitated attacks from the public that developed into a bizarre guerilla war along the line of the Michigan Central.

So long as the Michigan Central Railroad had been state property, the administration found it politically expedient to pay in full any claims for damages to stock or property along the line. An antique law that gave cattle the "freedom of the common" was cited to establish the railroad's liability for stock wandering on the track. When the line became private property in 1846 the legal basis for these claims was thrown in doubt, while the more frequent and speedier trains increased the number of such incidents. Brooks denied company liability for stock allowed to trespass on the railroad's right-of-way, but he agreed to pay one-half of any bona fide claim if personal hardship had resulted. Farmers along the line were outraged by this policy and charged that reckless operations by the company had made the Michigan Central "one gore of blood." In the spring of 1849 sporadic acts of violence quickly took on the appearance of an organized conspiracy. Throughout the summer, night raiders obstructed or loosened tracks and opened switches to derail Michigan Central trains. Woodpiles and bridges were burned, and night trains were pelted with rocks and debris—and occasionally gunfire. Efforts to resolve the issue proved fruitless, and farmers refused to fence their land at the price the company offered. The winter season curtailed traffic, and the violence subsided until the spring of 1850, when rate discrimination inspired renewed attacks.[31]

Confronted with another season of violence and bad feeling, Brooks hired undercover agents to flush out the "conspirators." Finally, after the Detroit depot was torched in November, Brooks took action. Working back from the Detroit fire, he assembled his evidence of a longstanding conspiracy against the railroad. Forty-four men were arrested in April 1851, and a highly publicized trial began that summer. The trial became a cause célèbre for the "locofoco" elements in Michigan society, and William Seward of New York was called in to conduct the defense. In a gothic twist, the chief "conspirator" died in the steamy Detroit jail August 14, before a verdict was returned. The railroad was vindicated in the courts, but the popular rancor ruined the company's image as a local benefactor. The political farce was complete when the Democratic state administration deserted its own partisans to defend the corporation, and the Whigs took up the cause of the martyred renegade. The whole affair defied rational explanation and convinced Forbes ever after that popular resistance to his railroad policies was the work of demagogues and madmen.[32]

While its popular image deteriorated in Michigan, the company was earning respect in the financial community. Forbes entered the money market several times for modest sums and succeeded in raising over $6 million for the road in the first three years. After the initial crisis over the down payment, funding had gone exceedingly well, and by June 1847, Forbes was fascinated with Michigan and railroads in general. The market was accelerating rapidly after long dull years of depression, and Forbes, along with everyone else, was caught up in the excitement. Discounts were so high by the autumn of 1847 that 7 percent bonds would not sell, and Forbes was forced to issue 8 percent convertibles in minimal amounts to carry on construction. With such high rates prevailing, Forbes was irritated by the reluctance of Europeans, and some of his American friends, to take up his offers.[33]

When the pressure broke in a short crisis in the winter of 1848-49, Forbes and John E. Thayer gave their personal notes at very high rates to the railroad to meet its interest and current accounts. By finally applying the December dividend to the construction account, Forbes preserved the credit of the road. Other firms did not survive, and Forbes's own losses in Reading Railroad stocks reminded him not to plunge into anything he could not control. His own Michigan Central was completed to New Buffalo on Lake Michigan in April 1849, but Forbes knew that inflation from California gold would derange the market again. To avoid selling bonds at a heavy discount he raised $700,000 in October on a short note for extension to Michigan City and further equipment on the line.[34]

Costs ran well ahead of estimates on the Michigan Central, but Forbes insisted his budget was conservative for a western railroad. In his report for 1849 he praised Brooks's achievement and explained that the $2 million worth of additional expenses arose from the company's policy of building for the future, with large depots, heavy iron, and substantial foundations. In order to stimulate demand in a new territory, a developmental road like the Michigan Central would first have to show an excess capacity. Immediate commercial success,

therefore, depended on garnering a large share of the valuable passenger traffic in the first years until the productivity of the country
increased. Severe price-cutting by established steamboat lines and an
outbreak of cholera that curtailed travel in the West cost the company its profits in the first year of service to Lake Michigan. Brooks
claimed that conditions in 1850 were so abnormal as to furnish "no
data by which to judge" the through traffic potential, while local
business was "just budding into a growth quite certain to more than
meet the most sanguine expectations" of the railroad's friends.[35]

Forbes was learning that these "sanguine expectations" were
easily frustrated. Regional economic growth stimulated competition,
and competition drove down the price of transportation. Carriers
were forced to do a volume business on the long haul, yet local trade
was the mainstay of a railroad line. Forbes's initial reaction to this
strategic dilemma was to avoid dependence on through business and
concentrate on steadily building that business that belonged exclusively to the Michigan Central. In the fast-growing West this was
tantamount to standing still, and Brooks quickly convinced him that
the company would have to promote through traffic in order to
spread rising costs outside the local territory. By 1851 Forbes agreed
that the Michigan Central must become a link in the "great chain of
communication" between the East and the West: "By doing so we
hope to be enabled eventually to reduce our local rates without de-
creasing our profits, and thus conduce to the interests of the country
adjacent to our line, and at the same time establish such a regular
business over our road, as will not be easily affected by short crops in
one state, or by any local causes."[36]

FIRST STEPS WEST

Forbes and Brooks had mastered the financial, commercial, and
technical affairs of their first railroad. They had kept it trim and
efficient, and they were finally paying the large cash dividends that
most eastern directors had expected from the start. Both men were
opposed to branch line constructions which all too easily burdened a
railroad and proved, according to Brooks, "universally disastrous."
Forbes was pleased to report in 1850 that private entrepreneurs in
Michigan were building several plank roads which "promise to give
us all the advantages of so many branches, without the inconvenience
and loss" that accompanied branch railroads. But even as a trim

stem line the Michigan Central soon needed a strategy for expansion. The sudden burst of growth and investment in the upper Middle West after 1850 drastically compressed the period when innovators could reap monopoly profits. Much sooner than Forbes expected, the "eventual" necessities of reducing rates and defending territory pressed upon the Michigan Central.[37]

The competitive pressure on the Michigan Central was caused by the mushrooming city across the lake. More rapidly than its promoters predicted, Chicago had risen from the swampy shores of Lake Michigan to become a booming center for the grain and lumber trade of the western Great Lakes. By midcentury the young city had been identified by merchants around the country as the next metropolis, and the inevitable race was on to open Chicago to rail transportation. Forbes assumed that the ferry connection with that western entrepôt must one day be replaced by rails, but he and the other eastern men had taken a leisurely view of their head start in the region. On the basis of Brooks's report in 1846, they had dismissed any route around the south shore of Lake Erie and across the old Southern line in Michigan as unattractive. By 1850, however, the formation of competing trunk lines west from New York City had confounded Brooks's earlier view. The Michigan Central was spurred to action when a group of New Yorkers bought the Michigan Southern and the Northern Indiana Railroad and began pushing an inexpensive trunk line straight for Chicago.[38]

Among the Michigan Central's owners, it was James F. Joy who first understood that the time for westward expansion was already at hand. A thick, broad-faced man, a promoter by temperament, Joy was the perfect western counterpoint to Forbes's Boston polish. He had lived in Detroit since the middle 1830s, and he was restless to develop the West. After arranging the sale of the Michigan Central, Joy had been retained by the new eastern owners to manage the legal and political interests of the road. Working closely with other promoters and with various state legislatures in the western region, he became a master strategist in the game of competitive construction. As early as 1848 he had arranged to purchase the Northern Indiana Railroad charter for $50,000. Brooks recommended the deal, but Forbes and the other directors insisted that the Chicago extension was premature. By the following year Forbes had seen his mistake, but the Indiana charter had already gone to the rival. Joy was stymied by Michigan Southern interests in the Indiana legislature and finally made an arrangement with the New Albany & Salem Railroad in October 1851. That line was empowered to build branches anywhere in Indiana, and for half a million dollars it agreed to build a priority "branch" around Lake Michigan.[39]

Forbes always claimed he had good reasons for balking at the Chicago extension, but in truth it was a serious mistake. The Indiana lease was inordinately expensive, and the new plan depended on a connection with the Illinois Central outside Chicago near the state line, which the Chicago city council promised to fight. Temporarily out of options and out of time, Forbes agreed to Joy's proposal, that they build six miles into Illinois without a charter in order to beat the Michigan Southern into Chicago. Crews worked all winter in 1851-52. The Michigan Central ran its first train into Chicago on May 21, 1852, just one day ahead of its southern rival.[40]

Forbes had slipped out of a tight spot, but not without engaging in the kind of business he openly condemned in others. He had built without a charter, exposing the company to damages without so much as legal standing in an Illinois court. He had contracted to purchase Illinois Central securities without director approval. For two years only his closest associates on the Michigan Central board knew exactly what he was doing in Illinois. Then in 1854 he blandly accounted for competition "carried on by us at considerable temporary disadvantage." The episode was laid to rest.[41]

By the end of 1852 the discrete boundaries that had marked the Michigan Central a mere six years earlier lay shattered by the combined pressures of competitive investment from the East, the precipitant growth of Chicago to the West, and the technological advantages of the evolving railroad system. The natural territorial monopoly on which the Michigan Central once depended was now threatened by hostility among local interests and the invasion of rival long lines connecting the major commercial centers. Forbes now acknowledged that no reasonable man could expect to monopolize so vast a flow of traffic as was destined to come out of Chicago. No single line, no matter how well situated, could expect to rest on its laurels one year and retain its share of the business the next. Control of the territory was a fleeting advantage at best; successful railroading required a constant commitment of time, energy, and money.[42]

Forbes was facing a turning point in his career. He could move into more intimate involvement with the management of railroads, but he preferred to go the other way. Anxious to draw back from details and regain his perspective as a general entrepreneur, Forbes hoped to make Brooks the "ostensible head" of the Michigan Central given that Brooks had "long since been its real Manager!" Part of this decision reflected Forbes's old impulse to retire, but it was also consistent with his growing conviction that a division of labor must exist between the capitalist and the technician, especially in "all enterprises carried on at an arm's length."[43] Forbes saw the business world in tiers, each more general than the one below. Atop the hierarchy sat the "large capitalist," the coordinator of responses to the opportunities of the market. This kind of generalist formed a bridge between the private corporation as an instrument of business and the natural rhythms of the economic system itself; he arbitrated the needs of the firm and the needs of the commonwealth. The recent race to Chicago doubtless reminded Forbes of the intrusions of reckless bounders in old Canton at the opening of trade. He knew from experience with cutthroat competition that the victory went to the entrepreneurs who tended to business and kept a cool view of the larger picture. Details belonged to technicians like Brooks and Joy; his own role was to balance the whole.

Forbes's qualifications for the job of overseer stemmed largely from his broad range of commercial involvement, which he maintained even as his railroad career unfolded. Investments in iron and coal complemented his railroads, and he used the transportation connections on occasion to speculate in foodstuffs. His old connections with the China trade also gave him a market in which to generate funds that were not otherwise linked to the fortunes of American industrial enterprise. Forbes made no secret of his outstanding record in trade when offering securities to reluctant investors at home and abroad. Especially as his pioneer railroads reached toward the Mississippi River and beyond, his personal assurances played a vital role in finance. He relied on a circle of friends whose resources he could tap and whose notes would sell "where the best Railroad securities would be thrown out." He frequently endorsed with his own name the notes of his weaker corporations in order to market them in the street—always taking his discount for the service. Sometimes he substituted his own notes if he could "get the money cheaper" that way. For his own protection Forbes made it a rule to buy stock as well as bonds of new railroads, symbolizing his confidence and securing his influence in the firm. Most importantly, Forbes established a pattern of selecting carefully, then plunging boldly to insure that "good things" were put through.[44]

Support for John Murray Forbes's developmental enterprises derived from a loosely organized team of experts in the field and capitalists in the East. The nucleus of this "Forbes Group" grew out of the Michigan Central adventure. Brooks with his technical skills and Joy with his political talents were the primary field men. They scouted the western scene for good railroad properties that offered strategic advantages. As information and advice streamed eastward Forbes gathered up resources to support his western hands. John E. Thayer and his brother Nathaniel, who managed many of the fortunes of Boston traders, often served as Forbes's brokers for securities. At the same time Forbes drew his personal connections from the China trade—John C. Green, George and John N. A. Griswold, and Edward King of New York, for example—into his regular circle of "friends." Edward L. Baker represented the interests of New Bedford capitalists, many of them friends and relatives of Forbes's wife, Sarah. Erastus Corning and later his son maintained a close, if always independent, connection with Forbes's enterprises. Finally, Forbes constantly attracted young men, new talent from old families who either needed a boost or wanted to invest their funds from trade and so took a place under the paternal umbrella of Forbes's favor.

The method by which Forbes guided this group was inspired by James F. Joy's original plan for the Chicago extension—and Forbes's mistake in not accepting the offer. Determined not to be caught short again, yet still unwilling to guarantee long lines through barren country, Forbes encouraged local investors to show him the way in a new territory like Illinois. By moving gradually into these struggling roads, Forbes could hedge his strategic commitments and use the ambitions of local businessmen as a lever against trunk line competitors, hostile legislatures, and reluctant eastern investors. This pattern became fixed policy west of the Mississippi River, but it originated in the formation of the Chicago, Burlington & Quincy (CB&Q) system.[45]

Even before the Chicago link was secured, James F. Joy had been looking for outlets toward the Mississippi River. Forbes was readily convinced that Illinois was the next bonanza and was soon tempting his London associates with its praises:

> Imagine a deep black soil, almost every acre of which can be entered at once with the plough, and an enormous crop secured the first season, but where the very fertility and depth of the soil make transportation on common roads almost impracticable at the season when produce ought to be sent to market, and this region now for the first time opened to a market by railroad.

Forbes quietly bought stock in the Aurora Branch Railroad; in February 1852 John W. Brooks was named a director of this tiny road with twelve miles of its own line and trackage rights into Chicago. The Aurora Branch was hardly a western outlet for the Michigan Central, but it was a base from which the Forbes group could discreetly maneuver more extensive connections.[46]

Local promoters had the next move. Joy was thoroughly acquainted with the railroad projects in Illinois, and he knew already that several towns in the middle of the state were locked in a contest to destroy each other. Three projects of interest were pending: the Peoria & Oquawka (P&O) and the Northern Cross, both through Knoxville, and the Central Military Tract (CMT), from Galesburg toward Chicago. In the spring of 1852 these lines were deadlocked without funds, when Chauncy Colton of Galesburg encountered Elisha Wadsworth of the Aurora Branch, and James W. Grimes, a director of the P&O from Burlington, Iowa, in a Boston hotel. The three men discovered that their interests could be joined by a railroad connecting the Aurora Branch, the CMT, and the Burlington Branch of the P&O. Sensing a breakthrough, they hurried off to present the package to John C. Green, George Griswold, and John Murray Forbes. The interviews went well, and the western men were sent to see Brooks and Joy in Detroit.[47]

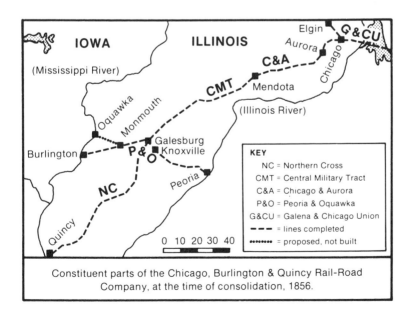

Constituent parts of the Chicago, Burlington & Quincy Rail-Road Company, at the time of consolidation, 1856.

Given the right terms, Joy could be satisfied with Colton's proposal, but some Illinois men saw another angle. In June 1852 Illinois
Governor William McMurtry, a CMT director, informed Colton
that "We have friends of the Chicago and Rock Island [Michigan
Southern] here and also the Aurora Branch road [Michigan Central]
striving with each other for our road, so I think we shall be able to
make a bargain with one or the other to our advantage." Joy played
his hand carefully. He knew that the Rock Island was only bidding
to block the Michigan Central. In late July he arrived in Galesburg
with a book of subscriptions already pledged to construct the Central
Military Tract. The money would be available as soon as local investors subscribed $300,000 of the stock.[48]

The figure was staggering. Chauncy Colton gathered $250,000
in pledges, but Joy would not accept this amount. Finally Colton and
fellow merchant Silas Willard pledged the balance. In October,
$800,000 of new stock was issued—the bulk of it already subscribed
by J. C. Green, George Griswold, J. M. Forbes, J. E. Thayer & Bro.,
Brooks, Joy, and a few others. Brooks and Joy and two other Michigan Central men were elected to the board. The directors met that
same day to amend the bylaws, issue mortgage bonds secured by
Forbes and others as trustees, and elect new officers. The Forbes
group had taken over, and within a year the Illinois stockholders
could not even hold a meeting until Joy arrived with the eastern
proxies.[49]

Eastern money now controlled the Aurora Branch and the Central Military Tract. These two corporations, in turn, subsidized the
Peoria & Oquawka to Burlington and the Northern Cross from
Galesburg to Quincy. Once completed, they would form a Y-shaped
system running southwest from Chicago and branching in the middle
of the state to touch the Mississippi opposite Burlington, Iowa, and
near Hannibal, Missouri. Starting in June 1853, construction and
traffic contracts channeled money from the main stem into the
branches. The Central Military Tract itself was completed by December 1854 and was placed under joint management with the Aurora (already named the CB&Q) the following March. The line to
Burlington opened later that year, and the Northern Cross reached
Quincy in late January 1856. Although corporate technicalities kept
the P&O and the Northern Cross legally independent for several
more years, the consolidated Chicago, Burlington & Quincy was approved by the stockholders on July 9, 1856.[50]

The evolution of the CB&Q showed the benefit of lessons

learned in the Michigan Central project. This time, in questions of strategy, Forbes deferred to Brooks and Joy "who thoroughly understand it *which I do not.*" As early as November 1852 Brooks was explaining to Forbes exactly how the pieces could be fit together—including even the Hannibal & St. Joseph in Missouri. Joy set up a timetable for construction of the separate units, and Brooks took care of such details as running several lines into Galesburg to get competition for depot sites and drive down the price of land. The two Detroit men arranged all the charter amendments, leases, and contracts, setting everything in order for eventual consolidation.[51]

The slow adaptation of local corporations was particularly important to Forbes's financial campaign. Local stockholders and directors were kept in the foreground as long as possible, both to quiet resistance to outside "monopolists" and to verify Forbes's assertion in the East that these were truly popular projects. Joy and Brooks personally loaned money to Colton and others for meeting assessments on their large subscriptions. The multitude of separate companies suited Forbes exactly. He used the bonds and paper of the CMT, which he controlled, to raise funds for the weaker units which he could not openly endorse. This procedure nearly bankrupted the CMT in the spring of 1854, and Brooks met the emergency by drawing on Forbes personally for cash while a second mortgage bond issue was readied. Forbes rescued the operation a second time in March 1855, when he cancelled $200,000 in CMT notes in exchange for a large package of new securities. Finally in 1856, the creation of a solid new CB&Q system strengthened the overall enterprise and replaced the securities of struggling components with those of a large new system.[52]

Complementary teamwork had created the CB&Q. The key to Forbes's method was the careful interaction of local ambition with outside direction. Brooks and Joy assembled the chaotic interests of small town entrepreneurs into a rational railroad network, and Forbes developed that plan into a financial promotion which eastern capitalists could accept. Sound in its logic and elegant in its division of labor, Forbes's method sought to rationalize the transportation revolution and launch an organized assault on space and time for the maximum benefit of East and West. At once conservative and visionary, John Murray Forbes tried to impose on his railroads the ordered systems of trade and investment that stood out so boldly in his mind's eye view of the capitalist system. If his efforts to temper the clash of interests in a free market proved frustrating, his insistence on keeping the long view would serve him well in the decades ahead.

Forbes himself, exhausted and ill from overwork, retired to Naushon Island for the coming 1857 summer season. In the year just past he had cleared out much of his personal debt, resigned his Michigan Central office, and brought his companies into stable condition. He proclaimed an end to his railroad career; yet even as he wound up the business of a decade, he was plotting his strategy for the next: "I am thinking a little of moving out some of my more saleable & settled R. Rd stocks in to the *wilder* & more promising ones having some *Land* basis attached."[53] He had joined Boston to the Mississippi River and now he faced the broad expanses of the trans-Mississippi West.

Both eastern and western men were now aware of the fact that a revolution in geography was at hand. The pioneer farmers who had crossed the "Father of Waters" in the 1830s once believed that they were nearing the limits of American expansion. Easterners, in turn, had once assumed that as the forests and the rivers disappeared from the landscape so too would the prospects for settlement, agriculture, and trade. But by the 1850s the incredible advances in steam transportation had cast the western prairies and the continent itself in an entirely new light. The wilderness state of Iowa was just four years old when California was admitted to the Union, and the sweeping faith with which men dismissed the barren miles between them foretold the future.

As early as 1854, two years before the railhead had even reached the Mississippi, both Forbes and his competitors had recognized the inevitable pressure to extend through the next tier of states. To be safe, Forbes took an interest in both the Hannibal & St. Joseph in Missouri and the Burlington & Missouri River in Iowa. Each of these projected roads fed the CB&Q at one of its Mississippi terminals, and the eastern investors needed time to see which would become their new main line. What they could barely sense and surely not yet understand was that here, in the great flat boundless West, the conditions, the pace, and the very idea of development would be radically transformed.

3

To the Frontiers of Settlement

FOR JOHN MURRAY FORBES and his generation, the West was the future. Certain greatness attended the continental empire of the United States; the glory of the republic was locked in the promise of interior lands. Like many eighteenth-century merchants, Forbes had built his house to face the sea, but now his gaze was fixed westward. His mind's eye pictured a vast region spreading before him, open and empty, yielding wealth and abundance to the advancing industrious American pioneers. Idealized in his view, the great West was inexhaustible, a storehouse of food and raw materials which merchants like himself might bring to the world according to the demands of the market. The key to this national treasure, for Forbes, was the regulated investment of eastern capital.

Developmental enterprise, as John Murray Forbes conceived it, was never truly popular in the frantic days of the American westward movement. Forbes's initial railroad experience in Michigan had already suggested the difficulties of coordinating investment with local aspirations. The Michigan pioneers' fear of dependency on outside capitalists turned to violence against their own much-needed railroad, and the problem of capital formation in a new country was only exaggerated as the railhead moved closer to the frontier of settlement. All driven by the chance of gain, pioneer farmers and townsmen spread onto new lands while railroad promoters stretched their iron tentacles into unspoiled country. Spontaneous settlement and competitive construction intersected at the Mississippi River in the 1850s. West of the river in Iowa, the broad expanse of unbroken prairie was at once a barrier to immigrants and an invitation to internal improvement unhindered by prior development.

Iowa was never the center of the Chicago, Burlington & Quincy route, but it presented Forbes with the first real opportunity for synchronized development according to a rational plan. Of course pioneer communities and other outside developers continued to scramble for control of this rich new territory, but there were far fewer interests already entrenched and there was no burgeoning Chicago on the other side to ruin the plans of a patient builder. If ever the railroad could set the pace of development, Iowa would surely be the place. Forbes would step into Iowa as he had Illinois, by offering aid to local promoters; but as quickly as their hopes would rise, so would these partners in growth clash over the speed and purpose of development in the American West.

PIONEER IOWA

American settlement on the west bank of the Mississippi began in earnest in 1833, when Indian titles to the "Black Hawk Purchase" were officially extinguished. Coming mostly from the south-central states, pioneers followed the river network into the rich lands of eastern and southeastern Iowa. Technically these immigrants were squatters living ahead of the government survey, so they created rude instruments of self-government to maintain the peace and administer their land system. Their number grew steadily. By 1837 more than 10,000 persons lived west of the river in the Iowa district; a new sovereign state was already in the making.[1]

Most early Iowa settlers shared a basic Jacksonian faith in their free and equal right to the opportunities abounding in their new land. Two attitudes marked these infant communities: a fierce dedication to local democracy and an equally intense attachment to individual free enterprise. Iowans portrayed their new home as a land of freedom and simplicity, more virtuous than either the urbane East or the sumptuous planter South, but their behavior was seldom as lofty as their self-image. Young James W. Grimes, one of the few early Yankees in the Burlington area, highlighted the incongruity in these pioneer communities: "Here is a fine field for any one who has industry, prudence, and economy, or a speculating turn." Land claims that were piously limited to the size of a single farm could be bought and sold without limit by local men, but speculation by "foreigners" was a "species of gambling" uniformly denounced.[2]

Despite this weakness for "dealing," the early settlers continued to observe the detailed protocol of moral economy that had once characterized traditional communities. Into their new land they invited only merchants "who trade on their own capital," and farmers and tradesmen with "energy of character." Iowa would be "a poor man's paradise." Once the broad agricultural foundation was laid, enterprising capitalists might raise up small mills and manufactories "at a trifling expense" and in time bring the economy into perfect balance. Here was the Jeffersonian hope reborn—a yeoman's society in balance with home manufactures yet free from urban decay and a planter aristocracy.[3]

By 1844 a partisan majority of Iowa's settlers was demanding statehood. Iowa Democrats were anxious to end the humiliation of territorial status and to share in the "liberal donations of land" that were promised from Congress for improvements, schools, and public works. Congress rejected the first application because of a boundary dispute, but on December 26, 1846, Iowa finally joined the Union. The partisan color of the new state could be seen in its constitution. The brief charter lodged almost all authority in the legislative assembly. State debts were prohibited, to protect the people from such "political gamblers" and "speculators" as had recently bankrupted Iowa's sister states in the Old Northwest. Banking was also denounced as a fraud perpetrated under the cloak of state authority. Special corporations were disallowed; credit and enterprise were expected to follow "natural channels." The Whig minority protested bitterly that these provisions introduced party creed into organic law, but the Democrats were not fazed. Their battle cry for 1846 was simple: "less legislation, few laws, strict obedience, short sessions, light taxes, and no State debt."[4]

The prohibition of banking, special corporations, and state debt made internal improvements practically impossible to finance in Iowa. Western states were understandably wary of massive public works after the recent financial disasters in Illinois, Indiana, and Michigan, but their reaction left no mechanism by which the work could be done. This political dilemma was longstanding. Since John Quincy Adams unveiled his monumental plan for national development two decades before, the party of Jackson had strenuously opposed both federal internal improvements and private corporations of privilege. By the time Iowa was admitted to the Union, western Democrats were hard put to reconcile their urgent need for transportation with the political creed of their national administration. Iowa Democrats looked to federal land grants for their salvation. Free land could be used to fund projects selected and administered by the local authorities without violation of the federal Constitution. Such a grant was made to Iowa in 1846 to improve the Des Moines River, but the project proved to be a long and scandalous failure. Moreover, the exciting and flexible railroad network had captured the public's attention; in the late 1840s congressional generosity shifted to the trunk line railroads. Perfection of the river system, once the great hope of the American Democracy, was not to be realized in the trans-Mississippi West.[5]

Shifting politics alone did not frustrate this water-based theory of "democratic" improvement. The prairies of Iowa were simply not endowed with an intersecting network of streams like the Ohio Valley. In fact, the very plainness of topography provided no key to the location of cities and towns and routes of trade: The real future of this new state depended on reaching quickly into the fertile plains and carving out farms and towns on the open prairie. Because geography played such a small role in determining where growth would be centered, a frantic rush of private interests in chaotic competition developed. Leading men in the principal Mississippi River towns along Iowa's eastern border, regardless of their political persuasions, abandoned their past theories of "natural" growth. It was these towns that pioneered the transportation revolution in Iowa.

BURLINGTON'S RAILROAD

Burlington was one of the river towns with a railroad future. In 1846 it was the largest town in the new state, but its future was in doubt. Situated on the Mississippi River near the southern border of Iowa, Burlington lacked an interior stream for gathering exports. Furthermore, a series of rapids in the Mississippi downstream at the mouth of the Des Moines River made Keokuk, not Burlington, the natural break point for river traffic. Burlington's merchants turned toward Chicago and the East in their bid to market the produce of the Iowa prairies. The railroad, not the river, would be their avenue. At the same time that John Murray Forbes was still hesitating to take up the Michigan Central, the editor of the Burlington *Hawk-Eye* was already proclaiming the great railroad route to Chicago. Burlington, he advised, would find its fortune along this iron axis.[6]

Vision matured well ahead of reality in the burgeoning communities of the West. By 1848, still four full years before a through line of railroad would reach Chicago from the East, the Burlington editor had worked out the details of his dream. Burlington was already the "converging point for an extensive trade," and when a railroad from the Iowa interior met a Chicago road at the river, "the produce of our farmers shall be forwarded to supply the instant orders, per lightning, from the farthest east." Anticipating a combination of railroads and telegraph, the editor imagined a market system that put Burlington into instant yet independent communication with the world trading community. The moment a ship landed in the Atlantic ports merchants there could ascertain "what produce they require in Europe which will bring remunerative prices":

> They immediately issue their orders to Iowa by Telegraph. These orders are received in Iowa in less than ten minutes after the arrival of the Steamship at the Boston or New York wharf. The produce is put into rail road freight cars, and in four days from the arrival they may be in the hold of the vessel; and in less than one week, on their way to Europe![7]

This picture of complex technology in the service of the existing decentralized marketing system was extraordinary. Readers were assured that they could "retain all the advantages of their natural position," and still profit from those "artificial means of prosperity afforded by the use of magnetic telegraph and the construction of rail roads." Belief that these improvements offered local advantages through local initiatives was not yet disproved; in fact, it was freely repeated in midwestern circles that the "idea that the railroad must be built solely by large capitalists is fast giving way."[8]

The home-owned railroad was the conceptual bridge by which western boosters connected their local ambitions to the image of a national marketing network suggested by the railroads. The concept suited the pride and jealousy of local capitalists who had come west to exploit the opportunities in an undeveloped economy. It frightened none but the most rabid antimonopolists, and it meshed perfectly with the assumptions of self-help and initiative that attracted cautious capitalists like John Murray Forbes. The strong tendency of railroads to centralize control of the market was not yet manifest: Railroadmen of the 1840s still spoke of the network as a "chain of roads."

The Burlington & Missouri River Rail Road (B&MR) was born of this local conception. It was Burlington's project, and it served that city's needs in the contest with neighboring cities for the interior trade. Obviously, an eastern connection was the key to capturing the hinterland trade, and outside capital was expected to play a part in the venture from the start. By 1851 many of the same men who were finishing a plank road from Burlington to Mount Pleasant were negotiating a branch line connection with the Peoria & Oquawka Rail Road (P&O), an Illinois company with access to Chicago. The city of Burlington agreed to invest $75,000 in the Illinois road, which prompted the interior town of Fairfield, Iowa, to join the Burlington men and forget Keokuk, "where they stand with their hands in their pockets waiting for the railroad to be built to their door." At the same time an appeal was formulated for a congressional land grant for the Burlington & Missouri River Rail Road as a link in the transcontinental chain.[9]

James W. Grimes was perhaps the most energetic promoter among the Burlington men. Born in New Hampshire, he had studied briefly at Dartmouth College, where his tutor was Forbes's railroad strategist, James F. Joy. Grimes left college to read law, then struck off west in 1836, finally settling in Burlington. From the outset he was an ambitious booster of his new community. He was instrumental in the plank road project and was at the center of the arrangements with the Peoria & Oquawka. When the subscription books of that road were opened in Burlington in April 1851, Grimes, together with his law partner Henry W. Starr, Judge Charles Mason, Senator A. C. Dodge, bankers J. F. C. Peasley and William F. Coolbaugh, and a dozen other leading men took blocks of shares between $500 and $2,000 each. In all, over 150 men in the city subscribed to stock in the Illinois road. Their interests were represented by Grimes and Charles Mason on the P&O board.[10]

With an eastward outlet apparently secured, Burlington's railroad rapidly took shape—at least on paper. The project was conceived as both a farm-to-market highway for interior communities and a vital segment of the transcontinental route. In January 1852 a committee was selected at a public meeting to draw up Articles of Incorporation for the Burlington & Missouri River Rail Road Company. The charter listed no less than forty-six incorporators, Whigs and Democrats alike, and was implicitly contingent on a grant of land. The new corporation was organized on January 17. Its first order of business was to send Grimes to Washington at the city's expense to press for federal aid.[11]

Iowa's bid for land grants was quickly snarled in old political conflicts in Congress, but the railroad enthusiasts were undaunted. At a massive railroad convention in Ottumwa, Iowa, in February 1852, delegates from fourteen Iowa counties pledged their full support to the B&MR directors. Local papers reported a determination among the people to build their railroad even "without the aid of a grant." Still, brave words did not put money in the treasury. While the land grant issue sputtered and died in Congress in the summer of 1852, the Burlington's rival line, the Mississippi & Missouri Railroad (M&M) prepared to strike west from Davenport. The B&MR needed a wealthy patron soon![12]

The Davenport line was being put forward by the Rock Island line in Illinois, itself an extension of Forbes's old nemesis, the Michigan Southern. Anticipating such a contest between rival trunk lines, James W. Grimes had placed himself in the confidence of James F. Joy and John W. Brooks on the Peoria & Oquawka board. Now with the land grant stalled in Washington, Grimes called upon Brooks to intervene on behalf of the Burlington road. Brooks went to work on Forbes and his friends while Grimes secured a resolution of support from the Iowa general assembly.[13] Local spirits in Burlington rose momentarily in early 1853, and before they could sag again John Murray Forbes's first offer of capital assistance was announced. Forbes and his associates stood ready to put in millions as soon as the people raised $600,000 on their own. Three-fourths of this sum could be county subscriptions paid with obligation bonds; the rest was expected from private individuals. At a special meeting of the B&MR directors on March 9, 1853, the board resolved: "Inasmuch as influential citizens of the east proffer to assist us with abundant means to secure the completion of the road, that we will proceed with all energy, means, and resources in our power; and that books of subscription to our stock should be opened in all the counties along the line of the road." The Burlington press cheered the news and concluded that "there is no use in longer wasting time by waiting on the slow and uncertain action of Congress."[14]

Iowans were quick to take up the challenge. At a convention in Fairfield on April 20 several counties pledged their share and petitioned the governor for a special session of the general assembly to authorize this form of public debt. When the governor refused, the citizens proceeded on their own authority to petition their county judges and approve by popular vote the necessary bonded debt. The directors of the B&MR voided all old subscriptions made in anticipation of the federal land grant, clearing the company books for investment on the new basis. Everyone seemed to understand and approve of the arrangement with the Boston men: Their local subscriptions and county bonds would not actually build the road, but they served as security to "capitalists who will furnish the money." Grimes privately worried that after "manufacturing a public sentiment" for the eastern men, the interests of Burlington might still be abandoned. But for most people in southern Iowa there was little sign of worry as they struck their bargain with the "foreign" money powers.[15]

To quell lingering doubts in Boston, Forbes sent his brother Bennet on a tour of Iowa and Missouri in early June 1853 to evaluate the country. Bennet was modest in his opinion of the Hannibal territory, but he praised Burlington and the land westward to the Des Moines River. "If going into the road," he advised, "depends on the capability of the country for producing, then it is sure to be a good operation." Forbes was satisfied with this report and the bargain was sealed. On July 2, 1853, James F. Joy and John W. Brooks filled two vacancies on the B&MR board; Brooks was unanimously elected president.[16]

FITS AND STARTS

Although the composition of the B&MR board remained overwhelmingly local, Brooks and Joy played a dominant role from the start. By October 1853 they had prepared a list of amendments to the charter that brought the concern into more businesslike shape. The books of the company were now closed to the public (except stockholders), and voting rights, which had been heavily weighted in favor of small holders, were placed on a one share-one vote basis. The original charter had limited subscriber forfeiture to the loss of capital paid in; the amendments allowed suits against delinquents for the full value of their subscriptions. Finally, a new article authorized the company to accept subscriptions from counties and municipal corporations. The amendments were reasonable improvements in the rules of business and were approved without dissent, but in time each of them would elicit hostility from the original subscribers toward their new partners.[17]

By the end of 1853 the first four counties in the line of the road had approved their allotment of bonds, and private individuals had subscribed for the stocks. Des Moines County, including Burlington city, took $150,000 in stock; Henry, Jefferson, and Wapello counties in turn subscribed $100,000 each. Preliminary surveys by a Michigan Central engineer were completed that winter. By March 1854 the directors announced the final route to Agency City in Wapello

County, advertised for bids for grading, and prepared to start the work. Towns along the announced route were elated, and property owners dreamed happily of real estate advances exceeding 100 percent. At their annual meeting near the end of March, the stockholders cheerfully reelected the directors and the officers of the railroad company.[18]

The green light was finally given to the Burlington & Missouri River Rail Road. In early May 1854 grading contracts for seventy-five miles were awarded to a long list of small bidders, and three monthly assessments of 5 percent were called on the stock. An additional $1.2 million of stock was offered for sale in the eastern states to fund construction to Ottumwa and beyond. Unhappily, the money market just then suffered one of its periodic "revulsions," and buyers proved unwilling to plunge. By early July the company slowed construction spending to the rate of payments coming in. John Murray

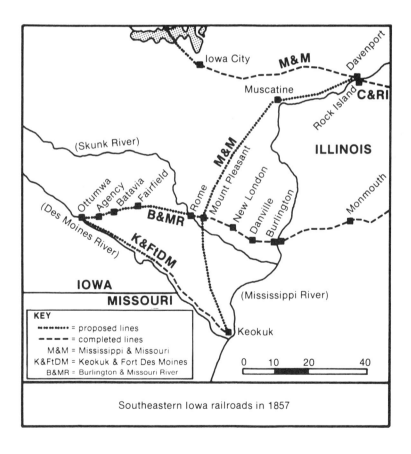

Southeastern Iowa railroads in 1857

Forbes advanced the road $25,000 cash in exchange for $37,500 in Des Moines County bonds, to be matched by local money. To encourage early payment the directors allowed subscribers 3 percent interest on their assessments paid *prior* to the opening of the line in their respective counties. In a region that was chronically short of cash, these inducements were simply irrelevant. Delinquency increased through the summer. More seriously, the county judges withheld their bonds pending actual construction inside their counties. Work was suspended for the winter while the search for funds stagnated.[19]

Time was not an ally of the Burlington railroad in the winter of 1854–55. While construction required cash, railroad promotions did not, and speculation in competing lines continued apace. As long as new ventures never reached the stage of collecting assessments, subscribers could be found for their stocks. The result was a steady fragmentation of the local market with little capital actually raised and few rails laid on the ground. Meeting so little response from the local investors, Forbes drew back his eastern support. The Forbes group was still interested in the Iowa line, to be sure, but it was simply not ready for a major commitment. John W. Brooks resigned as president of the B&MR in March 1855 to become executive head of the Michigan Central. Burdened by the urgent needs of the CB&Q in Illinois and the Hannibal & St. Joseph in Missouri, James F. Joy retired from the B&MR the following November. For the next two years the nominal management of Burlington's railroad reverted to local hands.[20]

Construction on the first section of the long-awaited road finally began late in the summer of 1855. A Burlington firm agreed to build thirty-five miles of railroad for $22,500 per mile, taking an assortment of city, county, and railroad bonds in payment for the work. The contractors would operate the line for their own profit until June 1, 1857. The first locomotive ran out of Burlington on New Year's Day, 1856, marking, if only symbolically, the inauguration of service on the Burlington railroad. What joy there was in that occasion was dimmed by the fact that the M&M already operated sixty-seven miles of line from Davenport to Iowa City, while a Keokuk railroad was pushing up the Des Moines River valley toward the B&MR's own target of Ottumwa. According to President J. C. Hall, there would be only $240,000 left of the capital stock after the contractors were paid, and the segment being built was already mortgaged at $350,000. Forbes would advance them nothing more until the interior stockholders paid up their assessments. The directors pushed forward bravely on a cash-only basis, but no major construction contracts could be let. The Burlington line was stalled once more, not yet to the banks of the Skunk River.[21]

A Reversal of Fortunes

The "home-owned" railroad was a product of local assumptions; and like most early improvements in Iowa, the B&MR had been specifically designed to suit the Democratic majority. The original charter would expire in just fifty years. Company books were declared *public* records. Stockholders could vote each of their shares up to fifty, but only one in five above that number. If large holders were thus penalized, delinquent subscribers were left free to forfeit their shares without liability for unpaid assessments. Power in the corporation was strictly limited and democratically distributed.[22] All in all, the B&MR was first conceived as a quasi-public corporation that favored small local investors with broad popular control. Forbes and associates quickly amended the charter in 1853, but popular feelings remained unchanged. Ideology, as much as the shortage of capital, blocked the fundraising efforts of the Burlington line.

In the 1850s ideologies were extremely unstable, and two broad movements were beginning to unseat the Jacksonian Democracy in Iowa. One was the steady drift of migration, increasingly from the northeast, decreasingly from the lower Ohio Valley and points south. The other was the disintegration of the Democratic program, as the national party sought vainly to steer clear of slavery and the sectional crisis. Iowa Democrats wanted railroad grants and a Homestead Act, but their national platforms consistently opposed them. Minority Whigs exploited their party's position on railroads and homestead policies to attract Iowans who were otherwise opposed to national Whigs, abolitionists, and antislavery sympathizers. Furthermore, the Iowa Democracy was mute on temperance and banking reform, allowing the opposition to build a core of support around these increasingly popular issues. The needs of the people and the composition of the population were changing in Iowa; by 1854 politics were unpredictable.[23]

When the Kansas-Nebraska controversy polarized the nation that year, the Iowa Democrats' position was untenable. Iowans had strongly supported the Compromise of 1850, but the turmoil in Kansas finally tipped the balance among a people whose local interests had been sacrificed too long to national politics. James W. Grimes led an awkward coalition of Whigs, Free-Soilers, abolitionists, and disaffected Democrats in a sweep of the October elections. When the General Assembly convened in December 1854, Grimes's party controlled the house and fell but one vote short in the senate.[24]

To balance his rhetorical focus on the sectional crisis, Grimes had shrewdly combined all the frustrations of the Iowa people into one package, which he laid at the feet of the national Democracy. Mercilessly he blamed his local opponents for the failure of railroad grants and homestead bills, for financial stringency, and for the shortage of cash. The Democrats were powerless to respond. Partisan intrigue and faithless leadership, thundered Grimes, had too long obstructed the will of the people. The Democratic Party was tyrannizing Congress! The alternative that Grimes offered was a local coalition, sensitive to the needs of Iowa voters without reference to creed or party. His stunning victory was recognized outside Iowa as a repudiation of the old party system and a victory for "that new party of the People" that was taking shape across the northern states.[25]

In reality, the Republican Party was not yet born, and the new governor of Iowa lacked either party or program. What he brought into power was a new philosophy of activist government. The "greatest object of the state," Grimes proclaimed, was to "elevate and ennoble the citizen." Republican government "would fall short of its design if it did not disseminate intelligence, and build up the moral energies of the people." Here was a higher calling for government that would bury the old Democracy. It was no longer enough, according to Grimes, for a free people to stand guard, jealously defending their rights against their neighbors. The real purpose of republican programs was to advance mankind through civic cooperation and vigorous moral leadership. Under Grimes's energetic administration, the people's government could—and must—encourage moral and material improvements in the name of progress.[26]

The political revolution in Iowa served to redefine issues like banks and railroads and homestead laws. No longer seen as departures from true democracy, such promotions by government became the central features of a new era. The idea was refreshing to a generation that was tired of Jacksonian politics. A fortuitous event near the end of Grimes's first term in office helped secure this new spirit—and Grimes's new Republican Party—at the center of Iowa politics. In May 1856, through no new efforts of the Grimes administration,

Congress passed the land grants for Iowa's railroads. With unmeasured fanfare the governor called his Republican general assembly into special session to accept the grants. No credit for their role in obtaining a favorable vote was given to the long-suffering sponsors, Senators A. C. Dodge and George W. Jones, both Democrats.[27]

Governor Grimes and his new Republicans were clearly more sympathetic toward corporate enterprise than any previous Iowa administration had been. When the passage of federal subsidies for the Iowa railroads reignited the interest of eastern men, this change in government viewpoint was not unnoticed. Still, when the Iowa General Assembly drew up the provisions for distributing the lands to railroad companies, their independence shone through. The act abounded with technical requirements and construction deadlines. Each road was required to interchange freely with intersecting lines, and all companies accepting land under this act were made subject to such "rules and regulations" as the legislature might some day pass.[28] These reservations were intended to preserve the integrity of these projects as Iowa railroads destined to advance the public welfare and not just the interests of outside capitalists. Ironically, the spirit of wild speculation, universally attributed to outsiders like John Murray Forbes, better characterized the behavior of the Iowa people toward their new railroad grants.

The ink was hardly dry on the bill when the rush began to buy up lands within the probable limits of the railroad grants. Iowans hoped to beat the railroads to the best parcels and ride the wave of inflation brought on by the railroad. Private speculators entered preemption claims even after the region was withdrawn from ordinary sale. Due to probable fraud, the Council Bluffs district, where most of the vacant lands along the Burlington lay, failed to close at all until the end of the month. Private duplicity was compounded by official abuses. The federal swampland act gave the states title to wetlands for reclamation. Iowa had given its swamplands to the county commissioners, who quickly seized large blocks of damp and unsettled territory lying in the path of the railroads. By early 1857 eastern capitalists like Forbes found themselves suing their own constituents for titles to lands clearly within the bounds of the grants. Furthermore, these same lands were often offered to the railroads in lieu of cash contributions. Local greed created the mess, but the popular mind readily saw the work of rapacious eastern capitalists.[29]

This was exactly the kind of trouble which Forbes's sequential strategy sought to avoid. Land grants, subsidies, and premature investments all brought chaos to a new territory. Having built the Michigan Central and the component parts of the Chicago, Burlington & Quincy entirely with private capital, Forbes was bitter over congressional largess. In 1853, while the Iowa grants were foundering, he wrote to Charles Sumner condemning the whole practice, not only because it demoralized private investors, but because it fueled the competitive scramble for railways where the territory could not yet support them. This constant pressure to expand into risky territory simply intensified Forbes's chronic fear that the bubble was soon to burst. By 1856 he was in no mood to take up anything new, but the Iowa grants were passed and the choice was gone. The Burlington directors conferred with Brooks and Joy over the winter. When Joy laid out his plan in the first months of 1857, Forbes took hold with a will.[30]

Forbes's idea was to issue enough new Burlington & Missouri River stock, distributed among the proper people, to control the enterprise now and then build it at his "leisure." Using the methods that had worked well in the past, Forbes told Brooks and Joy to recommend the stock to holders of Michigan Central and CB&Q in view of the railroad's potential as a feeder for those roads. Forbes then canvassed his personal friends and connections, placing large blocks of shares where he could. The new issue came out in March 1857, and $500,000 in new capital stock was subscribed before the month's end. When the stockholders met in Burlington on March 25, they elected a new board of directors. Grimes and Coolbaugh represented the residents; Brooks, John M. Forbes and Robert Bennet Forbes of Boston, Joy and John G. Read of Detroit, Erastus Corning of Albany, and Edward L. Baker of New Bedford made up the majority. President Coolbaugh proudly reported to the stockholders that those "prominent and influential eastern capitalists" would shortly raise their subscriptions to $1 million or more. The road itself was open twenty-eight miles to Mount Pleasant, work was progressing on time, and the contractor reported that operations were profitable on the open portion of the line. It did not seem to occur to anyone in Burlington on that March day that they had lost their railroad.[31]

Having established firm control of the corporation, Forbes turned his attention to fundraising, which proved more difficult than he had anticipated. His favorite brokerage house, John E. Thayer & Bro. of Boston, unaccountably declined to take the issue. Forbes went directly to work on his colleagues, explaining that his own well-known skepticism had been overcome by the "rich and populous

country, and its 300,000 acres of *Free Soil.*" Although progress was
slow, he urged Joy to take heart: " 'There shall still be cakes and ale
in the world, and ginger shall be hot in the mouth.' I have in my eye
another person in Boston, and one in New York, who can put the
thing through. One man in New Bedford would do it if he would
examine it. In short, it is too good to let go without a try!"³²

The New Bedford man did examine it, and at a directors' meeting in Burlington on May 18, 1857, Edward L. Baker was elected
president of the Burlington & Missouri River Rail Road. At the same
session the board amended the bylaws to allow the president or any
three directors to call meetings at any time and place. The board of
directors was thus effectively moved to Boston, where it first met June
9. The Burlington office was left in the hands of Oliver Cock, local
secretary and John G. Foote, local treasurer. The secretary–treasurer
of the company, John N. Denison, quickly requested that the seal of
the company be forwarded to his Boston office, from which the bonds
would now be issued.³³

Both ownership and management were in Forbes's hands by the
summer of 1857, and the Burlington & Missouri River Rail Road
had become a Boston enterprise. By a formula that granted rights in
proportion to holdings in the Michigan and Illinois companies,
Forbes distributed the Iowa securities in a predictable fashion. Surplus shares he placed among those selected investors who had bid for
more than their share. Forbes took 1,000 shares for himself and his
various trust accounts. Thayer finally came in for a like sum, and
other parties who exceeded their rights were awarded their full subscriptions. The system placed voting stock among gentlemen of
means who could, if called upon, pay in cash to keep the enterprise
afloat. Forbes intended, however, to pay in no more than half and
use the credit of the company, its lands, and the good names behind
it, to float bonds at a reasonable discount. By June 12 he was urging
the other large holders to increase their subscriptions 25 or 50 percent, in the hope of keeping down the number of assessments actually
called on each share.³⁴

Renewed construction on the Burlington & Missouri River Rail
Road had scarcely begun when panic swept through American financial circles once more. John Murray Forbes had long feared the
collapse of this railroad boom; now it was upon him. Construction
was stopped in October, and the reversal of fortunes so recently celebrated in Burlington fell under a different light. As the depression
settled over the agricultural Midwest, the Iowans began to rue their

bargain with Brooks, Joy, and Forbes. For many local people, ruinous prices, money shortages, and hard times followed the intervention of eastern capitalists too closely. The connection seemed obvious. Now the Iowans were being hounded to pay up their shares in a railroad they did not own and could not use. The ensuing tension and hostility between the local communities and the Forbes group in the next two years ruined forever that spirit of optimistic cooperation that had brought the two together.

SURVIVING THE PANIC

In 1857, the American financial structure once again collapsed. Since the middle 1840s, investment and commercial activity had intensified steadily. In 1854 the economy paused briefly; then it surged ahead at a record pace through 1856. Immigration, manufacturing growth, and newly opened western farms all contributed strong elements to the boom, but the leading sector this time was railroads. Completed railroad mileage leaped from 8,500 in 1850 to 24,500 in 1856, absorbing $600 million in new capital, roughly a third of which was borrowed abroad. The new rail lines of the 1850s not only brought the regional markets into closer interdependence, they were also large economic undertakings in their own right. The gradual emergence of a central market for railroad securities in New York attracted the reserve funds of country banks to New York vaults where they were loaned on call to securities buyers. While this generated large amounts of ready capital, such pyramiding of reserves was inherently unstable. The failure of the Ohio Life Insurance & Trust Company's New York office, on August 24, 1857, brought the structure down. The country banks frantically called for their reserves, and New York banks called their loans to cover; speculators quickly found the securities market glutted. Unable to liquidate their investments, the speculators defaulted, setting off a chain of failures that closed all but one of the New York banks by October 14. Unable to react quickly enough, and uncertain what to do in any event, banks and businesses across the nation went under, throwing hundreds of thousands out of work and idling the economic machinery everywhere.[35]

The panic of 1857 was severe but relatively short-lived. By midDecember the New York banks were paying specie again, and the credit system was in the early stages of repair. The more serious longterm difficulties resulted from excessive growth in capacity, which depressed agricultural and manufacturing prices, and from the tarnished reputation of large capital investment projects—especially uncompleted railroads. This combination of low prices for farm commodities and sluggish, high-cost investment in the critical transportation field left the Mississippi Valley still struggling for recovery well into the 1860s. For his part, John Murray Forbes was caught by both the immediate and the protracted effects of the crisis, and his responses illustrate the critical role played by the general capitalist in developmental enterprise.

After his successful capital drive for the Burlington railroad in the spring of 1857, Forbes had "retired" to Naushon Island for a long rest. He was still there, nursing his health, when the panic struck that autumn. On an urgent call from Brooks, the weary Forbes was pressed into service in October to save the Michigan Central from bankruptcy.[36]

Hoping for better rates in the bond market, the Michigan Central had run up a floating debt of nearly $1.5 million. The panic, of course, left the company embarrassed, and Brooks turned to Forbes to secure a loan in London. It was just the kind of chore Forbes relished; within twenty-four hours he was on board the steamer *Canada*, hatching his plan. He intended to "complete a party" to bid for as many of the company's $3.16 million mortgage bonds as were necessary to bring $2 million in cash. Forbes planned to bid very low for the entire issue, assuming that others would see a bargain and take at least half at somewhat higher prices. After maneuvering the best bids out of "Bond & Stockholders and outsiders," Forbes could take the balance at his low bid. With the loan thus secured, the market value of the bonds would naturally rise, and he could sell off his surplus at a profit. To pull it off, he was mobilizing every available dollar. He drew funds on his cousin Paul in China, which Paul might "repudiate by return mail" (which took several months) if he chose. In the meantime, Forbes wrote to Paul that he intended to use Paul's notes "to raise money or even if pushed *into a corner rather than fail* shall draw on you for *50,000* which you must borrow of Howqua or otherwise raise for me at some rate or other." He put up Milton, Naushon, Mt. Savage, and all his railroad and manufacturing stocks against fundraising; with some $300,000 in cash and receivables on hand, he would be all right unless nobody paid him.[37]

It was a bold plan relying on his own personal ability to obtain credit when others were failing. Yet in the midst of this risky gambit, he was plotting more complicated maneuvers to salvage the CB&Q and the western lines, should they be dragged down as well. On

November 8, 1857, he called for more China money to buy Michigan Central bonds. These he would sell after a small rise and invest the proceeds in CB&Q bonds as soon as they hit the market: "& when the last rise I may sell them & use the money (possibly) to take Bonds of the Iowa R. Road in case it continues to look well & in case the assessments are checked by the pressure of the times." These operations required careful timing, he explained to Paul, "& as the Western large stockholders & other small ones cannot be reached you & I & King & Griswold & Thayer & Green must step *in and do the needful* taking pay at panic rates."[38]

By the end of 1857 business was at a standstill in Iowa and Missouri, and crop failures in parts of Illinois had dried up local sources of revenue for the CB&Q. Heavily in debt from aiding construction of its feeder lines to Iowa and Missouri, the CB&Q planned a new $5 million, twenty-five-year mortgage. Over $500,000 in new bonds were sold in January 1858 at a heavy discount. These brought enough cash to pay the immediate bills but not the yearend dividend. With the Illinois situation stabilized, Forbes took advantage of panic prices to speculate in land along the lines west of the Mississippi River; but before many months had passed, "fire" broke out on the Hannibal & St. Joseph. Forbes feared as much as $1.5 million in cash might be needed to put the Hannibal line through and save that investment.[39]

Forbes had controlled the Hannibal company since 1854 by means of a fiscal agency, but the operating revenues belonged to the contractor until the whole line was completed. Construction delays simply padded the contractor's earnings while threatening the financial health of the company. After months of angry negotiations, Forbes went west in the spring of 1857 to exact a new agreement from the firm, but the panic that autumn further deflated the company's assets and forced default on about $500,000 million in private bonds and stock. By June 1, 1858, the Hannibal road was half completed with just enough money to pay its bills and no funds to finish the line within the land grant deadline.[40]

Forbes now faced the problem of raising $1.25 million or more in a market that was depressed in general and "very lukewarm" about Hannibal bonds. By this time rather testy toward those investors who hung back, he concluded it was for "the few who have *pluck & means* to take the Bonds at such a low rate as will be very tempting—& will warrant selling out of other things to go in." Once again, he bid for "all the Bonds there are and enough convertible ones, or stock to *make our rate.*" This would assure completion of the road without "having to *take all the* value out of the stock" by assessing shareholders for money "to finish it up." When the emergency subsided, Forbes would make the laggards pay in full to gain back their interest in stock and bonds. Such, he felt, was the price of weakness in the crisis![41]

One of the distinctive features of this series of refinancings was the use of the sinking fund, which Forbes subsequently required on all major bond issues. The practice of regularly setting aside money to redeem bonds was provided in the CB&Q loan of 1858. With $2 million worth of old bonds coming due in 1860, the Michigan Central followed suit the next year in the hope that its bondholders would exchange their mature paper for new bonds with this added security. The sinking fund not only gave the railroad companies a structured system of debt retirement, it also provided the trustees (usually including Forbes) with additional capital to invest in allied companies. The trustees held the bonds of one road in the sinking fund of another. This internal pyramiding of reserves was still risky, but under Forbes's guidance the CB&Q used the device successfully for the rest of the century.[42]

In light of the hectic demands made by the Michigan, Illinois, and Missouri companies, Forbes might well have let the Iowa road slide altogether in these years. It remained entirely a developmental proposition at a time when the territory was not producing enough business to pay the expenses on the lines already in operation. The B&MR ran through richer but less populated country than the Hannibal, and its land grant deadlines were not quite so pressing. Still, Forbes could not allow the Iowa road to languish. For one thing, the Iowa law regranting the lands specified at least seventy-five miles of construction by 1859. Another factor was Forbes's growing uneasiness about the future of railroad connections through slaveholding Missouri. Finally, he remembered the race to Chicago in 1851. That time Joy's vision had been right, and Forbes's hesitancy had cost them dearly. It would not always be so, but for the moment Forbes took his lesson to heart. Iowa must go forward or be lost.[43]

Crisis in Burlington

The people of Iowa saw the panic quite differently. From their perspective the eastern capitalists were responsible for the ruin. During the winter of 1857–58 the depression settled hard upon the region. Real estate prices plummeted. Scarce currency flowed eastward, leaving Iowans without the necessary cash to carry on business or meet their assessments on railroad securities. Excessive rains, early frost, and a hard winter exaggerated the hardship as if man and nature conspired together. Predictably, a people in despair turned their wrath on a clear and distant target—the eastern speculator: "We might ask who have been the principal movers in the real estate speculations of the West? Eastern men. If Tom, Dick, and the Devil from New York, New England, and every place else towards sunrise, had not puffed and blowed at these bursted bubbles, the West would have been all right to-day [sic]."[44]

This breakdown of confidence between East and West hobbled the new managers of the Burlington & Missouri River Rail Road as they struggled with the effects of the panic. President Baker begged the Iowa creditors to accept new stock at sixty dollars paid in exchange for old B&MR bonds; if these local bondholders would not help relieve the burden of debt, Forbes could not place any new bonds and the enterprise would surely fail. "If parties can see the thing in the same light we do," Baker reasoned, "they will doubtless be willing to turn in a portion of their Bonds."[45] But the "parties" would not see things in the same light. Western capitalists refused to dump more resources into the swirling funnel that was drawing money eastward to stem an emergency which they, in common with their poorer neighbors, believed was entirely of eastern origin. Despite the fact that men like Forbes were among the very few sources of real capital flowing *into* Iowa at this time, the local investors were sure, if the enterprise collapsed, that the public finger of blame would be pointed "towards sunrise."

After paying September interest, B&MR Treasurer John N. Denison ordered the Burlington office not to draw on him until further notice. Baker reported that notes in Boston with six names worth an aggregate of a million dollars would not raise money at 2.5 percent per month. The Boston directors were "powerless about raising money." The large stockholders, grumbled Baker, "enquire if our Western friends have paid up, put their hands in their pockets & keep them there." It was impossible to hire money in such a market: Were the directors expected "to steal it?" "If Iowa people are so anxious for the road," he concluded, "let them raise some money, pay their subscriptions or let it to us at a good rate of interest."[46]

Baker understood the sources of suspicion, and he urged Superintendent John G. Read to tell the Iowa people "that this hurricane came upon us too suddenly for us to prepare for it." The blame, he argued "must come on the New York Banks & Panic makers first, our delinquent Stockholders second, giving credit to our friend Forbes & many others." But the time for excuses was past. The company was out of money and materials. Work would be stopped, but Forbes hoped to do it quietly while still "urging men to pay." J.N.A. Griswold failed in his contract to deliver iron in October; with this excuse the directors notified their contractors to suspend work. They voted their last few thousands to pay off the laborers and halted construction October 30, 1857.[47]

Ill will prevailed everywhere. While the contractors contemplated suing for damages, local stockholders resolutely ignored their assessments. Governor Grimes resigned from the board to enter the U.S. Senate, leaving only one resident director. Finally, the eastern men were at each other's throats. Erastus Corning discovered that Iowa law held stockholders liable for corporate debts; with the company seriously embarrassed, he demanded release from his subscriptions. Griswold was furious at being made the scapegoat in the iron deal. He stopped paying on his shares. Forbes had been paid up all along, and Thayer was recently "fixed up," but now H. H. Hunnewell of Boston refused to pay. By the last week of November, Edward L. Baker was tired and disgusted.[48]

The extremely tight market eased in December, and hot tempers began to cool. Bernhart Henn of Fairfield, Iowa, who was special land agent for the B&MR, paid a visit to Baker in Boston and assured him that a large business was waiting for the line at Fairfield and Ottumwa. Forbes and Denison made the rounds, smoothing the ruffled feathers of their key supporters. James F. Joy came east to assure everyone that the personal liability law in Iowa, an artifact of the old Democracy, would be corrected the minute the Iowa general assembly convened. With this obstacle overcome, Forbes thought he could bring almost everyone back into line. As the new year opened, plans were once again laid for pushing the B&MR to Ottumwa.[49]

Restoring confidence and good will was a priority concern in 1858 as the company tried to get moving again. Rather than demand more money from impatient stockholders, Treasurer Denison approached a wealthy bondholder, William H. Starr of Burlington, for a loan of $7,000 to pay coupons and notes. Denison thought it was particularly important to meet interest on the bonds of those counties not yet served by the road. At the same time, Iowa men had grown complacent, and Denison warned that the eastern men would not do it alone. Working at the other end, Forbes tightened his control of the company. As an encouragement to easterners to come to the Iowa territory, the board changed the date of the annual meeting in Burlington from March to June. Baker hoped things would look so much better when they gathered in Burlington "that there will be but one opinion either at the East or West as to the importance of paying up assessments and pushing the work more vigorously than ever."[50]

No such harmony of interests was forthcoming. The people of Iowa had come to see the B&MR as a foreign corporation. The spring fundraising campaign, which began in April 1858, brought to the surface hostilities that had been festering all through the winter. Forbes was preparing a new million-dollar mortgage on the Iowa land grant to build forty miles of railroad to Ottumwa. Surveys were completed through the rest of the state, and local aid requirements were drawn up for each community. Baker's first letters to the West in April were both cheerful and optimistic. The far western Iowa communities were expected to deliver their swamplands as well as rights-of-way and depot grounds, while the city of Burlington and eastern Iowa towns were once more asked to pitch in to secure the through line. James F. Joy followed these letters with a personal tour to stir up enthusiasm and collect the donations. The result was a new series of bond referenda scheduled for May. Joy may have spoken too curtly in the West, but no one was prepared for the storm that broke over this new round of elections.[51]

Charges of tyranny sparked the revolt. Signing "justice" to his letter in the Burlington *Hawk-Eye,* one writer attacked agents like Joy "who make it a practice (warrior-like) of demanding tribute money every time they visit us, and threaten us if we do not comply with their request, with total annihilation [.]" "Justice" accused the eastern men of holding up construction on the B&MR while they speculated in land for their own profit. This was not the reason for construction delays, but it fell rather close to the mark nonetheless. From the beginning Forbes had intended to have "some Land Depot Speculations which will give good results to the Stockholders pro rata." From the eastern point of view, this was necessary to prevent profiteering by the local landowners; but even the suspicion of this activity in the West raised the old shibboleth of "speculation."[52]

Baker's patience was at an end. Forbes, Joy, and Brooks felt the same way. Word went out from Boston: "We cannot assess more, or begin work again, till people in Iowa have voted favorably." Full pressure was applied during the short campaign, and Forbes sent strict word not to use "a pound" of his new iron until things were put right. With their bluff so sternly called, the citizens of Burlington and Jefferson County backed down. Their bonds were approved on May 18, and work began to Fairfield at once. Construction beyond Fairfield would depend on the vote in Wapello County. Forbes and his friends were now playing the forceful role attributed to them in the western mind. No doubt it was impolitic, but as long as it brought results they pursued it. Baker bullied the judge of Montgomery County, whose offer would not build more than "half a mile of road": "To get a road through your county, it will be necessary . . . for the inhabitants . . . to make up their minds to prepare to aid the company liberally, in doing what will prove to be very much more to their advantage in every way, than it can possibly be to a non-resident." The same kind of pressure was used on Wapello County until the judge threatened a legal rejoinder.[53]

The original bond issues in Des Moines, Henry, Jefferson, and Wapello counties in 1853 had been a constant source of confusion since the eastern management took over the B&MR. They had contained complex provisions linking the issuance of bonds and liability for interest to the completion of different segments of the road. Furious over delayed construction and the abuse they were receiving from Baker, the judges of these four counties now refused to issue bonds to pay new assessments on their counties' stock. In August 1858 the directors considered formal action against Wapello and Jefferson counties; but before legal proceedings could be initiated, Henry County missed its obligation to pay the September coupon. Faced now with the possibility of real repudiation, Joy urged caution in preparing a legal strategy. Baker favored waiting until the road was opened into Wapello County, when there could be no doubt that the company had fulfilled its obligations. However, Superintendent Read in Burlington doubted whether the mood would improve, and on the last day of 1858 Joy gave the word to file suits.[54]

Despite the Forbes group's stubborn public posture, time was against them. The land grant, on which Forbes's new mortgage rested, was contingent upon reaching the Des Moines River by December first of the coming year. In January 1859 Baker quietly ordered work to begin toward Ottumwa in the hope that Wapello County would come around. This concession was too little or too late, for Wapello and Jefferson counties rejected all pleas to issue their bonds or pay back interest. When February coupons went unpaid a scandal broke in the public press. The Burlington *Hawk-Eye* denounced Jefferson County, damning "all repudiation and all semblance of it." The Fairfield *Ledger* responded bitterly that the railroad company alone owed interest on Jefferson County bonds until the trains ran into Fairfield. The editor listed several contract "violations," including the use of Jefferson County proceeds for work outside the county. Such hairsplitting allocation of funds was impracticable for the railroad, but the Jefferson County people felt no legal or moral obligation to pay back interest or issue more bonds. Wounded by the charge of repudiation, the Fairfield editor reminded the *Hawk-Eye* that when the county subscribed for B&MR stock, "the company had not yet been sold out to a few grasping eastern capitalists, who seem to regard the people of the west as having been made expressly to shovel dollars and dimes into the pockets of railroad monopolists."[55]

The repudiation controversy swept across other counties and other railroads in Iowa. Most local newspapers charged fraud and duplicity by the railroad companies, while the dissenters attacked the character of "repudiating" judges. After a month of useless debate, the *Hawk-Eye* published a lecture on the entire local aid question. The original bargains were perhaps a mistake, the editor felt, but primary blame must fall on local interests who would not wait for the railroads to be built with private capital. In a frantic rush to bend the line of the road to serve private needs, county and municipal leaders had burdened the people beyond their ability to pay. Communities had bid against each other shamelessly. The charge of absenteeism was true. The road, when finished to Ottumwa, would pay its eastern owners "at least ten, and we believe, fifteen" percent. The corporation would fatten its owners' friends and advance their interests, "of course." All of this would perhaps justify renouncing the bargain if it could be done "consistently with legal and moral obligations." But the *Hawk-Eye* could not see it as an open question: The people had bound themselves to pay—and pay they must.[56]

From the point of view of the eastern directors, abuses all lay in the western end. Since the passage of the land grant in 1856, Iowans had smugly retired from the enterprise, confident that the grant would build the road. The original grant of "about a million & a half acres . . . doubtless would have been ample," snarled Baker, but preemptions, swamp claims, and other prior entry by the Iowans had depleted the bounty to "one sixth of what was anticipated." Thus the company required swamplands, rights-of-way, and capital subscriptions from the counties in the west, and these demands were not negotiable. Iowa was entirely wrong, Baker continued, to assume that the Forbes group must build the road to protect their own interests. "Western people . . . must do something for themselves," he quipped. "Eastern men will not put both butter & honey on their bread, and carry it to their mouths also."[57]

As if to prove their venality to the Boston directors, the very Iowa communities that were repudiating their earlier bargains continued to bid for new lines to rival the Burlington. A convention at Oskaloosa on January 26, 1859, dissolved into an auction with towns offering pledges to get on a new line to the state capital at Des Moines. The B&MR was prepared to equip and operate such a line through Oskaloosa if the local promoters would build it, but the company flatly refused to be dragged all over the map each time the citizens held a meeting. Meanwhile Ottumwa, the long-deferred target on the Des Moines River, was testing its strength as a future rail center. The city council drew up a list of demands for the Burlington line and withdrew its aid. Baker advised the mayor and council that their policy was unacceptable, but he scaled down the railroad's demands: The road "ought not to enter your city at any cost whatever to our Company, for either right of way [sic] or Depot grounds." The concession was enough to give the city fathers an escape from their grandstanding, but the tone of confrontation persisted.[58]

While Denison and Baker labored to suppress rebellion in the counties west of the railhead, customers on the eastern portion of the line staged a rehearsal of the rate controversy that would occupy most Iowans in the decade following the Civil War. In the spring of 1859 shippers in eastern Iowa complained that the B&MR rates were excessive. CB&Q President John Van Nortwick agreed that the Iowa rates were driving away business that should continue to Chicago via his route. A decade earlier in Michigan, John W. Brooks had revised certain schedules on the Michigan Central to quell agitation among the farmers. But B&MR Superintendent Read, soured by the atmosphere of hostility in Burlington, had become belligerent. As long as his road had no competition he charged the highest rates he could get.[59]

Read's attitude did nothing to further the establishment of peace which the directors desperately sought. Nevertheless, once threatened with a shippers' boycott the directors responded with the same righteous dogma. Baker drafted the reply, and while he admitted the difficulty of establishing "the new relations" that the railroad created, he could find no role for local interests in the formation of company policy. The owners of the property could not respond to popular appeals without abandoning their rights as owners. If the people took direct action to "form combinations or use influences to injure" the railroad, they showed a lack of character deserving of no consideration. In short, while railroad construction was a joint effort of local and outside interests, the board of directors would be neither petitioned nor threatened on management policies.[60]

To punctuate deteriorating relations, John G. Foote of Burlington launched a personal attack against the absentee owners of the B&MR. Once local treasurer for the company, Foote had been removed under a cloud, and his office dissolved, in the first months of the panic. Now in August 1859, almost two years later, Foote published an open letter castigating the company's officers for their "hauteur" and their insensitivity to the needs of Iowa. He charged the company with illegally keeping books out of state, with mortgaging the railroad without the consent of the resident owners, and with all manner of corrupt deals and construction swindles. Most of the charges were technically groundless, but they forced the Forbes group to answer. The Iowa stockholders, they now pointed out, had freely and openly surrendered their railroad at a legal meeting in March 1857. Eastern men now owned over two-thirds of the stock. They had paid in hundreds of thousands of dollars, and they intended to thoroughly control their enterprise. There had been no fraud, but to the charge of absenteeism Forbes had no defense. William F. Coolbaugh, the sole resident director, bravely signed the letter of response, but the Burlington papers identified it immediately as dictation from Boston.[61]

At last, on September 1, 1859, a celebration marked the opening of the road to Ottumwa. Now seventy-five miles long and terminating on the Des Moines River, the Burlington & Missouri River Rail Road was finally tapping a large interior trade and collecting the receipts it had long expected. To avoid further controversy, Forbes asked James W. Grimes, now junior senator from Iowa, to refrain from involving railroads in Iowa's coming elections. Forbes complained of the difficulties of managing a thing "so far off," and welcomed Grimes's suggestions. But Forbes already had his own solution to the management problem. He placed a young cousin named Charles E. Perkins in the Burlington office to learn the business from the bottom up. With his own kin minding the store, Forbes would know exactly how things progressed in distant Iowa.[62]

Rhetoric of Confrontation

The controversies that raged in Iowa in 1859 were not against railroads per se; rather, they derived from a contest for relative advantages between eastern and western capitalists with different ambitions. While he feigned public indifference to the future of the Burlington line, Forbes needed the road for his larger design. Many Iowans, on the other hand, had gone too deeply into railroads in 1853, and they were looking for quick relief after the panic of 1857. Local acts of rebellion were designed to recover a flexible position for Iowa communities in their railroad negotiations. Forbes's responses, in turn, sought to neutralize those local interests and free his company to meet its own technological and strategic requirements within the railroad industry.[63]

Traditional ideologies regarding economic justice and public morality provided the rhetorical vocabulary for both sides, but these values served divergent interests. The merchant Forbes had lodged his personal interest in the railway system itself, and he understandably claimed the same rights and integrity for incorporated capital that he had always defended as a private trader. The interests of the Iowa merchants and farmers, while increasingly dependent on railroad services, were clearly distinct from those of the transport system. It seemed obvious to the Iowans that the "rights" of legitimate producers claimed a moral, if not a legal, precedence over the "rights" of privileged and protected corporations. Unable to recognize the gradual structural change that was shifting the balance of economic power, these producers and merchants identified the evil as the personal corruption of absentee eastern capitalists.

At the root of the trouble were the mysteries of railroad finance. Few Iowans understood or trusted the innovations in capital formation that were building America's railroads. When major stockholders issued fixed-interest bonds to fund construction while leaving their capital shares unpaid, the common observer saw fraud. Then, when county taxes were used to pay interest into the pockets of "foreign" bondholders long before the railroad began stimulating local incomes, the frustrated taxpayer concluded that the unfinished road exported more money than grain. In 1859 it was simply incredible that a company with one and one-half million in new capital stock, three hundred thousand acres of free land, over half a million in county bonds and untold thousands of real dollars paid in could be out of money after building less than fifty miles of railroad.

Yet this was exactly the condition of the Burlington & Missouri River Rail Road, and there had been no fraud. In order to "hire" money in the intensely competitive American market of the 1850s, Forbes had to offer stocks on marginal subscription, along with discounted bonds bearing fixed interest, in amounts far exceeding the actual cash raised by securities. In his role as a personal broker for the enterprise Forbes absorbed much of the risk, and therefore the stock, in order to upgrade the paper of the company. The panic of 1857 pushed this risk factor skyward while dropping bond prices and curbing payments on stock assessments. If Forbes's heroic efforts during the crisis earned him extra profits, they also secured the finances of the road.[64]

Ignorant of these financial concerns, many Iowans simply recoiled from their railroad enthusiasm altogether. What Iowa needed, they now proclaimed, was immigrants, not railroads—producers growing crops for the present, not speculators building dreams of the future. The argument was familiar and rested on traditional pioneer assumptions: Given a steady flow of energetic farmers, the new state would generate wealth and build its railroads in time.[65] This view was strikingly similar to Forbes's own ideal of natural development, and it was contradicted by the same forces. The pioneer concept of natural development was tied to the pace and character of the river trade network. Geographical reality was supposed to be static, and civilization needed only to remove those natural barriers that hindered its steady, incremental advance. But as soon as the railroads reached Chicago from the East both Forbes and the Iowans recognized the power of cross-country trunk lines to reorganize the human environment. This power was the focus of their struggle: Forbes needed it and the Iowans feared it in his hands. Long before the rate controversy lent statistical evidence to this power struggle, people in the West vaguely understood that whoever controlled the railroad governed part of their lives. From this perspective, Forbes's very success as a railroad builder was a part of his offense.

By the late 1850s violent resistance to economic change, which Forbes had encountered among the Michigan farmers a decade before, survived only as angry rhetoric in Iowa. The difference was perhaps due to a gradual recognition of the problems inherent in railroad development. Iowa Governor Ralph Lowe, in his inaugural address in 1858, reminded his constituents that the benefits of railroads extended to every class in the community in a permanent way. The country was indebted for their railroads to "the noble and self-sacrificing few, who manifest a willingness to peril much of their fortunes, to push forward a description of improvement that marks one of the great features of the age." Lowe's opponents could not dispute their reliance on "the great features of the age" but the terms of dependency worried them: Iowans should have their railroads, but they need not surrender their freedoms to the capitalists from the East. Communities could be generous enough with "foreign" investors without giving away their sovereign right to regulate business within their domain. The power of the railroads must be held in check. At the height of the contests of 1859, Ralph Lowe was sacrificed by his party for his outspoken support of state aid to railroads. His parting words raised the central question: "How are our railroad schemes to be carried forward?"[66]

In their desperate search for a principle of resolution, local supporters of Iowa's railways turned to theories of interdependence and harmony of interest. One Iowa mayor told a Boston audience that "Providence clearly intended us to be the complement and helpers of each other. . . . In a free and cordial interchange . . . lies our true path of honor and advancement."[67] Eastern investors like John Murray Forbes thundered their approval, but the harmony was illusory. Forbes's careful plans for sequential investment as the territory developed were upset at every turn by the impatience of the people, the competition from other rail lines and the generosity of Congress with public lands. Forced out to the margin of settlement, he could not finance such a road as the Burlington & Missouri River without the binding commitments of its future patrons. In 1859 the company could not yet pay interest on its first section of track; but the people of Iowa were in open rebellion, repudiating their bonds, threatening regulation of rates, and withholding their contributions until the line was finished. The ideal of a regional partnership had dissolved into absentee ownership and charges of tyranny.

By 1860 an apparently simple plan for opening the trans-Mississippi West to railroad communication had raised serious questions in the East and the West about technological and economic goals, financial practices, political ambitions, and general cultural values. The contest between Forbes and the Iowans was but a single example of the unsettling consequences of technological and industrial progress. The implications of such structural changes in settlement pattern and regional development as high-energy transportion engendered touched nearly every aspect of life in antebellum America. The historical identification of free enterprise capitalism with American democracy was severely strained by the integration of systems that concentrated wealth and power beyond the reaches of local democratic institutions. These concentrations of economic power were seen to imply social and political powers that threatened fundamental assumptions about American equalitarianism, regional diversity, and state and local rights. Taken together, a multitude of local disruptions like the Iowa railroad controversy created an atmosphere of tension that fostered the sectional crisis and the American Civil War. If the war drew attention away from the railroad questions of the 1850s, it was seen by John Murray Forbes *and* the people of Iowa to involve a host of their antebellum concerns as well. The implications of a plan to open the West and a war to "liberate" the South were strikingly similar.

4

Triumphant Union

FROM THE BEGINNING American railroad promoters had cherished the hope that the railroad system, "if advantageously applied and sufficiently extended," could so bind the "remote sections" of the nation as to perfect and preserve the Union.[1] Tragically, this hope for unity through transportation and communication evaporated as the steam railroad came to symbolize an attack by the industrial North on the agricultural South. Sharing both the agrarian outlook of the South and the progressive ambitions of the Northeast, the farming region of the new Middle West looked toward a day when its own fresh leadership might mediate the ancient hostility between the planting and mercantile states. Instead, the westward movement simply increased the competition between expansive systems of black slavery and industrial capitalism. The farmers of the Middle West had their own reservations about eastern capitalists, but they were at bottom uncompromising "free-soil" men. Forced in the end to choose between slavery and abolition, they would scarcely hesitate.

The Compromise of 1820 had postponed just such a choice by dividing the nation to the edge of the public domain, allowing slaveholding and free states to coexist. But by midcentury the accession of Texas, the Mexican War, the Oregon crisis, California gold, and the dream of a transcontinental railroad had redrawn the western map. Sectional balance was in jeopardy. In 1850 the aging titans of antebellum politics—Clay of Kentucky, Webster of Massachusetts, Calhoun of South Carolina—debated one last desperate compromise. The measure proved inadequate. The simple balance of sectional power that had suited the early republic was becoming unworkable in a dynamic continental nation. By 1854 the Pacific railroad schemes of Stephen A. Douglas had opened Kansas to slavery and reignited the sectional crisis.[2]

Like the vast majority of Americans in the Age of Jackson, John Murray Forbes had followed the middle road on slavery and sectional issues. He abhorred black slavery but took no actions against it. The 1850 compromises, however, threatened his view of progress in the North and the West; Forbes broke with the past and took his place in the new Republican movement.

By a similar course Iowa joined the northern cause. Before the early 1850s Iowans had no compelling reason to reconcile their feelings on slavery. But the threat of spreading the plantation system onto free soil drove them into the Republican camp. As southern leaders had long predicted, the closer commercial relations between the North and the West, made possible by the railroads, foreshadowed their ideological union. In 1860 the electoral success of the new and dangerously "northern" Republican Party raised the spectre of revolution in the Old South and sparked the final confrontation. Chanting "Free Soil, Free Labor, Free Men," eastern and western people rallied to subdue the rebel South. Their cause was now clear, but their common faith in Republican ideology only temporarily concealed their longstanding differences about the structure of power within the Union.[3]

BEWARE THE EXPANSION OF SLAVERY

Close observations of Chinese society in the 1830s had left John Murray Forbes cynical about the perfectibility of man. Forbes returned from Canton with a comparative perspective on the flaws in American society. He hated slavery, but he was equally impatient with abolitionists whom he identified with a "state of old maidishness." Following his instincts, he avoided the slavery question as long as it lay outside his personal interests. In 1846, however, when a crisis arose over David Wilmot's Proviso banning slavery in the trans-Missouri West, Forbes took a stand. The South's constitutional argument—that Congress was powerless to prevent slavery extension—he saw as a dangerous innovation. The great men of the North *and* the South had long recognized federal authority in the territories. There could be no "permanent peace or quiet," Forbes concluded, until that principle was recognized as "the settled policy of the country."[4]

Forbes's view was something of an innovation as well. In 1846 he had just embarked on his career in western railroads. As he expanded his vision of that region's future, his antislavery convictions could not fail to harden. Slave labor in the territories undermined those virtues of thrift and industry that buttressed Forbes's whole scheme for the growth of the West. Forbes traveled in the South nearly every winter for relief of a bronchial weakness, and his observations of South Carolina, Georgia, and Florida yielded increasing evidence of corruption and indolence in a slave-based culture. The planters were dissipated by pretension and leisure, while poor whites remained "frontiersmen, loafers, and hunters," content to fight with Indians for a soldier's pay.

A trip to Cuba in 1856 gave Forbes the most shocking view of a degraded slave society. The "laziness of the whites and the mere animal existence of the blacks" formed together the "most shiftless style of living that ever existed in a civilized land."

> How the picture rises up to my mind; the anxious overworked agent obliged to think of every plan and direct its execution; the unemployed white gentleman slowly puffing his cigar and never seeing a book or moving out of a snail's pace from the hall to the piazza and back, a walking oyster; the irresponsible, careless half-naked negroes and negresses; the swarthy (white) drivers with their swords on, sitting at table with us, then mounting their horses to go the rounds; the dirty court yard; the jerked beef hung in the sun to dry close to the house.

The natural beauty of the tropics could not counter Forbes's revulsion. He hurried back to New England, "the only real paradise."[5]

These images of slavery, compared with the industry and progress he had seen in Michigan and the country west of Chicago, left no doubt in Forbes's mind that slave labor must be excluded from the territories. The "absurdity of the slave institution" shocked his "logical nerves" and his "sense of fitness in this model republic." Conservative tradition called for nonintervention in slavery, but after what he had seen Forbes thought the steady "yielding of the strong growing North and West" to the demands of "the slave power" was "worse than a crime." It was the threat of slavery extension, even more than slavery itself, that governed his analysis of southern society and its pernicious influence on American politics and life. He might have allowed its continuation in the South; but by its presence on the frontier, slavery became a threat to the future of Forbes's own civilization.

When the Kansas-Nebraska Act of 1854 threw open the region to "squatter sovereignty," Forbes took the lead in organizing the

New England Emigrant Aid Society, which funneled well-armed
Yankee settlers into Kansas. "If you will only find me a million of
Dollars," he wrote to his partner, Amos A. Lawrence, "I could shew
[sic] you how to make *sure* of Kansas being free." "True safety" in
politics lay in "meeting the question now." He begged the "sound
and conservative men of the South" to find their own voice and "let
it be heard" in the North. Straining conventional logic, Forbes
sounded a call to resist revolution. Antislavery, he reasoned, had
reached the "laboring men, who fear and hate all aristocratic institutions": If Southern aggression were not stopped this year, the pas-
sions of the northern masses would rule in 1860![6]

Forbes's analysis was not far from the mark. The issue of slavery
extension now touched large classes of people who would never resist
slavery where it already existed. Even in a state like Iowa, where a
majority of first settlers came from slaveholding states, the territory
was assumed to be incontestably free. Resenting slave labor in their
native states, pioneer Democrats in new states like Iowa carefully
excluded both slavery and Negroes from their free-soil paradise. This
posture of avoidance was reflected in state politics. Iowa's congressional delegation rejected the Wilmot Proviso and accepted the Fugitive Slave Act because neither issue compromised Iowa's interests in
1850. Abolitionist agitators were as unwelcome in the state as blacks
and their owners.[7]

The turning point for Iowa came in 1854, when the Kansas-
Nebraska Act repealed the compromise line of $36°30'$ and raised the
threat of slavery on two of Iowa's borders. Suddenly the minority of
Yankee migrants, Free-Soilers, and abolitionists in Iowa found broad
support throughout the electorate. Strengthened by New England
missionaries, who laid the foundations for a popular movement, the
antislavery activists seized the Kansas-Nebraska issue. Their mouth-
piece was that ambitious Burlington Whig, James W. Grimes, who
capitalized on the moment and swept the state elections in 1854 with
his personal blend of Whiggery and antislavery. His triumph became
the basis for republicanism throughout the state.[8]

Although Grimes's progressive stance on banks, railroads, temperance, and constitutional reform had claimed a strong minority
following by 1854, it was his eleven-page sermon on the Kansas-
Nebraska crisis that galvanized the voters. Grimes assailed the historical and logical inconsistency of Stephen A. Douglas's "popular
sovereignty" doctrine. This repudiation of the boundaries of slavery,
said Grimes, was nothing less than the first step in a southern con-

spiracy to spread slavery into Iowa and elsewhere. It threatened the very foundation of law and freedom. Abolition, Grimes insisted, was not the issue; but he would "war and war continually against the abandonment to slavery of a single foot of soil now consecrated to freedom."[9]

The antislavery charge was sounded. Over the next six years events would further circumscribe political choices for the Iowa people. Yet despite similar antipathies, their path to the Lincoln campaign of 1860 was not the same as that taken by John Murray Forbes. The Iowans' position was defensive, more truly conservative, while Forbes's was subtly aggressive. Their resistance to slavery extension rested on fundamentally different arguments. Where Forbes insisted that Congress had the power to bar slavery from the territories, Grimes inverted the logic: "Slavery is a local institution, depending wholly on State laws for its existence and continuance. Freedom being the natural condition of all men, and no authority being delegated to the General Government to establish or protect slavery, Congress can pass *no law establishing or protecting it* [slavery] in the territories." [emphasis added] Free government proceeded naturally from free men. No power of government could create freedom: What Grimes feared was the ability of government to create slavery. The distinction was critical. Western people stubbornly clung to their states' rights federalism throughout the war. Even as Grimes departed Iowa in 1858 to enter the United States Senate, he sounded the warning that the states were "gradually losing their consequence" while the federal government was "fast becoming an elective monarchy."[10]

REPUBLICANS TO POWER

From his own point of view, all of John Murray Forbes's antislavery arguments were "conservative," intended to affirm the traditional order and resist "radical and dangerous experiments in government." Still, his ambition to spread his northern way of life was truly an innovation. The progress and industry of free northern society seemed clearly superior; in time it would liberate even the blighted South. In the face of such logic, the extension of slavery was simply "absurd." To demonstrate his confidence in the northern ideal, Forbes drafted a scheme for a model plantation in Florida, to be worked by free contract laborers imported from China. This experiment in the peaceful redemption of the South was denounced by a planter friend for introducing yet another "inferior race" and for posing an attack on the institution of slavery. Rebuffed in his peaceful overtures, Forbes was doubly angry when the southern extremists insisted on the right to spread their peculiar institution over new western lands.[11]

Through the campaign of 1856, Forbes assured himself that a large class of like-minded men in the South would rise up to silence these fire-eaters. He was shocked, just after Buchanan's election, when one "conservative" friend in Georgia informed him that "a dissolution of the Union is inevitable whenever the free-soil principles of the North shall in any instance be enforced." Forbes's resistance to slavery extension was now absolute. If the South must engage just that question, there was no middle road. His relentless logic bound slavery's corruption of free society to the South's conspiracy to increase its power, proving to Forbes that the southern design was to corrupt the nation or destroy it. At stake was the future of American civilization.[12]

For James W. Grimes and his antislavery following the question was less dramatic. While their principles were secure, their political power still rested on the fleeting excitement of the popular temper. There was little the governor of Iowa could do to insure a free Kansas, but Grimes kept his one-issue following inflamed with belligerent rhetoric. William Penn Clarke, an old Grimes friend and radical Free-Soiler, organized the Iowa Kansas Committee, and Grimes soon saw to it that a new shipment of arms in the Iowa arsenal was "stolen" to outfit an expedition into the territories. Enthusiasm ran high, but some new political structure was needed to secure the antislavery power. In January 1856, Grimes called a state convention to organize a Republican Party dedicated to Free-Soil principles.[13]

To strengthen their base of political power, the Iowa Republicans balanced their antislavery message with traditionally "Whiggish" political economy, temperance, and the localist principles of the Free-Soil Democrats. Still, by early 1858, despite the Kansas agitation and some strategic redrawing of congressional districts in Iowa, the Republican movement began to wane. The effects of the depression, the embarrassments from nativist Republicans in New England, and the growing animosity toward railroads in Iowa threatened to break up the new party. Grimes once more turned his attention to the escalating crisis in Kansas. In desperation he concluded that the adoption by Congress of the proslavery Lecompton

Constitution would be "the only thing that can save our party."[14] This cynical wish was quickly granted. Douglas Democrats across Iowa broke ranks with the Buchanan administration over the Lecompton affair. In 1858 the Iowa Republicans again rode to victory on the waves of public outrage. Grimes went to Washington to enter the Senate, and Iowa stepped into the ranks of solid Republican states.

If direct antislavery agitation in Iowa had heretofore enjoyed little success, the effects of the Kansas crusade and the tales of atrocity that streamed in from the frontier were now electrifying. Iowa presented the best "free" route to Kansas for combatants from the eastern states, while contributions of men, supplies, and moral support from the Iowans themselves grew steadily. John Brown's campaign of bloody justice in Kansas, financed by men like John Murray Forbes in Boston, made Brown a folk hero across Iowa. The national movement for a free Kansas, again funded in Boston by Forbes and Amos A. Lawrence, gathered its rank and file from among the neighbors and communicants of the Reverend William Salter, William Penn Clarke, Josiah B. Grinnell, the Reverend George B. Hitchcock, and the Reverend John Todd—community leaders in Iowa with strong New England ties. Around the image of John Brown, the Holy Warrior, these accomplices in violence forged an interregional brotherhood of good works that paralleled the emergence of the national Republican Party. As sectional patience expired after 1860, this bond of blood helped strengthen the party and provide a unifying spirit between the East and the West.[15]

As he did everywhere, John Brown strained the loyalties of his Iowa friends with increasingly maniacal plots. In 1859, shortly before leaving for Harper's Ferry, Brown led a gratuitous raid into Missouri, killing a white slaveholder and freeing twelve blacks. The backlash was severe, and Brown was hurried out of the state by Grinnell and Penn Clarke. The denouement at Harper's Ferry later that autumn left many believers stunned and dismayed. Forbes in Boston feared the raid would drive "timid" conservatives from the Republican cause. Iowa Governor Samuel J. Kirkwood's remarks, praising the spirit if not the method of Brown's crusade, brought a storm of protest from the incensed opposition. But the time for retreat was past. Massachusetts and Iowa rallied in the Lincoln campaign. Victory at the polls in 1860 drew them closer together; the outbreak of war the following April cemented the bond in a spontaneous response to Lincoln's call for troops.[16]

The Republican coalition in 1860 could have formed only under the intense pressures of the sectional crisis. Its ideological program seemed refreshingly clear when compared to the confusion and pettifoggery of political debates in the decade past. The virtue of free labor, long celebrated as a cornerstone of American life, was being threatened with degradation by the oppressive class system of Southern slave culture. The free-soil corollary bolstered the American dream of material advancement and social mobility. If the fruits of free labor were the acquisition of land and independent middle-class status, then slavery threatened to expropriate the just rewards of the white laboring class.

Recalling the revolution of 1776, Republicans cast the planter elite as an illegitimate aristocracy, a parasitic class. Popular hostility toward "the appearance even of aristocracy," as Forbes often put it, was genuine: Free men in the North were not about to stand by while arrogant slavocrats turned the federal government into a private club. According to this view, the Republicans cause in 1860 was a reaffirmation of the American Revolution. It was the "party of the people" preserving their freedom, reclaiming their power, and conserving the meaning of the federal Union.[17]

Yet there was an alternate reading of Republican ideology, one that subtly reflected the dynamic changes in the industrializing North while it reinforced the paranoid style of southern politics. The new Republican Party embodied the powerful values of nationalism and industrial capitalism that were melding the federated republic into a single unit. Once freed from the confines of sectional politics, which alone had balanced diverse ambitions within the Union, the combined operations of large national economic and political structures would consolidate power and wealth in the hands of northern industrial leaders. For John Murray Forbes, this triumph of his own class was the "conservative" ideal; but from the southern point of view, this was *real* revolution, perpetrated by northern capitalists and their abolitionist henchmen. A northern triumph would bring, not an end to slavery alone, but an end to all local autonomy and self-government.[18]

The argument was not lost on western men who cherished their independence. James W. Grimes warned ominously, in 1858, against the "centralizing influence of the Government." "The liberties of the people," he proclaimed, "can only be preserved by maintaining the integrity of the State governments against the corrupting influences of Federal patronage and power." But the threat to local self-government that was inherent in industrial progress and economic growth was not clear to Iowans in 1860. The degradation of slavery, on the other hand, was an old and familiar evil. Recent history had shown centralization and abuse of power to be southern sins while Republicanism was grassroots democracy. Disgusted with the politics of sectionalism and confident that Republican principles would not only serve their interests, but also bring the belligerent South to heal, Iowa and its midwestern neighbors risked their hopes for the future on the election of Abraham Lincoln.[19]

DESCENT INTO WAR

One of the great tragedies of the American Civil War was that it distilled a host of social and political issues into a death struggle over slavery and secession. America in 1861 little resembled the infant republic of 1789 in its physical environment, social structure, or intellectual climate, and a generation of Americans who were born in a smaller, simpler world were still struggling with the enormous energies of change when the war came. After April 12, 1861, the nation was at war with itself over one question that symbolized, all too imperfectly, the great issues of the day. Institutions of control, already crumbling from inadequacy, collapsed in the face of crisis. Decisive actions of "practical men" took precedence over fine points of theory and constitutional law. Power gathered in the hands of unquestioned "Union men." The initial consensus was illusory; it would not last the year. But the terms of loyalty were set. Throughout the course of the war and the decade to follow, political opposition would desperately challenge the emerging order. Still, the centralization of power in the nation, which began with the siege of Sumter, was not reversed.

The unwitting beneficiaries of the wartime crisis were just such progressive entrepreneurs as John Murray Forbes. Forbes had had little influence over the course of public policy before 1861. Once hostilities began, however, governments at all levels needed men of Forbes's class for their skills at simplifying the complex and doing the needful. Heroic entrepreneurs in service to the nation, men like Forbes stepped forward in April and May of 1861, then slipped back to advise elected officials in the years to come. For John Murray Forbes, the experience first clarified the "meaning" of the war, then strengthened his assumptions about efficiency and order in the "true democracy" of the national state.

The idea of domestic warfare horrified Forbes and raised in him
the conservative's fear of revolution, anarchy, and mob rule. As he
viewed the secession of southern states one by one in December and
January, his analysis of the crisis became less coherent, his appeal for
common sense more frantic. Forbes pleaded for time to cool tempers
and reestablish a calm national forum. He abandoned with entrepreneurial candor all points of "Law and Learning and Logic" over
which men might "argue for a century," and he narrowed his objective to the security of Washington and the federal Congress. Forbes
begged a Baltimore friend to lay aside the "broader view" and help
meet the emergency. Surely two "right-minded honest men" could
contribute to a solution "by looking the facts straight in the face."
Once the Lincoln government was safely in power, Forbes promised
to urge it toward "broad grounds . . . to effect a permanent settlement." If, in a cooler moment, the true majority of southern voters
wished to secede, a separation must be arranged. But Forbes would
not accept a "compromise made in the midst of a revolution, and
offered to a faction" of southern slaveholders. Forbes was treating the
subject as a merchant, "entirely in its practical bearing upon the
present and future, . . . and leaving the clergy, the abolitionists and
the Calhounists to contend about its moral aspects."[20]

In his effort to isolate the immediate concern, Forbes had jetti-
soned virtually the whole substance of the argument between the two
sections of the country. He looked "straight in the face" of only those
facts he chose to see; beyond minor technical amendments he would
brook no compromise of the victorious Republican platform. His
curious offer of eventual separation suggested his faith in a loyal
southern majority rather than any willingness to divide the Union.
Forbes denied being an abolitionist, even as he denounced his State
Street colleagues, the old "Cotton Whigs," for their spineless endorsement of the Crittenden Compromise. These proposals formed the
agenda for a peace conference in Washington in early February, to
which Forbes had been appointed by his friend and confidant, the
radical Massachusetts Governor John A. Andrew. While these citi-
zen-peacemakers tried one last time to resolve their differences,
Forbes idled away the dreary debates by plotting schemes for the
relief of Fort Sumter.[21]

Rumors of an invasion of Washington had abounded since late
January. On February 1, 1861, with almost unseemly anticipation of
armed conflict, Governor Andrew began mobilizing his militia.
Forbes took unofficial charge of provisions and transportation for the

mustering regiments. He determined the location, cost, and availability of steamships in the various New England ports and quietly laid the groundwork for action at the right time. On April 15, 1861, when the call came from Lincoln to defend the capital, Massachusetts's response was swift. Forbes recommended sending one regiment to Fortress Monroe and two to Washington, all by steamship. In a flurry of activity he chartered the *Spaulding,* a Baltimore steamer then in Boston harbor, and the *State of Maine,* at her home berth in Fall River, Massachusetts. Both vessels were loaded and under way by nightfall on April 17. Within forty-eight hours the first Massachusetts soldiers set foot on Southern soil.[22]

Forbes served as quartermaster for the men in Virginia until the federal government could muster them in. When the generosity of the merchants of the Quincy Market outstripped their good sense, Forbes suffered the embarrassment of shipping three hundred tons of ice, together with fresh meat, vegetables, and Baker's chocolate, to the front. Putting the best face on this "appearance of amateur war," he directed the meat to the troops and the ice to the benefit of the hospitals of the Washington camp. This minor comedy notwithstanding, the operations came off quite well, if not according to any strict authority. Implicitly trusting entrepreneurs over government placemen, Forbes urged his governor to find a "working *business man*" for the commissariat, since this would save money now and credit later, "after the enthusiasm boils past." By early June a regular appointment had been made and Forbes turned to other fields of service.[23]

In war, as in business, Forbes followed his instincts. From his brief experience in provisioning he realized that the "modern art of war" would be "largely indebted" to the systems of supply and care of the troops. While this was a tactical problem for the North, the want of military and civilian manufactures was the great weakness of the agricultural South. The merchant strategist quite logically turned his attention to blockading the enemy and defending the shipping lanes for loyal trade. During the first days of the war, when communications with Washington had been cut off, Forbes had purchased two steamers for the Commonwealth of Massachusetts with funds from private subscription and a loan from the Boston banks. Armed with borrowed navy ordnance, the vessels were intended for transport service and coastal defense, but when Forbes tried to commission them into federal service in May, he "got only the cold shoulder from the Government." Caught with a pair of warships that no one wanted, and for which he had no regular authority from any government, Forbes ordered them out as privateers. The government finally bought one and issued a letter of marque to the other, which was sold to Bennet Forbes, but the snarl of red tape was just a preview of things to come.[24]

Forbes saw the northern states as essentially a naval power. The improved technology of the American merchant fleet, together with the large body of experienced seamen, constituted a readymade volunteer navy, wanting only commissions to set up an immediate effective blockade of the Atlantic coast. Because political patronage and "old fogyism" had enfeebled the regular navy, Forbes launched a plan in April to build seven modern steam sloops that he would sell to Congress when it met in July. Financed by a large number of small subscribers, this kind of democratic enterprise seemed above reproach and promised modern ships at a fair price in the shortest possible time. Meanwhile Forbes wanted the president to commission agents in Boston and New York to secure merchant ships for immediate service in transport and defense. He pressed his plan on everyone in Washington. "We can doubtless buy and equip vessels . . . cheaper than the department can," he wrote to Navy Secretary Gideon Welles, "but when it comes to using them for war purposes, . . . it is safer to have them under your well-digested regulations." Time was of the essence. The rebels had already claimed the army's weapons and the best West Point officers. Only prompt employment of Forbes's seaborne militia could neutralize this advantage.[25]

The need for an effective navy was doubly important in the face of British ambiguity about trade and diplomatic relations with the northern and southern states. While Forbes never doubted that England was the natural ally of the Union, he feared that careless policy on both shores would squander that goodwill. Queen Victoria had already proclaimed her own neutrality, allowing her merchants to trade freely with the rebel states. The wise Union course, according to Forbes, was to control the southern coast and force the British to deal with the Union alone. Once occupied by loyal forces, the cotton ports might be opened "at our pleasure" to soothe the British interests. In the meantime, public relations work with England was essential. Forbes transformed his private correspondence with leading English liberals into a personal diplomatic mission, alternately wooing and cajoling the peckish John Bull. The liberal sympathies of the English people, he reasoned, together with their antislavery attitudes and their industrial sisterhood with the American North, must all be flattered at every turn to keep pro-Union pressure on the British cabinet.[26]

As the first year of the war drew to a close, Forbes reconciled himself to the prospect of a long, debilitating contest. The government's want of energy and decisive force in the first months had allowed the renegade movement to mature. But that was history now; there was nothing left but to organize a proper war effort to achieve the victory. His own definition of the objectives of the war, temporarily confused during the spring crisis, acquired a new clarity. Sweeping away forever the complexities of the prewar debates, and with them a great body of antebellum thought, Forbes identified his cause as simply resistance to domestic revolution. The root question was whether "a government once republican can go backward in these modern days," toward the rule of an oligarchy. Drawing a curious analogy to the British suppression of the Indian Mutiny, Forbes complained to English economist Nassau W. Senior that "you do not properly appreciate the fact that we are not fighting to subjugate the South, but to put down a small class who have conspired against the people." Elsewhere Forbes expressed his view that an unleasing of the slaves might be only a military expedient: "I confess to being one of that average class which constitutes the majority of our people, who as yet hesitate at the dreadful experiment of [slave] insurrection; [but] if it becomes necessary, an alternative to the subversion of republican institutions, we should not hesitate a moment."[27]

There was a deep irony in Forbes's interpretation of the war. His entire "conservative" impulse rested on the revolutionary assumption that even before the crisis the United States had been a national industrial union. When Nassau Senior republished an old essay that supported this view, Forbes applauded the conclusion "which everybody here long since arrived at except Calhoun and his gang of conspirators." What Forbes saw before him was a war between "the people and a small class." There were ten million people in the slaveholding states, Forbes argued. Two million were "avowed loyalists in the border States"; four million more were blacks "ready to help us when we will let them"; three million more were poor whites "whose interests are clearly with us." The illusion of a rebel majority would evaporate once the suffering of the war had performed "an operation upon their *eyes!*" The North must "conquer the arrogant slave-owner classes" or submit to being dragged into a "grand slave empire." It was a war for modernity, for the triumph of progress over feudal despotism.[28]

Forbes's argument accomplished at a stroke what two decades of controversy had failed to. Such a triumph of the national state during the Civil War became a bitter point of contention for the political opposition in the North—and for some western Republicans as well. But the sentiments of loyalty neatly protected men like Forbes from their critics. Having seen his mission, Forbes marched boldly through the rest of the war, expedience and victory his sure guides. The fate of the nation was now cast in terms an entrepreneur could understand, and Forbes adopted the model of the corporate boardroom as his measure of government performance and public policy. The people were stockholders in a nation that was managed in trust by elected officials. Whenever political sensitivity hindered the Lincoln administration, Forbes saw it as a weakness in management—as if the farmers had gained control of the trains. To Forbes, the meaning of the war was simple, the goal was clear, the mandate was absolute. The popular democracy should be flattered in its virtue, educated in its errors, but resisted in its misguided demands.

THE BUSINESS OF WAR

Forbes sought to express his understanding of the war through practical efforts to advance the Union cause. At every turn, however, he encountered the inefficiency and corruption he had come to associate with irrational government and petty democracy. In business Forbes had always found relief by cutting red tape and suppressing "harmful" competition. Now he saw the Lincoln administration in need of the same kind of reforms. Politics aside, Forbes insisted that a government at war must function like a systematic business enterprise.

The navy department was the first target of Forbes's many attacks on the federal bureaucracy. Offended to find a ship that he had personally inspected and purchased for the navy being stripped and rerigged in the Boston Navy Yard, Forbes suspected "rats nibbling at the public cheese." He could not prove theft, but he urged Congressman Charles B. Sedgwick and Assistant Navy Secretary Fox to investigate the probability of profiteering by yard agents. Graft and delay in military procurements continued apace, reaching scandalous proportions by the last years of the war; Forbes demanded that businesslike systems be adopted and these rascals be "gibbeted to public opinion if the real hemp cannot reach them!"[29]

The whole system of public economy concerned Forbes, and he poured torrents of detailed advice on Treasury Secretary Salmon P. Chase and the Senate's financial expert, William P. Fessendon of Maine. As soon as a long war was evident, Forbes outlined a comprehensive funding plan that relied on taxation for ordinary expenses and interest, long-term bonds for the whole of extraordinary war expenditures, and short paper, bills, or treasury notes for "expedients only." He opposed legal tender greenbacks as both bad policy and bad principle. Arguing in January 1862 that the "currency" and the "patriotism" of the country had been tapped, but "the capital hardly at all," Forbes explained how long bonds at good interest, possibly tax exempt, could bring in the abundant capital that was otherwise fueling inflation. The capitalists must be brought into the government loans to secure the government's credit and relieve the pressure on the laboring classes. Greenbacks, he insisted, were a boon only to the "stock jobbing and broker and debtor interest." They encouraged profiteering without really aiding the public treasury; they drove solid capital away while grinding down the laboring poor. Forbes included tax penalties as well as incentives to force rich men into the public debt.[30]

Secretary of the Treasury Salmon P. Chase pursued exactly the opposite course throughout the war, and by December 1862 Forbes was denouncing "lawyers" and "politicians" and the want of a "business man" at the Treasury. Chase "stupidly" refused to sell long bonds at high prices. "Like some country farmers," Forbes chided, "he seems to think if his goods (bonds) are worth 104 to other folks they are to him!" Forbes worried that a combination of laborers and capitalists would soon demand peace if inflationary policies were not reversed. The country "demands more taxation," he proclaimed. "Rich and poor, all see it, except Congress. The rebels and their allies, the copperheads, alone oppose it."[31]

Forbes had grown accustomed to the incompetence of politicians in the field of finance, but the same display of ineptitude in the prosecution of the war astounded him. War was a technical, not a political, problem. Someone like John W. Brooks, "the Napoleon of R. Road Men," could "take the war by contract and put it through." Forbes lobbied for the appointment of "practical business men in those departments where promptness and knowledge of prices and system are required." Sentimental abolitionists were unfit for the cabinet, although Forbes saw "no danger of our having too much of that element in our Armies!" Secretary of War Simon Cameron's mismanagement and "mischief" was exasperating. Personally wounded by Cameron's charge that he was meddling in Missouri to protect his railroad interests, Forbes joined in the clamor to unseat the secretary, suggesting James F. Joy, his railroad strategist, for head of the War Department. The nation wanted "uncompromising" leadership in this "battle for National life." Instead Forbes saw weakness and corruption in Washington and softness on the field of battle. "We have never hanged . . . a single spy," he complained in 1863. When General Butler obliged him the following month, Forbes was elated. Growing almost vengeful, he opposed the lenient parole of prisoners: "[L]et our men remain on rebel fare until exchanged, and very few of them will willingly risk capture!" Obstructed in every effort to do "anything practical" on the military front, Forbes grew "sick and discouraged" as the war progressed. "[A]fter you leave Washington," he complained in 1864 to Iowa Senator James W. Grimes, "we shall sink into a stagnant sea of red tape."[32]

Forbes's instinctive response to official barriers was to circumvent them with private enterprise alternatives that he could organize and direct as he saw fit. An example was the bounty system of army recruitment. "It has bred up a race of swindlers," wrote Forbes, "dealers in men—worse than slave traders, and another class of men who sell themselves for the bounty." While advising the government to adopt a centralized system, Forbes took remedial steps of his own. In partnership with Amos A. Lawrence, who had joined with Forbes in the Kansas crusade, he established a brokerage that monopolized Massachusetts bounties and contracted with local governments to fill recruiting quotas. Forbes figured the cost of a green recruit "laid down in the South" at $450 and sent his agents as far away as Iowa and California in search of bodies for the Massachusetts regiments. He proposed to his old friend Joshua Bates, at Baring Bros. in London, that he contract for emigrants among the British unemployed, excluding "rigidly" the young, the old, and the lame. "Take the chance of their enlisting," he advised, "and I will have somebody on board the ship who shall get some of them into our service." Now a bounty hunter himself, Forbes steadfastly believed that his class of broker could drive out "ruthless" speculators and reduce the wasteful competition among middlemen. He did reduce the cost of a soldier by two-thirds at least, reserving profits for further recruiting, the regimental band, and "other useful purposes."[33]

Perhaps a better example of the entrepreneurial response to wartime problems was the Port Royal experiment in which Forbes played a more financial role. In the late autumn of 1861 Union forces captured the Sea Islands near Charleston, South Carolina, leaving the federal government in awkward possession of several thousand black slaves. The opportunity was seized by abolitionists in Boston and New York, who set up charitable societies and, on March 4, 1862, dispatched a band of missionaries to educate and prepare the Sea Island blacks for freedman status. By chance John Murray Forbes was sailing on the same steamer to visit his eldest son in the army camp at Beaufort. At first this "villain-tropic" band of "odd-looking men, with odder-looking women" reminded Forbes of the "fag end of a broken-down phalanstery!" Once on the ground in South Carolina, however, he quickly recognized the potential for a great experiment in emancipation and free labor agriculture—a scheme similar to his Florida plan some years before. Forbes saw this "noblest" of experiments as the beginning of that "social revolution" he believed would substitute "a Democracy for the beastly Aristocracy" now ruling the South. The following January he was readily persuaded to take part in a private partnership that purchased 8,000 acres of plantation land at tax sales in order to continue the free labor experiment on a businesslike basis. This intervention of big business was bitterly denounced by those missionaries whose ideal was the independent black homesteader, but Forbes insisted that wage apprenticeship was a necessary first step to ownership. A scattering of large efficient plantations run by "liberal men at the North" would teach industry and economy to the black freeholders and prevent either government dependency or ruthless speculation and exploitation of the free blacks.[34]

The Port Royal enterprise was a great success from its first year. Although Forbes's profits were restricted by agreement to 6 percent on his capital, he thought it a stunning example of the blessings of free enterprise. The experience of Port Royal proved that the "right sort" of men should be encouraged to do a large business in the cotton South. Still, Forbes's faith in free labor doctrines was not totally naive. He insisted on the rapid division of the land among *proven* small farmers to insure a permanent structure of freehold agriculture. Recognizing the vulnerable position of the newly freed slaves, he wanted a freedman's bureau to protect them from exploitation and reenslavement by either army officers or unscrupulous employers.[35] But the important question had been solved: The blacks would work in a free labor system. The corollary remained: Would they fight for it?

The conjunction of his work as an army recruiter and his observations at Port Royal brought about Forbes's final conversion to "radicalism." The "military necessity" of freeing and drafting the slaves at Port Royal set an excellent precedent for "expedient" abolition. Forbes returned home from the Sea Islands in May 1862 an ardent believer in emancipation and the use of black troops. "Trebly conservative as I am," he declared in June, "I sometimes get so disgusted with the timidity and folly of our moderate Republicans that I should go in & join the Abolitionists." Research into the revolution in Haiti convinced him that blacks would fight; in fact, a well-chosen regiment of fugitive slaves should "fight like devils!" By the end of summer Forbes was chairing the Committee of One Hundred, a Boston group dedicated to promoting black troops and raising the first black Massachusetts regiment.[36]

Now that Forbes had reached his own decision on a great question, he could not comprehend why others held back. If Lincoln could not grasp the slavery question "on so easy and practical a point as Pt. Royal," he complained in December, "we may as well give in!" Noting the "absurdity of buying men at the cost we do," when blacks were willing to fight, he equated emancipation with "self-preservation." By coupling abolition with black recruiting, even those who would not war for the "benefit of the negro . . . will be very glad to see Northern life and treasure saved by any practical measure, even if it does incidentally perform an act of justice and benevolence." Emancipation was proclaimed on January 1, 1863, but a host of objections to black troops remained. The army was racist and bitterly opposed to accepting black comrades. Even sympathetic men were afraid that black troops would incite brutality and mayhem among the rebel forces. Forbes met every objection with stubborn confidence, and by the end of May the first free black soldiers of the war, the 54th Regiment of Massachusetts, set sail for Beaufort, South Carolina. Elation in Boston turned to mourning a short month later when the 54th was badly cut up at Battery Wagner, and its commanding officer, Robert Gould Shaw, a favorite son of the city, slain.[37]

The loss of young Shaw, followed quickly by the draft riots in New York City, only strengthened Forbes's dedication to black troops, freedom, and total victory. He was outraged when the government failed to give equal pay to black soldiers. The differential defied common sense: "Who is to be the judge of a man's descent?" By 1864 Forbes's radicalism was complete: land reform, abolition by constitutional amendment, Negro suffrage, equal justice and equal pay, and the total subjugation of the planter South. Yet he had come to his views without recourse to "abstract principle." "I am not good enough to be an abolitionist," he wrote. "I am essentially a conservative." He had no more love for the "African" than for the "low-class Irish." But you cannot "steal one man's labor . . . by law," he argued, "without threatening to steal . . . every man's labor, and property and life! Hence to be anti-slavery is to be conservative." Through the whole intellectual muddle of the Civil War Forbes had reduced the most elusive principles of freedom and justice to the "practical" language of liberal capitalism. Confident that he had found the true meaning of American life, Forbes's last great service to the nation at war was to propagandize these views as the foundation of loyalty to the Union.[38]

Since the summer of 1862 Forbes had been working out plans for a propaganda machine designed to "sink these old [party] distinctions, and to put before the voting and fighting masses . . . the real issue" of the war. The plan was to reprint and distribute short articles of sound "doctrine" on a large scale, feeding material to loyal publishers and directly to the troops in the field. By February 1863 he had organized the New England Loyal Publication Society and was urging friends in New York to form a similar body on the national level. Loyalty to the principles of "true democracy" was the guiding idea, and Forbes warned against serving "any political friend or clique." For full effect the enterprise must be independent and "broad as the Union." In addition, Forbes wanted a serviceman's journal or "Army Punch" to feed the army "upon more wholesome diet than it has had in the New York Herald and other poisonous affairs." He quickly tied these plans in a loose fashion to the new "non-partisan" Union Leagues, giving the Publication Society a base outside the Republican Party. The stated objective of both organizations was to counteract the effects of political dissenters, who had already survived extraordinary suppression by the government and, by 1863, threatened to defeat the administration and sue for peace.[39]

Throughout 1864 Forbes continued to slip toward open manipulation of the electorate. Lincoln was "in no proper sense a pilot," he reasoned. Should the summer fighting bring more disasters the people may "demand a *Leader*" by election time. Forbes wanted the freedom to name a winner. The North was full of "Secesh" and

Copperheads who would "vote and pay for McClellan's election," unless loyal men could invoke the "popular element." On the surface this was simply campaign strategy, but Forbes had in mind the monopolization of political power. Failing in April to postpone the Republican convention, he threw the entire energy of the Loyal Publication Society and the Union Leagues into a "Union" campaign for the reelection of Lincoln. "If we can do this successfully," he wrote in August, "we can laugh at our enemies north and south, and we will found a nation . . . instead of the mere confederacy which these people pretend that we have been and are." Forbes arrogated to his party the whole defense of republican institutions and urged it to "widen itself" into the party of "True Democracy," which should "rule this country for fifty years to come." Forbes's America was clearly a modern nation state.[40]

IOWA HOME FRONT

John Murray Forbes could well afford to take the broad view of the Civil War that led to these nationalistic conclusions. His role near the councils of government was exhilarating; his private fortune and his personal point of view were truly "broad as the Union." For millions of Americans, however, the war years were not grand. For the ordinary citizens of Burlington, Iowa, they brought mounting irritation. This was a defensive war for the Iowans. Their interest in the slavery crisis was the protection of their homes from the advance of black slaves. Their stake in the Union was in free access to the ports of the continental nation. Their Republican ballots in 1860 had not authorized a revolution in government, economy, or society. On the contrary, the hope of western Republicans was to strengthen their relative independence in a government dominated by eastern business interests and southern slaveholders. Their commitment to the Union, once hostilities began, was perfectly sincere; but their perspective on that Union was sharply different from that of John Murray Forbes.

On January 14, 1862, Iowa Governor Samuel J. Kirkwood delivered a stirring appeal to prepare his constituents for a long and difficult war: "We must give up the idea of money making to a great extent until this war is over. We must be content to devote to the preservation of the country a portion of all the surplus we have been accustomed to lay up in years gone by. We may be required to return to customs and expedients for many years abandoned."⁴¹ The impulse to sacrifice was not wanting among the Iowans. Their response to the April crisis was as prompt and enthusiastic as that of Massachusetts or any other loyal state. Yet even as Kirkwood spoke, there was growing in the West a justifiable sentiment that the sacrifice fell disproportionately upon their shoulders. While industries in the northeastern states anticipated high profits in war supplies, trade in the Mississippi Valley collapsed. Money disappeared from the region once more. The Mississippi River was closed at New Orleans by the federal blockade. Iowa's line of export now lay solely through Chicago. Deprived of the river markets, the harvest of 1861 overwhelmed the transport system. Freight rates to New York quickly doubled and the price of corn at Chicago fell more than half. By early 1862 the shippers' cruel dilemma had returned: Iowa producers once again had a crop and no market. What surplus they might have devoted to patriotic ends was devoured by the eastern railroads. The inequities of this railroad market came to symbolize, for many Iowans, the whole unjust impact of the Civil War.⁴²

The impact of the war on the railroads themselves was not unmixed. New construction fell off sharply while tremendous pressures bore on the existing network to upgrade facilities, consolidate operations, and increase productivity. The sudden demands on Chicago roads like the CB&Q to absorb the ordinary commerce of the Mississippi River as well as the extraordinary wartime traffic focused the attention and resources of railroad men on these strategic links. Developmental projects like the Burlington & Missouri River Rail Road in Iowa were deferred. During the war the CB&Q was almost entirely rebuilt with new rail and heavy ballast. Freight- and grain-handling facilities in Chicago were doubled; a new stockyard was begun and eventually merged into the Union Stock Yard in 1865. Expenditures on the roadway alone increased fourfold between the first and last years of the war (including inflation), and dividends were suspended until late 1862. By that time the CB&Q was finally equal to the task, and its earnings rose embarrassingly through the remainder of the war. The CB&Q emerged from the war one of the "largest earning and best-paying roads in the Country," but the success of the Illinois company and the revenues that piled up in Chicago simply sharpened the contrast, for the people of southern Iowa, to their own languishing railroad.⁴³

John Murray Forbes actually gave little personal attention to railroad matters throughout the war. The B&MR management had just embarked on a conciliatory policy toward the people of Iowa when the secession crisis broke out. The company treasurer, John N. Denison, wanted to add four local men to the directory to regain the sympathy of Iowa communities. Then the war intervened and no changes were made. The abrasive superintendent at Burlington, John G. Read, did resign to enter the army, leaving the local office to the somewhat more popular Charles E. Perkins. The company also gained a measure of goodwill by offering free transportation to Iowa troops. But by midsummer of 1861 the impact of the war and the competition of a new rival had ruined business on the B&MR. Receipts did not cover interest on the bonded debt. From a business point of view the company suffered as much the following winter as its Iowa neighbors.[44]

The economic contrast between Chicago and Burlington helped fortify the opinion in southern Iowa that the Burlington & Missouri River Rail Road had been hopelessly burdened with stock and bonds by its absentee owners and was now being systematically bled dry. The company had not completed a mile of new track since September 1859, and many of its strongest supporters now doubted that the line would ever be finished. Competitive traffic running eastward through Illinois on the old Peoria & Oquawka line, which the CB&Q had largely subsidized but did not own, sparked rumors of a conspiracy to starve the Iowa line. Ironically, when the CB&Q finally foreclosed on the Peoria & Oquawka to relieve competition on the Burlington line, the city of Burlington rebelled. In November 1861 the citizens resolved to support the independence of the old P&O in hopes of breaking the Forbes group's monopoly hold on the city's commerce. "Every embarrassment that human ingenuity could devise," the people protested, "has been resorted to by these conjoint owners of the Chicago, Burlington & Quincy and Burlington & Missouri River Railroads." Working "in combination," the two roads had made "every distinction in rates of freights, which could embarrass our commerce." This time, discrimination was condemned by such original B&MR supporters as Henry W. Starr and former company president J. C. Hall.[45]

The old suspicions between local and eastern supporters of the Burlington road were raised to a new level of hostility by the frustrations of the war. Rate discrimination was a reality at Burlington, and it did serve the interests of the CB&Q by increasing through traffic to interior Iowa points at the expense of the Burlington terminal. Viewed from the perspective of the Forbes management, this was a reasonable policy for Iowa business under the pressures of the moment. Had the Iowans "kept control of the road," argued John N. Denison, "it could not have saved Burlington from the fate of all western cities & towns." The logic of systems that emerged, however, clashed with prior conceptions of the B&MR as an independent Iowa line. Both in rate structure and in strategic design, key eastern directors including Forbes already saw the Iowa road as a subordinate part of the CB&Q—and an unimportant one at the moment. B&MR President Edward L. Baker was frustrated by the neglect of his line, while Charles E. Perkins, Forbes's young cousin in the Burlington office, innocently urged extension as the only way to save the road. There was no money "here at the West," he admitted, but was it "simply absurd or not, to think of extension at present with Eastern Capital?" Forbes thought it was.[46]

Wartime unity notwithstanding, the Iowans prepared to resist the subordination of their interests to the large views of eastern investors. Convinced that the railroads were exploiting the disruptions of the war to their own advantage, the Iowa General Assembly was determined to pass some new regulations. In January 1862 the old Burlington antagonist John G. Foote, now a state senator, organized a campaign to place railroad lands on the county tax rolls. Governor Kirkwood lent his support to the movement, noting that none of the land grant roads was in strict compliance with the terms of the 1856 Act. Respectful of the now powerful Foote, Treasurer Denison argued for an income tax upon "productiveness," rather than a property tax that acted as a "prohibition upon Railroads." Edward L. Baker was less conciliatory. He promised to withdraw all eastern money from Iowa if the land tax were passed.[47]

In this early battle against state regulation, Forbes's management team revealed two strategic principles that foretold the future course of industrial politics: withdraw the issue from local government and withhold the blessings of industrial progress. For example, an income tax collected by a central state agency on the basis of company reports was infinitely preferable to property taxes levied by "petty" politicians in the towns and counties. "It would be more reasonable," cried Denison, to "pass a bill confiscating the whole of the property . . . than to deliver us up to be tormented & stung to death by a swarm of malicious or thirsty" assessors. Outside men would put no money into railroads "over which they have no representative control," if that property were subject to unchecked taxation by the local democracy. On the other hand, representatives from the western half of Iowa were treated to an unending stream of threats that no further rails would be laid in Iowa under such hostile conditions.[48]

These strategies reflected both the economic power and the distrust of democracy that marked the new industrial leaders. Investors in the large scale structures of a national economy dared not submit to home rule in local communities across the country. The Iowa land tax was defeated in 1862, but the victory for the B&MR was a fleeting one. The more critical question of completing the road was no closer to resolution. Hostile legislation, unpaid western subscriptions, repudiated bonds, and the steady erosion of the land grant through unfavorable judgments in swamp claim suits, in addition to the general uncertainties caused by the war, left eastern investors resolutely determined not to spend another dime in Iowa. On the other side, the people of Iowa would neither pay up nor shut up until the company renewed construction as a demonstration of its intention to carry the road through. Deft leadership at the top might have broken the deadlock, but Forbes was so preoccupied with war work that Denison and Baker could not "see him upon our matters at all."[49]

By 1863 economic hardship in the agricultural Midwest had been somewhat relieved by price inflation, strong demand for foodstuffs, and increasing competition in the trunk line carrying trade. The Iowa State Agricultural Society reported real prosperity by the end of the year, for which Governor Kirkwood promptly congratulated his industrious constituents. But the roots of midwestern anxiety ran deeper than the immediate balance of trade. Federal tariffs and excise taxes continued to bear most heavily on the agricultural West, driving up the cost of supplies and machinery faster than the world prices for grain and meat. More important, the poor showing of eastern armies, together with the apparent favoritism of Congress toward eastern industrial interests, raised grave doubts in the West about the commitment of their seaboard comrades to the winning of the war. Deprived of half its male population, the state of Iowa had turned in record crops only to see its gains eroded by inflation and taxes. Western armies had reopened the Mississippi River by the middle of 1863 but federal regulations, licenses, and fees still crippled that competitive outlet for western produce. The mounting human casualties of the war added deep emotional anguish to these feelings of inequity. In all, the conduct of the war, the policies of Congress, and the manipulations of the railroads seemed calculated to reduce the whole West to "little more than a province of New York."[50]

In such a climate of aggravation, the completion of the Burling-

ton & Missouri River Rail Road as an independent Iowa line became a symbolic as well as an economic demand. Forbes turned his
attention to the Iowa stalemate in 1863. A circular was issued October 7 requesting the holders of bonds from the first three B&MR
mortgages to exchange their now worthless securities for new 7 percent bonds and preferred stock, secured by a $6 million consolidated
mortgage. Private letters to large eastern holders explained the measure as an effort to keep the company out of receivership, where large
county and municipal stockholders in Iowa might exercise their
rights to "ruin" the property. The campaign was successful outside
Iowa: The majority of bondholders had agreed to the plan by March
1864. However, William F. Coolbaugh, the company's long-suffering
resident director in Burlington, rebelled at this last piece of financial
manipulation. As a result of his influence, a number of second mortgage bondholders in Iowa refused to accept the offer.[51]

Technically Coolbaugh objected to the values assigned to the
old securities, but beneath this complaint lay a more serious problem.
As sole resident director he had not been consulted in the reorganization. He saw this as another of the eastern owners' calculated efforts
to silence the local voice in management. When Iowa bondholders
applied to him for advice in the matter, Coolbaugh denied knowing
anything about it and refused to recommend the exchange. Implicit
in his reservation was the fear that the Burlington line would be
swallowed up by the CB&Q to serve only the larger interests of
Forbes's railroad system.[52]

Carefully observing the new power struggle from Burlington,
Charles E. Perkins concluded that Forbes's personal neglect of these
delicate relations was at fault. "I am satisfied," he confided to Forbes,
"that if Coolbaugh had been attended to properly from *head-quarters*
the second mtge would have 'come in' ere this." Yet it is difficult to
see what Forbes might have done because Coolbaugh's fears were
well founded. In April 1864 the CB&Q directors adopted a plan to
subsidize construction of the Iowa line, taking new B&MR securities
in payment on the joint traffic account. Except for the second mortgage holdouts, everything was in place for extending the road out of
profits due to the CB&Q. This is exactly what Coolbaugh had
feared. Before the annual meeting in June he offered to resign his
directorship. Embarrassed by the appearance of conspiracy, the eastern men rejected his letter. Coolbaugh must either be brought into
line or personally discredited.[53]

Mounting political pressure further threatened the Burlington
railroad. The Iowa General Assembly had opened in January 1864

with talk of reclaiming the land grant under the terms of the 1856 Act. Perkins lobbied feverishly, but to Forbes he made it clear that persuasion would no longer serve. "The B. & M. *needs* you," he pleaded in May. After *"drifting"* long enough, the people no longer had faith and would "only believe that we mean to extend when the spade is actually at work." The company had already lost its competitive advantage in western Iowa trade and land sales; now it risked losing the land grant itself. By October 1864, although business was steadily improving, Perkins saw the B&MR "being ground to death" by local competitors and even by its sister line, the CB&Q.[54]

Not even Perkins's pleas for the Iowa road would move the eastern men. The final solution to the stalemate in Iowa came instead through additional federal land grants that transformed the local Iowa line into a potential competitor for transcontinental business. Hoping to make up for lost swamp and preemption lands, the Iowa land grant roads had returned to Congress in the spring of 1864. Forbes was in Washington pressing for relief of the Burlington line. A grant of June 2, 1864, promised over 100,000 additional acres if the B&MR were extended twenty miles in the coming year. More important, a vast tract of Nebraska land was offered the following month to construct a branch of the Pacific Railroad to the one hundredth meridian. These were powerful inducements, but the directors stalled for time, using Coolbaugh's bonds as their public excuse.[55]

By the first months of 1865 even the company's friends in Congress were out of patience. Iowa's Senator Grimes and Congressman James F. Wilson refused to support another time extension for the road. Perkins tried in vain to move Forbes into action. The Iowans wanted to *"push* you up to extending the B.&M.," he explained. In March Perkins warned that the people of southern Iowa were planning a "perfect network of railroads," chiefly because of discrimination and delay on the B&MR. On April 9, the day Lee surrendered at Appomattox, Perkins declared the time was right to "make the beginning." Still Forbes lingered in Washington, where he had taken up housekeeping to await the exchange of his imprisoned son. The excitement of the recent peace was captivating, and Forbes busied himself with building grandstands for convalescent soldiers, that they might watch Sherman's and Grant's return to the capital. Only later that summer, when Forbes was back home and the war clearly over were preparations made for the continuation of the Burlington & Missouri River Rail Road.[56]

Eight years had passed since John Murray Forbes was welcomed in Burlington as the patron of the Iowa line. For six of those years the road lay dead on the banks of the Des Moines River, abandoned to war and other interests. The people of southern Iowa had utterly lost faith in the project; they suspected now that if the line ever resumed its westward course it would not be the local railroad they had imagined a decade before. Neither was it still the railroad that attracted John Murray Forbes in 1853. Iowa had grown up; other roads had opened the region and filled in the network to the east. The intervening years had seen new concepts of integration and consolidation in railroad management. Forbes's sequential model of "natural" development along stem line railroads was no more viable in Iowa in 1865 than the local conception of a home-owned railroad. The economics of combination and competition that marked railways as a special case in the laws of trade were spreading to western lines. The Pacific Railroad would soon be built, and the Nebraska land grant made the B&MR an interstate trunk line before it had fully evolved as an Iowa feeder. In 1865 the era of large railroad systems was dawning.

Forbes would soon recognize the compelling analogy between the new national union and a consolidated, integrated railroad system, but the Iowans wanted no part of it. What Forbes understood as the logical realities of national economic progress were seen in Iowa as abuse and neglect at the hands of absentee masters. In a larger sense the whole impact of the Civil War was related to this shifting framework of ideas. The plight of the Burlington railroad was a single dramatic example of the shift in emphasis from particular interests to broad systems of progress—from sectional rights to national goals. During the war, some western Republicans like Grimes of Iowa bitterly defended their sectional interests, but the debates dissolved into regional slanders on the "effete" East or the "uncivilized" West. Expecting to dominate the victorious party, most western Republican leaders remained in the fold. Then when the moment of triumph came, the objective of keeping the "Union" party in power set limits on political diversity in the new American nation. The postwar political vocabulary suited the views, not of James W. Grimes, but of John Murray Forbes: one class, one party, one nation united. The American republic had been transformed.

5

Localism Under Siege

IN MAY 1865, barely a month after the signing of the peace, Major General Quincy A. Gilmore asked John Murray Forbes if he would build a railroad on the sea islands off South Carolina. Forbes responded with a firm negative: "I hope my labors in the way of railroad building are done," he explained, "having been one of the pioneers in such enterprises, and being now entitled to a rest." But he urged the general to press forward his scheme before the government of South Carolina could be reinstated and the army's jurisdiction curtailed. Reconstruction for Forbes was the act of forcibly bringing the South into harmony with the industrial integration and progressive outlook now favored in the North, and no procedural stumbling blocks, like the resurgence of stubborn local democracy, should be allowed to bar the way. Throughout the Reconstruction era Forbes begged his wartime friends not to split the Republican party by intrigue and plotting, because "upon the unity and cohesion" of that party depended the "successful restoration of industry and order . . . for years to come."[1]

In May 1866, a little over a year after the signing of the peace, Senator James W. Grimes rose in the U.S. Senate to denounce the continued proliferation of federal agencies. "During the war," he lectured, "we drew to ourselves here, as the Federal Government, authority which had been considered doubtful by all, and denied by many of the statesmen of this country." Grimes reminded his colleagues that the extraordinary powers exercised in war were justified only by the state of emergency: "That time," he thundered, "has ceased and ought to cease." The only honorable course for the victors, according to Grimes, was to go back to "the original condition of things, and allow the States to take care of themselves." For Senator Grimes, Reconstruction was an act of restoration. He did not acknowledge what men like John Murray Forbes believed was the

111

primary truth in the Civil War: that the consolidation of power to and the administration of progress from the center was the meaning of the victory. Between Forbes and Grimes lay the great unsettled issues of the American Civil War.[2]

For more than three decades Forbes had tried to bring order to his changing world, first in a small commission house at Canton, then in ever expanding railroad lines, and finally in the government of the nation. Despite his addiction to conservative, paternalistic postures, Forbes's successes depended on emerging liberal systems of business and government. His personal interpretation of the war left him a thorough nationalist, and he feared any return to antebellum ways. Unrepentant Southerners would naturally seek to reverse the outcome of the war by a return to states' rights heresies; and if loyal Republicans like James W. Grimes could relapse so completely, there was much to be feared in the West as well. The Republican party's work was unfinished. Forbes envisioned his party as an army of occupation not only in the South but in the house of government itself. "We owe it to the living and the dead," he wrote in 1868, "to keep together until we have absolutely secured the fruits of our dearly bought victories."[3]

It was to watch and assist in this continuing revolution that John Murray Forbes "retired" once more from active business. Ironically it was business, not politics, that brought the great questions back into focus in the postwar years. The hegemony of the Republicans stifled debate and turned the electoral process into a factional exercise that corrupted partisans and in time repulsed men like Forbes. At the same time, ideological issues gave way to bread-and-butter complaints emanating from the economic distortions of the war and its aftermath. Outside the South, two issues transcended partisan quarreling: currency deflation and railroad regulation. On the money question there was no simple, clear division among men, but the railroad question resolved itself into a challenge by the advocates of localism to the encroachments of national interests.[4]

The public vehicle of protest in the postwar struggle for railroad control was a farmers' movement called the Grange. Men like Forbes called it agrarian reaction, but the Grangers were often inspired and led by local merchants who were threatened by emerging national markets. Remembering with James W. Grimes the reservations they had about the party of Lincoln, western farmers and local moguls rose up in the early 1870s to defend the ideals of the early American republic. By now the story of Forbes, the Iowans, and the Burlington

Route was but a single example of a larger phenomenon that was regional in scope and so complex in nature that no contemporary understood the problem well. Forbes could not understand the West's devotion to antiquated theories of business and government while the Iowans only dimly perceived that they had too great a stake in the new age to go back to "original conditions."

LANGUAGE AND THE LAWS OF TRADE

The problem with "original conditions" was that they belonged to a preindustrial, prerailroad world. By the end of the Civil War the shape of American business and society had been irreversibly altered by three decades of railroad development, and the return of peace brought an explosion of new construction in the West that would reach the Pacific Ocean before the decade's end. Adam Smith's eighteenth-century model of merchant capitalism still supplied the language of political economy for most practical-minded Americans, but the conditions of trade scarcely resembled the markets of England ninety years before. Railroads had brought isolated markets into competition with each other in ways that local entrepreneurs were powerless to address. At the same time, competition between carriers in the railroad network was governed, not by commodities markets, but by the capacity of the system and the demand for transportation. Competition—the "invisible hand" that regulated Smithian markets to perfection—was threatening local enterprise all across the railroad system while it seemed to encourage the railroad's assumption of monopoly powers. Railroads were a centralizing force in the American economy, and by the end of the war it was clear that something was "wrong" with the laws of trade.

The evolution of economic language itself made it hard to respond to the tendency of railroads to accumulate power. For example, back in 1846, when John Murray Forbes took up the Michigan Central, railroad transportation was universally seen as an "artificial" advantage in the commercial environment. Western boosters like the editor of the Burlington *Hawk-Eye* were confident that these "artificial means of prosperity" would complement and preserve the natural advantages of their own commercial centers. But for two decades thereafter progressive entrepreneurs like Forbes had dedicated their energies to eliminating just those barriers of time, space, and physical geography that defined the "natural" commercial network. By 1865 this sense of conscious intervention in economic geography had been lost among railroad men. They saw the railroad system as a natural environment in its own right, obeying the same natural laws of trade. Those who suffered under the new system and sought to defend the priority of geographical location or the old river routes were now charged with "artificially" obstructing progress. This adaptation of old language by the forces of change rendered traditional economic rights meaningless in the postwar world.[5]

As a merchant, John Murray Forbes had been raised to believe in the natural laws of trade. He easily transferred his theories from foreign commerce to his new railroad enterprises. However, few merchants and farmers at the local level in the West were prepared to embrace all the changes wrought by the transportation revolution. For Forbes, new developments were inevitable and resistance was futile. Local western interests saw the same developments as corrupt and threatening to their economic independence. It was this contrast of perspective that caused B&MR Treasurer John N. Denison to defend rate discrimination at Burlington as the "fate of all western cities and towns." To the towns this fate was a "return to serfdom."[6]

The rhetoric of natural and artificial markets was misleading from the start. All economic systems reflect the exploitation of nature by human society; at issue in postwar America was the arrangement of that exploitation and the tools by which it was accomplished. The spectacular growth of Chicago as the premier midwestern entrepôt offered striking proof that new technologies were gaining the upper hand. Between 1840 and 1850 Chicago grew from an outpost of five thousand souls into a booming city of thirty thousand. Another decade boosted Chicago over the hundred thousand mark—the eighth largest city in the country and close behind St. Louis. In volume of trade, Chicago's exports (mostly produce) rose from $5.3 million in 1851 to almost $73 million in 1860. Total trade at Chicago just before the Civil War rivaled the great western mart of Cincinnati; during the war Chicago passed St. Louis forever as the trading capital of the upper Mississippi Valley.[7]

How had this been accomplished? St. Louis lay at the meeting of two great rivers in the geographical center of the nation, the natural focus of prerailroad trade for the north-central region. The general faith in St. Louis's natural advantages even fostered a complacency among the city's merchants toward the new railroad developments. The energetic drive of Chicago promoters, however, reversed the downstream flow of trade. Railroads, lake steamers, sophisticated storage, handling, and marketing systems, and abundant commercial credit were the instruments of the Chicago victory. The railroads led the way in transforming Chicago's commercial systems.[8]

During the 1850s eastern trunk lines met at Chicago, then feeders radiated into the rich farming districts to the north, west, and south of the city. Although the first rails to the Mississippi fed produce into the downstream trade, the superior facilities at Chicago were already reversing that flow by 1861. To capture the bulk agricultural business, the railroads built grain elevators at convenient collection points, often creating new towns for the purpose. Managers tapped their personal and financial connections in the East, through telegraphic communications along the railroad rights-of-way, to offer the latest price quotations to merchants in the country. Faster service, better credit, and fewer handling charges frequently outweighed a slightly higher ton-mile rate for carrying grain. Furthermore, aggressive Great Lakes steamship lines kept long-haul New York charges competitive for either water or rail transportation. Chicago soon became the better market even for eastbound grain from Michigan and Indiana. While St. Louis dealt in bagged grain that was loaded by hand, stored outdoors, or hauled across town in wagons for storage, Chicago grain merchants pioneered the bulk elevator, ran rail spurs directly to the docks, devised automatic systems for loading freight cars and steamships, and implemented uniform systems of grading, pricing, and warehouse receipts. Two elevators built by the Illinois Central Railroad in 1858 exceeded the storage capacity of the entire St. Louis market. In the 1850s, grain exports from Chicago by water and rail rose from 1.3 million to 26 million bushels; flour jumped from 100,000 to 700,000 barrels. By 1860 the vast majority of this freight came *into* Chicago by rail.[9]

For a host of smaller towns in the Mississippi Valley the success of Chicago was a mixed blessing. Prairie towns in Illinois and Iowa river ports like Dubuque, Clinton, Davenport, and Burlington all entertained visions of their growing importance in the railroad network. Unprepared for the streamlined integration of the Chicago market, most of these centers found their own growth quickly stunted by rates and services that made Chicago more attractive to interior shippers. By offering more attractive rates than the hometown buyers, Chicago railroad agents were soon in a position to dictate terms to the interior as well. The legitimate advantages of the commercial system through Chicago brought powerful examples of centralization and integration with eastern markets to the heart of the agricultural

Midwest. The outlines of the new system were evident when the war closed the Mississippi River in 1861; the absence of meaningful river competition during the war allowed the rapid consolidation of this power and opened the door to monopolistic abuses.[10]

The central element in the railroad's power to manipulate the flow of trade was the rate-making process, yet the "science" of rate making was makeshift at best. Overall levels and average rates meant nothing to particular shippers; it was the relative structure of rates that mattered. Dozens of variables influenced the rate on any class of freight at each station on the line, and freight agents were expected to adjust the published schedule of tariffs whenever necessary to maximize revenues at their stations. High fixed costs called for increased volume to spread these costs more widely. Because terminal and handling charges did not vary with the length of trip, short hauls were substantially more expensive per mile. Interregional "through traffic" passed at far lower rates than local freight in order to compete at distant markets. Seasonal fluctuations and a chronic imbalance between bulk agricultural exports and compact manufactured imports resulted in periodic car shortages, "deadheading," and frequent underemployment of equipment throughout the system. Finally, the presence of rail or water competition at a terminal pressed rates downward, while single-service "way points" were charged all that "the traffic would bear." Given the circumstances, railroad freight agents quoted charges that varied wildly.[11]

Even a perfect rate structure would have seemed unfair to the western shippers because the objectives of the railroad network were different from those of local producers. Rationalization of a national market necessarily discriminated between primary and secondary centers of trade. Furthermore, the laws of supply and demand, as they bore on the transportation business itself, often contradicted the behavior of commodities markets. High demand for transportation resulting from a good harvest, for example, made transportation dear just when the price of grain was lowest. On the other hand, crop shortages that raised grain prices also raised the price of transportation, except at the most competitive points, because carriers had to recover fixed costs on the reduced volume. At such times more expensive corn would bear the higher charge. If this was unfair to certain captive shippers, it was the price to be paid for large regional advantages in the new transport system. Unable to store their services or withdraw from the market, railroad managers followed shifting rules of competition that baffled the shipping public—and many railroad men as well.

These serious problems were aggravated by ignorance of the real cost of transportation by rail for any given service. In their struggle to show an overall profit, most railroad men disregarded questions of equity in the rate structure. Citing the time-honored principle, "what the traffic will bear," they constantly intervened to manipulate the supply of traffic and the rate it would bear through monopolistic agreements with grain merchants, wholesalers, manufacturers, and steamboat companies. Collusive agreements among the railroads to divide the business further curtailed competition. By the late 1860s these practices resulted in wild distortions of the competitive environment and "unjust" discrimination against individuals and localities. Large shippers depended on the favor of their railroad friends. Intermediate cities rose or fell in response to the structure of local rates. Certain shippers and towns made unprecedented gains while the majority of small merchants and farmers in the Mississippi Valley lost all control over where and how and at what price they sold their crops. If railroad rates were often fair and equitable, they were always arbitrary. The threat of destruction, even more than actual abuses, focused public hostility on the arrogance and power of the railroad managers. While the best of these managers proclaimed the virtues of the "natural laws" of supply and demand, they constantly defied those laws from necessity or from habit.[12]

Ironically, free competition had created the problem both for the midwestern shippers and their railroad rivals. Rate discrimination grew out of competitive pressures, from consumers and railroad promoters, to build developmental lines faster than the territory could support them. For two decades John Murray Forbes had been preaching the gospel of patient development, but his argument fell on deaf ears. Neither railroad builders nor anxious pioneer patrons would be stayed in their frantic rush to the West. As a result, conflict was built into the original bargain and proved almost impossible to overcome. Distortions in the rate structure reflected the railroad managers' understandable need to raise immediate income while building a revenue base for future defense against competition. Techniques of operating efficiency that made possible reductions in interregional freight rates favored long- over short-haul business. Furthermore, aggressive merchants in those local markets blessed with competing rail service encouraged the rate wars that so heavily taxed their less fortunate neighbors. Railroad defenses against ruinous competition were indistinguishable in character from monopolistic abuses. Western interests therefore unfailingly pressed for *more* competition to recover their independence. At the same time that eastern capitalists like John Murray Forbes were condemned for dominating the western economy, they were forced to expand their investments in response to the demands of western people. If Forbes refused, others would invade the territory he already controlled.

A "FIT" YOUNG MANAGER

Charles E. Perkins was located uncomfortably at the center of all these contradictory pressures. Perkins had come to Burlington in 1859 as a clerk on the B&MR. As the war drew off his immediate superiors, he took on the duties of land agent, assistant treasurer, and assistant secretary. Forced to sit out the war in Iowa, and finding little employment as yet in selling railroad lands, Perkins became the principal liaison between cousin John Murray Forbes, the Burlington company, and the people of Iowa. His considerable talents as a manager together with the circumstances of his confinement in the Burlington office cast young Perkins in the mold of a company man, a role that in time would make him an invaluable resource to the Forbes group and the Burlington railroad.

Born in Cincinnati, Ohio, in 1840, Charles Perkins was the oldest son of James Handasyd Perkins, himself a cousin of John Murray Forbes. The elder Perkins had rejected the commercial life of his family to take up an intellectual calling in the West. Briefly recognized as a lecturer, writer, and Unitarian minister in the Cincinnati region, James Perkins died suddenly in 1849, leaving young Charles to care for his mother and four brothers. The youth managed to stay in school until he was sixteen, when he took employment with a wholesale fruit grocer in Cincinnati. From this position he applied to John Murray Forbes for advice and direction in selecting a career. "There is a great want of good, trustworthy businessmen for the management of our railroads," came the reply. "I can help you on better in that direction than any other, and if you can fit yourself to manage such matters well . . . you would certainly stand a good chance of having your services recognized by pay and promotion when the proper opening comes." In July 1859 the eighteen-year-old Perkins accepted an offer to assist Charles Russell Lowell in the land department of the Burlington railroad. It proved to be the most successful of John Murray Forbes's many efforts to place willing young men on the path of the future.[13]

If Forbes wanted a manager for his western railroad, Perkins was determined to "fit himself" to be the best. He took to the Iowa country and the railroad business immediately. The outbreak of war brought added responsibilities which he gladly shouldered, but the lure of battle promised high adventure and stimulated his sense of ambition. By the summer of 1862 Perkins threatened to take a commission in the army for "$1,300 besides the glory" unless Forbes could get him a substantial raise in pay. While most young men of his class and generation were distinguishing themselves on the fields of battle, he complained, he was marking time on a stagnant railroad. Forbes finally convinced him that he could better serve his country and his widowed mother by staying alive in Burlington. During this isolation Perkins formed an increasing attachment to the Burlington company. When, in the last years of the war, he desperately urged Forbes to extend the Iowa line, Perkins felt that his own future along with the Iowa business was at stake.[14]

In the beginning Perkins was both a paid company manager and the personal agent for the Iowa Land Association, through which Forbes and his friends speculated in real estate along the line of the road. The Boston men may have viewed him for the moment as a hireling, but Perkins's own ambition was to accumulate knowledge and property and rise to partnership among them. For this reason he carefully exploited the family connection with John Murray Forbes, writing privately to Forbes to insure that his views would cut through regular company channels. He thought of himself as a spokesman for the eastern men in their western mission, and he tried to interpret events and attitudes at each end of the network for the benefit of the other. Like the younger John Murray Forbes in the Canton commission house, Perkins gradually made himself indispensable to all parties interested in the Burlington road. He was placing himself at the center of an emerging Burlington railroad system.[15]

Perkins believed that the Iowa line was the key to the postwar success of Forbes's whole railroad network. Forbes was inclined to agree, but he paid little attention to its development. Immediately after the war Perkins persuaded Forbes and four other eastern directors to visit Iowa to examine the prospects for themselves. Perkins argued strenuously for the old developmental ideal, but with a quickened pace. Both the value of the land grant and the steady traffic of

the Burlington road depended on rapidly and systematically planting a friendly population in southern and western Iowa. Since local
fundraising for new construction was no longer promising, he placed
more faith in the contract with CB&Q to finance construction from
Iowa earnings. By the end of summer 1865 those earnings were "very
large," and Perkins was secretly investing his eastern friends' money
in depot lands just beyond the railhead. As winter approached plans
were laid to bridge the Mississippi River at Burlington. At long last
things were moving on the Burlington railroad.[16]

Time was the enemy for Charles Perkins. Throughout 1866 he
pressed for bonuses to speed construction, and he fumed about delays. Contrary to Forbes's traditions, Perkins asked for a cheap road
quickly in order to get the line open and catch his competitors.
Forbes and the Boston men remained deliberate in their methods. In
October 1866 the CB&Q directors agreed to finance another sixty
miles beyond Chariton. Slowly the work progressed. By June 1867
the line had advanced only forty-seven miles, while the Chicago &
North Western (C&NW) had completed its line to Council Bluffs,
complete with bridges at the Mississippi and Missouri rivers. Still, the
Burlington line had earned nearly half a million dollars in the past
fiscal year, and less than half had gone for operating expenses. This
kind of revenue would service construction debts for perhaps another
year, but Perkins knew only too well that finished lines to the north
would draw off his traffic and drive down prevailing rates. When the
Burlington line finally reached the Missouri River its profit margin
was sure to be slim. Construction from current earnings must be done
very soon or not at all.[17]

Perkins's efforts to finish the line were hindered at every turn by
public impatience with the B&MR. He turned to local politics for
relief, cultivating members of the state legislature with free passes
and correspondence. An open lobby "of R.R. men at Des Moines,"
he reasoned, "could turn some honest members against us, who, by
judicious behavior on the part of our friendly members, may be
brought to us." Whenever he could, Perkins reminded his western
Iowa "friends" that rate regulations favored only those eastern Iowa
interests, "who having the road care nothing for the interests of the
State at Large." When it seemed prudent, he issued a friendly line
expressing his "interest" in some local election. At one point he asked
Forbes to send out a man with money and doctrine enough to buy
out the Burlington *Hawk-Eye*, whose current editor was hostile. Perkins's politics, however, were not entirely insincere. He made positive

efforts to secure the city of Burlington against commercial losses resulting from the new Mississippi River bridge. Even as the superintendent of a "foreign" railroad, Charles Perkins was deeply attached
to Burlington and worked conscientiously to develop his adopted
community.[18]

Because of his field experience and his growing commitment to
the Iowa road, Perkins was the first to recognize weakness among his
eastern supporters. James F. Joy was the chief doubter. Without coal
and timber, Joy reasoned, Iowa could not be settled. Perkins thought
this a mistake in judgment, but in time he came to suspect that Joy
had "so much else on foot that he pays no attention to us." Naturally
the Burlington's lands would not be settled, he argued, "till the road
is built." In fact, Iowa courts would soon *"decide our lands Taxable"*
unless the railroad were finished and the lands sold. As Joy turned
against him, Perkins warned Forbes that endless delay "not only
makes the heart sick, it sometimes makes men mad!!"[19]

By 1868 the pressure on Perkins had become intense. Rumors
were flying that the CB&Q intended to absorb the Iowa road. (Perkins asked Forbes, was it true?) In January 1868 the Iowa legislature
began debating the resumption of the Burlington land grant. Characteristically, Perkins bristled at this kind of threat, even when it
indirectly served his interests: "Would it be wise or dignified to be
whipped into doing what a parcel of black-mailing cutthroats . . .
want us to do [?]" Perkins wanted to press forward, taking no more
local aid and making no promises to local communities. Still Joy
dragged his feet, keeping the Iowa road at arm's length from the
CB&Q.[20]

While Forbes and his friends dawdled on their Iowa project they
might have lost the property altogether. A recent contract for aid
from the CB&Q called for B&MR bonds convertible into preferred
stock, which required the approval of two-thirds of the voting shareholders. But the nonresident directors held only a simple majority.
By February 1868 it was evident that Iowa stockholders would use
their voting strength to block the new issue. Perkins devised a scheme
to corner the full-paid shares of the city and counties whose bonds
had not been honored. He pressed for judgments against the remaining bonds, forcing an auction of full-paid shares that he then secretly
bought. Forbes was cool to the idea at first, but the ease with which
Perkins was acquiring shares at fifteen and twenty cents on the dollar
brought him around. When the marshall's sale took place in Burlington in July, Perkins captured 750 shares at less than seventeen cents

per share. Systematically B&MR attorney Henry Strong foreclosed
on public delinquents. United States District Judge David J.
Rorer, a former company attorney, then ordered the sale and Perkins's agents
bid off the stock with funds supplied by Forbes, Perkins, Counselor
Strong, and Senator James W. Grimes. By this method another 3,250
shares were acquired before the cover blew off in August. In the face
of charges of fraud and a possible injunction, Perkins transferred
certificates to the real owners of this new stock as quickly as possible.[21]

This entire operation had been Perkins's initiative, designed
both to strengthen eastern control of the company and to improve his
own position with the eastern directors. When Forbes finally scolded
Perkins for his constant complaints about the directors, Perkins was
ready with his defense. He had more faith in Iowa than all the rest.
He had gone out on a limb to secure control when others were indifferent. "You know," he told Forbes, "what a queer man Judge Rorer
is—It was all I could do to bring him to sell. . . . I had to *give* him 43
shares!" Perkins's maneuvering had profited everyone in Boston, but
if "Mr. Thayer & others think I would turn my hand over to put
money into their pockets (possibly) without a 'consideration,' they
are mistaken." Without wealth of his own, Charles Perkins was capi-
talizing accomplishments which John Murray Forbes was bound to
respect. It was risky for so young a man to cross powerful opponents
like James F. Joy and Nathaniel Thayer, but Perkins would soon be
rewarded.[22]

By the autumn of 1868, B&MR stock had begun to rise, and
completion of the line to the Missouri River was nearly assured.
Perkins figured the cost of the finished road of 300 miles at just over
$10 million. Nine million of that sum was interest-bearing debt, but
the earnings record suggested that the B&MR could pay all of its
interest plus a 7 percent dividend in the first year of operations to the
Missouri River. The stock rose to par in June 1869, and the line itself
was completed to Plattsmouth on November 26. After sixteen years
the Burlington & Missouri River Rail Road was finally completed.
In the next twelve months its earnings exceeded Perkins's wildest
predictions—over $200 million.[23]

DIVERGENT STRATEGIES

In his struggle to finish the B&MR, Charles Perkins had proved
himself to be an able "descendent," though not simply a copy, of

John Murray Forbes. He pursued the basic theory of development that Forbes had laid out before the war, even though Forbes now paid entirely too little attention to his sprawling railroad interests. Perkins subtly adapted Forbes's ideas to the postwar environment, but the old merchant himself blindly followed James F. Joy into an explosive new period of railway expansion. Convinced that nothing could shake his confidence in Joy, Forbes had given that Detroit promoter essentially free reign over the management and strategy of the CB&Q and its allied western lines.

Forbes's confidence in Joy was based on two decades of successful cooperation. At the beginning of the postwar boom, the CB&Q was a solid Illinois road of four hundred miles, doing some $6 million worth of business per year. Roughly half that sum was consumed in operating expenses; the balance easily serviced $6 million of funded debt and returned 11 percent on a capital stock of $8.4 million. Thus situated, the CB&Q was a perfect anchor for more speculative ventures to the West, and the Boston directors perhaps understandably took their dividends from Joy without complaint. Expansion from earnings was always safe, and presumably Joy would come to Boston if the need arose for new inputs of capital. What Forbes did not consider was that Joy had acquired new financial supporters of his own, chief among them Moses Taylor, president of the National City Bank of New York and one of the richest railroad investors in the nation. This alternative source of capital gave Joy a measure of independence from the cautious conservatives in Boston, just when western railroads entered the fiercest round of competitive construction the industry had seen. Less deeply committed to sequential development than Forbes, James F. Joy was easily attracted to those manipulations of grand systems that marked the "looser" side of railroading. As president of the CB&Q and a leading executive in the Michigan Central, the Hannibal & St. Joseph in Missouri, and the B&MR in Iowa, Joy was in potential control of much of the interstate rail traffic in America's heartland. Neither he nor Forbes recognized how treacherous a temptation that was.[24]

By manipulating the rate structure, railroad managers could often divert traffic over long and inefficient routes without serious loss to the company's revenues. The mischief that resulted from such practices was well recognized before 1865. John W. Brooks had complained in 1863 that any rule other than "even and uniform rates would produce utmost chaos." Brooks knew, however, that as long as two roads connected the same two points, any physical difference in their routes would be counteracted by the rate structure. Security lay in having the most efficient route and keeping rates up to a paying level. For this reason Brooks came to share Charles Perkins's impatience to finish the Iowa railroad and establish steady, efficient through traffic over the long western line. Both Brooks and Forbes identified sequential development—working westward along with the settlers—as their best defense against wild competition.[25]

James F. Joy was formulating a different plan made possible by the wartime development of the transcontinental railroad. Leaping ahead of sequential investors, the federal government was creating a trunk line through barren lands from which all transcontinental traffic must flow to the half dozen carriers in the Mississippi Valley. It took no special insight to recognize that whoever controlled the first and most numerous connections with the Union Pacific Rail Road possessed an immense source of immediate wealth. Because the bottleneck at the gateway created this opportunity, further development of far western lines would be counterproductive. This prospect led Joy to concentrate on connecting the existing Hannibal & St. Joseph with short lines up the Missouri River to meet the Union Pacific at Omaha. The deep contradiction between Joy's opportunistic strategy and sequential development in Nebraska was not immediately recognized by the Boston directors.

The true friends of the Iowa railroad made two perceptual errors that gave Joy his opening. Forbes, Brooks, and John N. Denison allowed their disputes with the Iowa people to assume such importance that they almost believed their own threats not to finish the line. While these men adhered to their theories of local aid and territorial development, CB&Q President Joy treated his whole board of directors to endless statistics that proved that the Hannibal road was a more profitable feeder for the Chicago company. Charles Perkins recognized the game, but his word was not enough. Joy spoke favorably about the Iowa line in his CB&Q reports, but he implied a choice between quick profits in Missouri or expense and hostility in Iowa.[26]

Forbes's assumption that the Nebraska land grant promised the B&MR its own transcontinental connection was another error that played into Joy's hand. Though clearly safer in the long run, this developmental strategy meant even longer and larger commitments before really handsome profits could be expected. It had been difficult enough to get CB&Q directors to approve the pay-as-you-go aid to the B&MR. By November 1866 Joy was subverting that agreement with unfair comparisons between the completed Missouri line and the truncated Iowa road.

Kansas City was the focus of Joy's new interests. His sudden large investments in land, railroads, bridge stock, and cattle in that region drew off the capital of Nathaniel Thayer and others into a field that would one day compete with the direct Iowa line. Finally sensing trouble in late 1866, Forbes tried to scold Joy back into line: "I have not any interest on the southern line," he pronounced, *"and shall not have any."* Forbes had placed B&MR bonds among "old fashioned people with my own *individual guarantee,"* and he would not "give it the go by." Thayer would do both if Joy presented them jointly; but if Joy persisted in offering "alternatives" to Iowa, Forbes would break with him and "shoulder it alone with Brooks and a few" others. Unlike the Hannibal, the B&MR brought business only to the CB&Q. "It has become to me what the C.B.& Q. once was when I alone had pluck enough to endorse its notes," Forbes concluded. Joy agreed to speak up for the Iowa road, but he made no withdrawal from his southwestern design.[27]

Awakened to the danger, Forbes outlined a transcontinental strategy of his own. The Pacific Railroad Act of 1864 designated Council Bluffs, Iowa, as the eastern terminus of the Union Pacific (UP). However, the section of the Union Pacific from Kearney, Nebraska (on the one hundredth meridian), to Council Bluffs was technically one of several branches authorized by Congress to compete for interchange at the Kearney gateway. The B&MR's Nebraska grant authorized another such branch. Because government engineers had identified Bellevue, Nebraska—midway between Omaha and the Burlington's western Iowa terminus—as the preferred site of a UP bridge, Forbes planned to meet the UP at Bellevue on equal terms with the roads coming into Council Bluffs. This would give the B&MR the short line to Chicago and postpone construction in Nebraska until the volume of traffic demanded the new Burlington line. Omaha merchants and Forbes's Iowa railroad competitors wanted an Omaha bridge instead, with a single connection at Council Bluffs for all Chicago roads. These interests had the upper hand in 1867, partly because of close financial relations between the UP's Omaha branch and the Chicago & North Western Railroad in Iowa. Executive control of the Union Pacific was in the hands of old Forbes competitors whose "friends" in Congress stoutly opposed the Bellevue bridge. After repeated unanswered calls for help, Forbes was told by

Omaha Gateway ánd Missouri River region, c. 1870

Iowa Senator James W. Grimes to come to Washington and "attend to your bridge yourself."[28]

Forbes's position was only technically reasonable. Omaha was the obvious commercial center in Nebraska and a bridge between that city and Council Bluffs was more useful even if less desirable from an engineer's point of view. Besides, in 1867 the Chicago & North Western line was nearly completed to Council Bluffs while the Burlington had almost two hundred miles to build before reaching Bellevue. Nevertheless, Forbes hired a lobbyist to press his case in Washington and sent his own engineers to survey a bridge at Bellevue or Plattsmouth for his independent connection with the Union Pacific. By early summer 1867, the company surveys had revealed the Bellevue crossing as no better than Omaha, but by then Forbes was too deeply committed to back down.[29]

At Bellevue Forbes was trying to force his ideas on an issue that was already lost. Joy, on the other hand, was manipulating completed lines and short connectors into a quick, if roundabout, route to the Union Pacific at Council Bluffs. His immediate success encouraged the notion that railways could triumph over geography. Forbes and his closest allies knew that the lay of the land would never be irrelevant to the cost of transportation—that a circuitous route could not hold the business. But Joy stressed the immediate needs of the Illinois railroad over the Iowa line. Treating the CB&Q directors as short-line investors, he was splitting their interests from the system as a whole, at the expense of Iowa's B&MR. After June 1867 he openly opposed the Iowa project; Forbes finally understood Charles Perkins's complaint.[30]

Forbes now turned his whole attention to the Burlington & Missouri River Rail Road. He ousted Joy from the Iowa presidency, putting Brooks back in charge, and he shored up his support on the B&MR board. The climax came at a CB&Q board meeting in August 1867. Forbes was presenting his argument for the immediate extension of the Iowa and Nebraska lines when Joy announced that the subject would not be discussed. Erastus Corning called for adjournment. The meeting was gavelled right in the middle of Forbes's speech.[31]

Joy had overplayed his hand. His strongest supporters were also holders of B&MR bonds. Joy's demonstration in August started a rush to unload the Iowa paper. "[I]nstead of buyers," complained Treasurer Denison, "I have sellers of bonds after me." If the B&MR failed to meet its obligations Forbes would see to it that angry investors discovered the true source of their losses. Joy backed down enough to endorse a circular on September 18, 1867, recommending more Iowa bonds to the CB&Q stockholders. Forbes then committed his Iowa directors to extending their line to the Union Pacific. By the first months of 1868, Forbes had regained the initiative in Boston: A new circular called the Iowa road the *main line* of the CB&Q; Hannibal & St. Joseph was a *feeder*.[32]

Two distinct strategies had taken shape within the CB&Q directorate. Forbes, Brooks, and Denison were determined to stay with Perkins on the main east-west line of development, pouring money into the B&MR in Iowa and Nebraska. James F. Joy, backed by Thayer, Corning, and Moses Taylor, was drawn by competitive intrigue into trying to control every branch line or route southwest of Chicago that might invade his territory or divert through traffic. Easy money and a booming market for railroad securities allowed both sides to pursue their objectives for a while. A network of branches was clearly needed to retain local traffic in the Burlington's territory, while steady westward extension and consolidation of the east-west lines offered the strongest defense in the overall contest for trunk line business. At least Joy and Forbes agreed on one thing: It was "impossible to remain stationary."[33]

Joy's System Unravels

Despite steady progress throughout the West, all was not well within the Burlington "family" of roads. By 1870 Joy's program of "defensive" expansion had taken on a distinctly aggressive appearance. Joy's system of roads included the CB&Q, the B&MR, the Hannibal & St. Joseph, and a number of short lines along the Missouri River. His branches in Illinois were beginning to invade the territory of the Chicago & North Western and Rock Island railroads. C&NW President John F. Tracy thus proposed an Iowa pool to divide the traffic of the Union Pacific and avert rate war with the fast-growing Burlington. Joy agreed to the pool, but he continued "stealing" transcontinental traffic at less-than-paying rates by means of his Missouri railroads. Charles Perkins retaliated with a cheap Iowa rate to St. Louis, which was absurdly roundabout, until Brooks commanded him to give all business "to the shortest route." Then Forbes intervened, ordering all St. Louis traffic to Hannibal and all Chicago traffic to the Burlington, which was fair to "family" but still cheated the pool. Joy continued to run Chicago business over his southern line—until Perkins stopped paying his bill to the CB&Q. The young Iowa manager demanded either a strict short-route principle or free competition. Joy finally backed down and closed the Hannibal route to Chicago.[34]

Joy was in a tight spot. By the summer of 1871 his personal financial interest lay in Missouri, not in Iowa, and thus not in the pool. Forced to keep peace in Iowa, Joy suffered losses on his southern roads, whose owners began to turn on him. Cutthroat rates, rising costs, and widespread construction were straining the budgets of all the companies, yet Joy was as often as not the instigator of these burdens. Finally, in a surprise raid, Wall Street speculator Jay Gould captured the Hannibal. By November Joy and five other Burlington men had been removed from the Hannibal board. Then the Council Bluffs road missed the first of a series of interest payments that would end Joy's management there as well. The situation was getting out of control.[35]

Brooks refused to believe that his lifelong partner was responsible, but John N. Denison saw through the problem. Joy had become "dictatorial" in his management of the overlarge empire. He still had the "unqualified faith" of the Boston men, but "it stings them to the quick," Denison wrote, "to have you call them into question." He begged Joy not to let "irritating words break up agreeable and profitable relations." Charles Perkins thought the conflict was "irrepressible." You "cannot ride two horses in opposite directions at the same time without producing some soreness," he explained. "And this is practically what Mr. Joy is attempting to do." By the end of 1872 the loss of the Hannibal, together with the consolidation of the B&MR with the CB&Q, effectively returned Joy to a single mount. But his "soreness" was not relieved.[36]

While struggling with his southwestern network, Joy had also involved the CB&Q in a series of branches leading northwest from the main line into Iowa and Minnesota. His customary instrument for branch line expansion was a traffic contract under which the CB&Q controlled the stock of the branch and used a portion of the profits from interchange with the new line to purchase its bonds. To complete this particular design, Joy needed control of three Iowa companies, known together as the River Roads. Their stock, however, was already pledged to construction companies. In April 1871 Joy persuaded Brooks, Denison, John A. Burnham, Nathaniel Thayer, and Sidney Bartlett—all CB&Q directors—to join him in buying those construction companies. The affairs of both the railroad and construction firms were then left in the hands of J. K. Graves, a local capitalist in Dubuque, Iowa.[37]

The following August, Charles Perkins warned Forbes not to put his money, or *"anybody elses,"* into the River Roads without careful examination. Perkins's fear was strategic. These lines ran through the heart of Chicago & North Western territory: Building there seemed to Perkins like "couching another man's wife."[38] Still ignorant of Joy's deep involvement, neither Perkins nor Forbes suspected how financially treacherous the deal was. The construction contracts for the River Roads did not even require the contractors to finish the lines once they had spent all the money and received all the stock. J. K. Graves, as president of each, drew money from the railroads through the construction companies as fast as it came in, paying interest to Joy and his fellow creditors. In turn, the CB&Q directors recommended River Road bonds to their constituents with the same assurances they gave to B&MR and other inside issues.

By the summer of 1872 almost $6 million had passed through Graves's hands, plus a quarter million in advances of cash and equipment from the CB&Q. A few months later the construction companies exhausted their funds and stopped work on the unfinished lines. With no earnings and no more securities to sell, the River Roads would surely default on their coupons. On April 19, 1873, the CB&Q directors voted to quietly pick up the tab for River Road interest, taking 8 percent notes from Graves's railroad companies. At this and each prior meeting in which aid was extended to the River Roads, John Murray Forbes, John C. Green, and J.N.A. Griswold had been absent. If the market had held, they too might have overlooked these arrangements. But the railroad boom was finally collapsing, and the panic brought this unfortunate episode to light.[39]

Forbes's instincts were already giving him pause by the New Year, 1873. So far as he knew his properties were sound: CB&Q stock commanded a high premium in the market. But market price meant nothing if the boom ended, and the intrinsic value of his railroads was unavoidably slipping. In the six years since 1867 total investments in the CB&Q alone had more than doubled. Earnings per mile of road fell from $17,000 in 1868 to $10,400 in 1872, as the system exceeded twice its postwar size. Operating expenses continued to rise as the composition of traffic shifted to include more through freight at marginal prices. In 1867, local business at rates nearing four cents per ton-mile comprised one-half the freight tonnage and 82 percent of freight earnings on the CB&Q. Four years later the local share had dropped to one-fourth of total volume, although it yielded two-thirds of freight earnings. As through rates continued to fall, this disproportionate burden on local shippers engendered public hostility. By 1871 Illinois had already enacted restrictive rate legislation, and other legislatures were discussing the subject.[40]

Aware of the danger in these developments, Forbes paused in June 1873 to analyze the condition of his western roads for a worried stockholder. He blamed too much prosperity for the years of reckless expansion. "With roads building and threatening in all directions," he explained, "Joy, a good lawyer and bright man, not much of a merchant, but honest and bold, had to lead a company which trusted him implicitly." Backed up by "unlimited credit, & an easy money market, and the prestige of success," Joy bought or built numerous branches for profit and defense. All were not "wise nor all economically built, but looking at it in the large," Forbes thought the road was better off now than had it "lain still."

Forbes knew that the CB&Q was overextended, but thought there was nothing "fatal in the mistakes so far." The firm had $7 million worth of branch line commitments plus its own debt to service. Then there was some moral, if not legal, obligation to cover "*the worst blunder of Joy's administration*"—the River Roads bonds. These debts could be refunded, Forbes believed, and the "*spenders*" brought under control. If the "*loose era*" of railroad building was finally ended, then "*good economical management in the future*" would return the CB&Q to its old prosperous condition. Confident that recent mistakes were legitimate business errors and nothing more, Forbes invited the stockholders' investigations: "The more you criticize the better I shall like it, but you had better fire at the Executive officers, and if they don't satisfy you, you have your recourse through the Press, to which now Railroad officers, under a cloud, are sensitive."[41]

Still trusting Joy in spite of Perkins's many warnings, Forbes shifted blame for the recent mismanagement of the CB&Q to its new president, James M. Walker. To get the jump on irate stockholders, Forbes privately asked John C. Green to demand an inside investigation. "I *do* think the time has come," he argued, "for us to know something more about the property if [of] which we are the managers than any of us here at the East do know." Because of Walker's intimacy with Nathaniel Thayer, with whom Forbes's relations were no longer "cordial," an old critic like Green could best fire the first shot. Gradually Forbes discovered more evidence of neglect and conflict of interest in the Joy-Walker regime. By October 1873 the financial panic had struck; the River Roads were bankrupt, and Forbes was deeply embarrassed by his apparent responsibility. With his trusted old colleague John N. A. Griswold in tow, Forbes set out in November to meet Brooks in Burlington and see for himself what was wrong in the West.[42]

Forbes expected to find James M. Walker at the bottom of "irregular" deals with the River Roads. He was shocked to find that Joy, Brooks, and other directors of the CB&Q were leading stockholders in J. K. Graves's dubious construction companies. He confronted Graves with the evidence. The interview revealed the astounding practice of paying money to officers and directors without so much as a treasurer's record. Forbes learned this much when Graves, sensing his mistake, refused to say more. Stunned by what he had heard, Forbes dashed off a letter to Sidney Bartlett, attorney and director for the CB&Q. Describing the situation as the "most remarkable condition of things which I have ever found upon any living railroad," he asked Bartlett if Graves and his directors might not be personally liable to innocent bondholders. Then, ordering Graves to send a full accounting to the eastern directors, Forbes steamed back to Boston.[43]

Still ignorant of the extent of involvement among his Boston colleagues, Forbes went home expecting sympathy and a speedy resolution of the River Roads scandal. Instead he found cool resistance. The only directors as ignorant as Forbes were John C. Green and J.N.A. Griswold. Unable to command a majority, these two urged Forbes to avoid public exposure. Brooks and Bartlett privately censured Graves; but the latter, with Joy's support, denied any wrongdoing. Forbes and Perkins, said James F. Joy, "were no friends of mine." With genuine horror Forbes faced the New Year knowing that public disclosure would show his own company corrupted, his pious disclaimers hollow. While he pondered this misery, the gathering storm of the "farmers' revolt" broke out on the Burlington's Iowa line. The year 1874 brought the toughest contest over public control of railroad rates that Forbes had ever seen.[44]

THE ORIGINS OF PROTEST

Cutthroat competition and uncontrolled railway expansion had produced exactly the results Forbes had worked all his life to avoid. Yet western people saw the "loose era" of railroad construction in the opposite light. Tradition taught them that *too little* competition, not too much, was the great evil. Their experience during the Civil War only reinforced that principle. Postwar prosperity was unevenly distributed. If interregional freight rates had fallen dramatically, the vast majority of producers and merchants continued to pay high local rates at noncompeting points. From their perspective only monopolistic middlemen enjoyed cheap transportation. Railroad owners like Forbes might complain about costs, but as company revenues soared the public refused to believe that the margin of profit was falling. Citing dramatic examples of profiteering, like the Crédit Mobilier of the Union Pacific, people easily condemned large capitalists for fattening their purses at the expense of the commonwealth. In September 1873 the failure of Jay Cooke & Co. and the subsequent collapse of American finance seemed to verify that the swindlers and stock jobbers had struck once more.

At the core of this unrest was enough real injury to western business that the charges of hardship could not be denied. What was not so evident was the degree to which injured merchants represented their own interests or those of the commonwealth. As early as 1860 the mayor and aldermen of Burlington, Iowa, for example, had petitioned the legislature to set maximum rates for freight and passengers in the interest of "Iowa commerce."[45] During the Civil War there were new demands for canals to the Great Lakes to compete with Chicago railroads. After 1865 meetings of river town merchants repeatedly memorialized Congress and the state legislature for water competition and railroad rate regulation. Dubuque, Davenport, Clinton, Muscatine, and Keokuk joined Burlington in a campaign for statutory rates that would reestablish their role as the marketing centers for Iowa produce. These towns demanded, not pro rata equity, but legal maximum tariffs fixed at or below prevailing Chicago rates.

Interior communities rightly saw these demands as special pleading: "The time has passed," argued one state senator, "when the river towns can hold the enviable position of commercial agents for all the counties lying back of them." In 1870 most interior interests still agreed that the railroad had "brought a better market to every man's door than the river towns could possibly have afforded." Schemes to protect these local centers were undoubtedly selfish, but they sounded an important warning against the loss of local marketing power. Burlington, for example, was already in serious trouble by 1869. Less than half the city's commodity exports still passed through the hands of Burlington dealers. Over 90 percent of southern Iowa livestock moved directly into the Union Stock Yards over the Chicago railroads. Burlington's merchants still handled much of the iron and coal and manufactures coming in from Chicago, but almost three-quarters of the lumber and salt business rolled through town in bulk. A short three years later, in 1872, nearly 80 percent of all CB&Q shipments to and from Iowa passed through the Burlington market without pause. The following year, the consolidation of the B&MR with the CB&Q reduced the city's commerce to strictly local proportions.[46]

The cause of Burlington's problem was rate discrimination. Short-haul rates to Burlington were nearly twice as high as the long rates to Chicago; in 1873 the differential reached a high of two-and-one-half times the through tariff. One hundred pounds of first class freight could be shipped the twenty-eight miles from Mount Pleasant to Burlington for twenty-five cents (18¢ per ton-mile), or it could go

Through Traffic at Burlington
(percent of total)

	IOWA EXPORTS					
	Corn	Hogs	Cattle	Flour	Fresh Pork	Packed Meat
1869	58.2%	92.4%	93.3%	5.3%	40.5%	67.4%
1872	66.6	99.4	97.6	47.2	90.8	65.6
1873	71.4	99.9	98.9	57.6	69.6	91.6
1874	64.6	99.9	99.9	70.3	93.3	42.5

	IOWA IMPORTS					
	Lumber	Sundries	Iron	Coal	Salt	Agricultural Implements
1869	71.7%	41.1%	3.2%	13.7%	76.4%	91.2%
1872	96.7	73.8	82.3	56.8	81.7	90.2
1873	98.7	82.7	69.3	72.4	80.6	92.5
1874	99.3	88.6	90.7	99.0	88.0	97.4

	1869	1872	1873	1874
Total export/import average:	54.5%	79.1%	82.1%	86.4%

Note: 1872–74 data include BCR&M and B&MR.
Source: Iowa State Agricultural Society *Reports*.

through 248 miles to Chicago for eighty-five cents (7¢ per ton-mile). Long-awaited improvements, like the bridge over the Mississippi in 1868 and the completion of the B&MR in 1869, simply accelerated Burlington's decline. Interior cities like Ottumwa, which had lured competing lines during the decade of railroad promotions, received the lowest rates. Burlington's loyalty to the B&MR was proving the ruin of its commerce. Thus, in late 1872, the announcement of impending consolidation with the CB&Q sent shockwaves of concern through the community.[47]

A year later Burlington had had enough. An angry committee of citizens accused the company of "absorbing everything and contributing nothing" to the Iowa town. CB&Q President James M. Walker insisted that his policies were "dictated solely on account of economical reasons." Strict economy of operations alone would reduce charges, he argued, so these measures were ultimately in Burlington's interest. Burlington was not impressed. Local stockholders pushed a hostile resolution through the annual meeting in February 1874 charging violation of contract by the CB&Q. The community was outraged: One citizen renamed the company "Cursed, Bursted & Quarrelsome." Even the supportive Burlington *Hawk-Eye* warned the railroad that Burlington was the "natural and geographic" center of their territory. Sooner or later the owners would "regret the loss of her help and good feeling, which will then be gone to rival railroads."[48]

These harmful effects of consolidation and integration in the railroad network were not long restricted to river towns like Burlington. After 1870 farm prices began falling faster than interior freight rates, and the hardships of local discrimination spread to noncompeting "way points" across the state. More and more voters identified with the complaints of the river town merchants against the railroads. Iowa's Republican leadership, having opposed rate regulation since before 1860, now endorsed antidiscrimination measures in the face of diminishing trade. By 1872 the General Assembly was overwhelmingly in favor of some form of regulation, but the deadlock between river town supporters of maximum rates and more moderate proponents of an advisory commission prevented action that year. The economic impetus for railroad regulation had reached full proportions well before the panic of 1873, but the motive was not well focused. It remained for a second source of western temper to unite the victims of injustice in a campaign against "railroad abuses."[49]

Clearly private interests had blended into a public cause, and the Patrons of Husbandry—the Grange—became the reluctant vehicle for a massive regional protest against railroad and industrial power. Oliver Hudson Kelly, founder of the Grange, intended an agrarian fraternity dedicated to education, social intercourse, and the improvement of the farmer's life. But the Grange touched a raw nerve in thousands of frustrated producers in the upper Mississippi Valley. The bitter western critique of economic policies in the Civil War had returned in the early 1870s and found its clearest articulation in this new farmers' movement. Blending traditional moral and political economy with the modern concepts of combination and cooperation, the program set forth in Grange conventions across the region gave a momentary coherence to the desperate complaints of western men.[50]

In Iowa, the Grange reflected exactly those values of political economy that had carried James W. Grimes and the infant Republican party to power two decades before. Progressive local development within the context of the "natural order" was supposed to be the goal of the people and their government. During the Civil War Iowa's State Agricultural Society had denounced every attempt to "violate and set at nought the laws of trade and exchange . . . which

God impressed on this continent when He created it." By the end of the war Grimes himself came to criticize government aid to monopolistic railroads. The "true" objective of Republican government, he declared, was to insure that every man was "the owner of his own soil, the owner of his own tools, the owner of his own labor, and his own machinery."[51] Another spokesman accepted the railroads as the "revealers" of American greatness; but as the "entire relationships of the country" were "revolutionized" by the "annihilation" of space and time, Iowans feared being kept "merely as an agricultural population." With a cry of betrayal, the Iowa farmers were called to organize:

> We are furnished with the theoretical elements of agriculture, and the dignity of our calling has so bewildered our ideas that we have allowed huge monopolies and fat corporations to form around us un-noticed, and now they go strutting about carrying State Legislatures [sic] around in their breeches pocket, with their extortionate rates and unjust discriminating power between places and individuals, while hundreds of honest practical farmers in the State of Iowa stand today on the verge of financial ruin.[52]

The response in Iowa was electric. The number of local granges increased from forty in early 1871 to three hundred one year later and eighteen hundred by November 1873. The order peaked ten months later just one unit short of two thousand. The Grange program of cooperative buying and selling was an important attraction, but antimonopoly and antirailroad rhetoric was the symbolic and emotional core of the appeal. The voices of popular protest were blended in January 1873, when the State Agricultural Society, the state's Republican governor, and a massive convention of Iowa Grangers all proclaimed their outrage in identical terms.

On the morning of January 8, 1873, Agricultural Society President John Scott warned his audience of the perils that now threatened the "natural" primacy of the farmer. By "combinations which easily grow out of their occupancy of the great centers of population," he argued, the urban interests—merchants, carriers, and laboring mechanics—had suppressed competition to insure their profits. But the farmer, in his "so called market," was "but the sport of bulls that toss and bears that squeeze," while everything he bought "from the cradle to the coffin" came to him "priced by a board of trade."[53]

Scott's address proved to be but an introduction for a stunning oration that evening by Governor Cyrus Clay Carpenter. The governor was a short, solid, stubborn-looking man with thick, cropped hair and beard, perfect in appearance for his role as reformer. Convinced that rebellion was brewing, this surveyor and land-trader-turned-politician was determined to "take the lead . . . on this question of transportation." His speech, carefully studied, exquisitely phrased, opened with this dramatic blast:

> If . . . today, there is a shadow resting upon the prosperity of the Great West, which it is no exaggeration to compare with the fleshless fingers, the rattling joints, the eyeless sockets, and the grinning teeth of a skeleton, it is found in the cost of exchanging commodities over long lines of communication, by expensive agencies, and at exorbitant charges for transportation. *This is the skeleton in every Western farmer's corncrib.*[54]

Carpenter argued that the farmer had become a lowly tenant with no voice in determining the share of his crop to be taken in "rent." Wasting no time debating the existence of railroad abuses, the governor considered the avenues of redress. He urged more feeding of livestock, compressing exports to ten times their value per pound of freight. Diversification of crops and the development of home markets were obvious aids, but he cautioned against too much reliance on the latter. Iowa was naturally agricultural: Iowans must bring "their industrial habits, their social theories, and their political policies into accord with the evident designs of the Creator of all things." Government regulation was the key. Carpenter ordinarily rejected government "interference" with individual freedom and enterprise, but the new transport system bore such an "intimate relationship to the very existence of organized society," that it now presented a "towering" monopoly. The government "which proves unequal to its control," he reasoned, "abdicates a power for which it will be held responsible at the bar of an enlightened and aroused public opinion."[55]

What, then, was the course of action? Carpenter denounced efforts to stimulate more competition among existing railways; such efforts resulted in "a greater oppression" by larger, unreachable combinations. "What the people want is *stability, certainty.*" Rate ceilings must be established. Discrimination against individuals and locations must be stopped. Federally owned and operated trunk lines should set standards of service and tariffs that private interstate lines would have to meet. Carpenter denied the assertions of men like Forbes that public enterprise would fail. Pointing to the number of railroad failures since the panic of 1837, he insisted that private capitalists with decades of experience had no better record than the experimental public works of the 1830s. Finally, Carpenter predicted that radical reductions in freight rates would so boost the volume of business that the railroads would increase their revenues.[56]

The governor had addressed nearly every aspect of the railroad question with clarity and intelligence. His plan was comprehensive, yet believable; his tone, determined. Even James S. Clarkson, editor of the Iowa State *Register,* railroad favorite and boss of the state Republican party, put his seal of approval on Carpenter's words. Three weeks later the Iowa State Grange held its convention in Des Moines, with a turnout that astounded editor Clarkson. Nearly one thousand delegates convened in the capital city despite the heavy snows of an Iowa winter. Astonished themselves at the growth of their order, the Grangers found little to add to Governor Carpenter's address. They petitioned their legislature and begged Congress to restore the farmers' "God-given rights." The presence in Des Moines of a thousand angry Grangers did stir the special session of the General Assembly to take up the railroad question, but reform was still a year off.[57]

THE GRANGER MOVEMENT

By 1873 the midwestern agitation for rate law reform had received national attention, and the protest was destined to intensify. Illinois and Minnesota had already enacted rate regulations, and the legislatures of Wisconsin and Iowa repeatedly debated the issue. CB&Q General Manager Robert Harris readily conceded that "wild and unreasonable and unnecessary [rate] cuttings and discriminations" were "at the bottom of all this noise." Had railway managers taken a sincere interest in an equitable solution, one might have emerged. In most of the cases of injustice brought before the bar of politics, it was the arbitrary nature of the rate, not its magnitude, that hurt the most. Even Governor Carpenter's plan rested on the assumption that "stability" and "certainty" were what the people wanted. The railroads were no less desirous of stable rates, but the image of farmer-legislators dictating policy to private corporations so offended men like John Murray Forbes and Charles E. Perkins that they made little effort to reconcile. Dogmatic views of political economy and prejudicial assumptions about regional character only sharpened the confrontation that began in railway economics.[58]

John Murray Forbes blamed the Grangers' rebellion on the persistent failure of western men to comprehend the postwar world. He sought desperately to educate what he patronizingly called the "slow agricultural mind." The farmers "don't mean to do wrong," he conceded, but they failed to understand the cause of differential rates. With "time and patience and with such timely concessions as steel rails and close management will warrant," Forbes thought he could show the farmer that "good economical management aided by such competition as he can get up will give him his best and only chance of getting his local transportation cheapened."[59]

Forbes saw the Grangers in the light of the unfinished revolution that was begun during the Civil War, and he was fully confident that the emerging systems of industry and commerce would eventually benefit these misguided farmers. Therefore he counseled patience, and he urged the locals to instigate harmless competition. Charles Perkins agreed with Forbes that it was time to start "educating the popular mind" on the question of railroad regulation, and he admitted that the railroads had a credibility problem. "It wont [sic] do," he argued, "to try to prove that all RRd men are saints." Still, the principles of corporate freedom had to be defended by the roads to keep the farmers from "going on the wrong track." It was E. L. Godkin of *The Nation,* a New York weekly that John Murray Forbes had financed just after the war, who finally put into words the larger issue presented by the Grangers' complaints: "The locomotive is coming in contact with the framework of our institutions. In this country of simple government, the most powerful centralizing force which civilization has yet produced has, within the next score years, yet to assume its relations to that political machinery which is to control and regulate it."[60] For Godkin the question was rhetorical: Like Forbes he assumed that the framework of political nationalism and corporate economy already taking shape in the United States was the true and proper response to the locomotive's challenge. For western men, however, that was the whole question.

The midwestern railroad protest quickly broadened into a contest of regions and cultural values that added more heat than light to the questions. Grangers linked the farmers' problems to corruption among businessmen and politicians in the Grant administration in Washington. Stung by the charge, easterners blamed western demagogues for all the special pleading in Congress that was demoralizing public life. Charging "spoliation as flagrant as any ever proposed by Karl Marx," editor Godkin once stamped the Grangers with the mark of communism. More often he simply belittled western complaints with a patronizing detachment. If farmers lived a thousand miles from the eastern cities, for example, that was the natural consequence of moving west. Godkin even condemned the farmers for losing their "rugged" virtues: Clinging to the railroads, the "modern frontiersmen" demanded all the conveniences of church, school, newspapers, and magazines; his wife and daughters "must have a piano and silk dresses . . . and their minds, instead of being intent on the homely joys of the forest and the prairie, are vexed by the social and religious discussions of the East." It must have seemed unfair to many a western reader to be criticized by cosmopolitans for wanting those elements of culture by which the East defined its own superiority.[61]

The western press replied in kind; with each exchange the chasm widened. Iowa spokesmen roared their denunciations of Crédit Mobilier scandals, congressional corruption, and the nest of thieves on Wall Street. By association with rich and powerful speculators all railroad men were turned into scoundrels. Charles Perkins struggled vainly to produce a comprehensive, balanced discussion of the railroad question which "*everybody* would read"; but such a short course in complicated economics was not forthcoming. Out of the East came more invective, culminating in the insufferable charge that without " 'railroad speculators,' there would not be any West at all."[62]

Gross insensitivity to regional culture simply hardened the Grangers' animosity toward the new commercial systems. The Chicago Farmer's Convention in October 1873 called on its brethren to withdraw wherever possible from interdependent markets, avoid debt, buy home manufactures, oppose tariff protection, and organize farmers everywhere. The bitterness in Granger rhetoric was unmistakable. One correspondent in the Iowa *Homestead* complained sadly that the farmer considered himself "but a beast of burden." With the "whole load upon his back he has neither profit nor honor. Those who ride despise him." Shifting from the language of economy to political liberty, Iowa Grange Master A. B. Smedley rallied his brothers to the defense of "free Republican" institutions: "If that eternal vigilance which has been called the price of liberty is not exercised, if this aggressive power is not boldly met and restrained by wise and reasonable legislation, all the industrial interests of our country must languish."[63]

At the threshold of organized mass political action the Grange took sudden pause. The founder of the order had strictly enjoined the granges from official involvement in partisan politics. The Grange program was admittedly "full of pure politics," but it was "*partisan* NEVER." The farmers' movement was not to be used as a "cat's paw to drag political chestnuts out of the fire either for parties or for individuals." The rule was well made, if poorly followed. Local Iowa granges launched an antimonopoly third party movement in April 1873 that was quickly captured by cynical leaders of Iowa's old Democracy. Holding its nominating convention at the height of the August harvest, the new Anti-Monopoly party offered a slate of old Iowa Democrats and drew up a platform that was little more than the antebellum program of the party of Jackson. Ending in betrayal, the Grangers' partisan efforts did nevertheless force the Grand Old Party to take a vigorous antirailroad stand. A very close election returned chastened Republicans to power.[64]

The reelection of Governor Carpenter probably saved the issue of railroad reform. Forced to break with his railroad friends, party boss James S. Clarkson agreed to redeem the pledge on railroad regulation. Carpenter introduced a plan combining the maximum rate bill of the river town merchants with a classification of roads by earnings that protected small or weak lines. Ironically, by the time the assembly settled down to work in February 1874, the Iowa State Grange had endorsed an advisory commission with antidiscrimination guidelines as the most reasonable and effective remedy for the farmers' complaints. The experienced voices of commercial interest had little trouble steering the river town plan, with Carpenter's classification, through a legislature overwhelmingly controlled by farmers. Less dramatic than an ironclad tariff, the Grange proposal was quickly tarnished by association with railroad men like CB&Q President James M. Walker, who earlier had sponsored such a bill as a substitute for maximum tariffs. Furthermore, President Walker proudly announced record earnings for the CB&Q just at the height of the Iowa debates. Charles Perkins bitterly thanked the directors for conferring "a favor upon the long suffering public which it will not [soon?] forget!"[65]

The Iowa tariff bill passed on March 8, 1874, and was signed by the governor on March 23. Essentially protective of the river town merchants, the new law indirectly promised stable rates and relief from discrimination in the interior as well. Having finally struck at the railroads, Iowa's mood turned sober. Carpenter himself had grave doubts that the benefits would meet popular expectations. The Iowa Grange insisted that the wrong bill had been passed, but they hoped for the best. All that was left was to wait and see. Editor James S. Clarkson put it best: "Our Iowa people are now nearing the real railroad crossing, and Gov. Carpenter, even before he hears the bell ring, may as well be looking out for the cars."[66]

By 1874, Illinois, Iowa, Wisconsin, and Minnesota had each passed restrictive railroad legislation. The term "Granger Laws" was fixed almost immediately, but these measures were neither radical nor agrarian. The important rights claimed by western legislators were entirely customary. American judicial tradition and the common law consistently upheld such local regulations of franchises and carriers. The farmers alone would have settled for equitable rates, had not the western merchants exploited their anger to secure favorable adjustments in the rate structure itself. Yet even this flagrant protection of local markets fell within the framework of traditional American political economy.[67]

Cultural differences help explain the interpretation of the Granger Laws in the centers of eastern commerce. In part, John Murray Forbes saw the movement as a personal affront. His style of business was paternalistic, and his patient efforts to develop the Iowa country had been repaid with hostility. Furthermore, because Forbes and his class of entrepreneurs assumed that the new corporate order was already triumphant, they could not understand these resurgent defenders of local autonomy. When western tempers flared, eastern capitalists attributed the anger to agrarian reaction or alien communism—thereby concealing their own assault on local democracy and traditional American values.[68]

Caught in the middle, reflecting the ambiguity of the moment, was the Grange. By 1874 the movement had acquired its final, awkward position as an instrument of protest in modernizing America. In its celebration of the soil, moral economy, and divine social order, the Grange was romantic, backward looking, and nostalgic. At the same time the Patrons' program of cooperation, combination, and class solidarity showed a realistic willingness to "fight fire with fire." Only a deep resistance to the alien principle of combination in the end stood between Granger rhetoric and effective Grange action. Brought up as independent producers—free enterprise capitalists—few Iowa farmers could embrace either the organic unity of a former age or the class solidarity of a modern trade union. Allowing for all the confusion, it was the very liberalism of the farmers' demands that forced their eastern critics to sketch them in caricature.[69]

Beneath the agrarian rhetoric of the midwestern Grange there lay two demands to be met before the farmers would join in the new national economy. First, they wanted their fair share of the profits. They would not go back, as E. L. Godkin advised, to simpler ways just to enrich urban America. Secondly, even if they abandoned the "original conditions" of James Grimes's early Republicanism, farmers and merchants alike refused to be governed by undemocratic combinations of capital. The arrogance of railroads like the CB&Q, which openly ignored the new Iowa tariffs, was a "direct insult to the sovereignty of the state." Such behavior was "without precedent."[70] On this point the Iowans would press their case to the United States Supreme Court. In 1877 the high court upheld their sovereign rights—at least for the moment. The main point vindicated, the people were then free to repeal the obnoxious law and start anew. In the Middle West, the passage of the Granger Laws marked the end of traditional economic order and the beginning of a struggle for recognition within the new industrial systems.

6

Adjusting to the Changes

THE GRANGER MOVEMENT marked the end of an era in agrarian Iowa, and what followed after 1874 was an interlude in which farmers, merchants, and carriers alike adjusted their views and their actions to a new situation. The frustrations of the Grangers had been rooted in the prerailroad world, where local governments and local interests had fancied themselves supreme. But even at the height of the agrarian crisis almost everybody knew that the railroads had already restructured American geography; the whole framework of enterprise and society would have to conform. National systems of transportation and commerce were taking shape, and western farmers and merchants had to seek new ways to exploit these larger markets. No one felt much constrained any more by that "harmony of interests" that had dominated the rhetoric of progress for a generation. The emerging order was more bluntly contractual and bureaucratic than the old, and interest groups responded to changes with bolder motives and sharper political skills. Harmony as a theme was replaced by negotiations and the threat of confrontation. While the railroads sought protection in the legal rights of property, western shippers maneuvered to improve the terms of their dependence on powerful corporations.

For John Murray Forbes the triumph of corporate capitalism did not come without a price. From the simple tenets of merchant capitalism he had fashioned new instruments of enterprise, but the changes that they had wrought could no longer be measured by the standards of the old Boston countinghouse. Competition in railroad building had ruined his model of planned development; his interregional partnership with the pioneers lay shattered. Neither business nor society seemed to follow a design any longer. Forbes tutored his cousin, Charles E. Perkins, in the ways of the model entrepreneur, that his own vision might be perpetuated; but the student was not

145

like the mentor. Where Forbes saw in railroad development the aspirations of the American people, Perkins found primarily the logic of the firm and the needs of corporate systems. Forbes was a dreamer with a passion for business and a lust for building, his verbal pragmatism notwithstanding. His younger cousin was a more practical man, a scientist who banished empathy to the private sphere. The difference was a sign of the times.

Between 1874 and 1881 the Chicago, Burlington & Quincy completed a series of reorganizations that resulted in stable leadership for another twenty years. During the same period the shippers and consumers along the line of the road took stock in their own positions and began laying plans for the future. Rather than resist the course of development, as some Grangers had tried to do, local interests in Iowa turned their attention toward controlling the carriers' influence in the new market systems. Sometimes the justice of local complaints was difficult to discern, but the purpose of the uproar was unmistakable. The new "artificial means of prosperity" might make Iowans rich, but not at the cost of their independence.

LEADERSHIP AND VIRTUE

From the start, leadership in American industry had been divided between gentleman-merchants and "ambitious" speculators, and nowhere did the contrast stand in sharper relief than in the battle between John Murray Forbes and James F. Joy over the Iowa River Roads. Forbes's hope for a quiet resolution to that problem had been frustrated by the refusal of the interested parties to confess their sins. Joy and his colleagues were powerful and respected capitalists in the richest of American business circles: They would not readily surrender their positions to suit the delicacies of Boston pride. Even J. K. Graves, River Roads president and chief culprit in the piece, enjoyed the enthusiastic confidence of his local Dubuque, Iowa, public. Not even the possibility of embarrassment for the CB&Q seemed to bring these men around.[1]

In the year since his first interview with J. K. Graves, John Murray Forbes had looked for an ordinary business solution to the River Roads problem. Now the depth of embarrassment was exhausting his patience. Reflecting privately on his efforts, Forbes saw but one way left to restore faith among the innocent investors. Those directors who owned the construction companies and at the same time offered bonds to their clients and friends should pay off their victims and surrender their stock to the outside bondholders. This would eliminate both the reality and the appearance of conflicting interests within the CB&Q directorate. Such repentance was not forthcoming. When the River Roads went into receivership in January 1875, Forbes was astonished to learn that the stockholders wanted Graves, the man who had squandered the funds, appointed to be the receiver! Local speculators were determined to make Forbes and the outsiders look the villains, and this time the involvement of Joy, Walker, and the other Boston directors gave the charge a color of truth. After "30 years of confidence & admiration" in James F. Joy, Forbes reluctantly declared himself at war with his rambunctious western partner. At a bondholders' meeting February 3, 1875, Forbes called for an end to delays and equivocation. Under Joy, the shareholding managers of the River Roads continued to "*divide* their interest" from that of the bondholders, and those interests would remain contradictory. The "best and only satisfactory answer," Forbes concluded, was to offer the bondholders whatever stock and remaining assets there were, "cheerfully and of our own motion."[2]

The issue was now one of pride and principle. Forbes pleaded with John W. Brooks to spare him the "heart-burnings and antagonism" which a "rupture with old friends" must cause. He would share in the blame and the loss, if that would preserve "harmony in our circle." Still Forbes was stung by the fact that his friends had led him to "join in causing the mischief." Brooks was equally grieved by the estrangement, but he could not accept the personal responsibility Forbes proposed. The River Roads, he argued, were no different from earlier deals in which Forbes had heartily joined. The real point for Brooks was the success of past contracts and the failure of the present one: "We who do not claim to be immaculate, beyond expediency, but are content with right intentions and good results . . . will not be so much troubled about our defense."[3]

The rift between Brooks and Forbes was the more bitter for being narrow. Brooks would not assume the penitent role Forbes tried to assign him, but he did admit the injury to investors caused by his negligence. Now retired in Boston, he blamed his servants in the West and denied culpability beyond personal neglect. James F. Joy was the real villain—"chief Sinner," Forbes called him. Between these two men lay the greater contrast of the business cultures of antebellum Boston and America's Gilded Age. Scorning Brooks's defense as "unmanly," James F. Joy insisted that the Burlington direc-

tors, including Forbes, had known exactly what they were doing—
and there was no wrong in it. Joy's position was that of a Chicago
business lawyer. The roads had offered a good line and would have
gone to the competition if he had not acted. His contracts had saved
the Burlington's traffic, with unanimous board approval. Strategy
aside, the construction contracts were perfectly legal. Iowa law did
not require contractors to finish their work once the money was gone,
"and all, therefore, which Mr. Forbes said about the form of the
contract has no meaning to it." Reaching for general principles, Joy
defended any scheme that furthered the work at hand.[4]

Nothing in John Murray Forbes's conception of the corporation
or the entrepreneur could justify applying such a narrow legal right.
Throughout his career Forbes had condemned the barely legal practices of western promoters and their New York brokers. The conservative Boston style was above such methods. When Forbes first welcomed James F. Joy into the community of State Street capitalists, he
assumed that the western man had adopted Boston ethics. Since the
early days on the Michigan Central, Forbes had given his personal
endorsement on the strength of Joy's word. "I should have considered
it an insult to him," he explained, "if I had said to him, 'Mr. Joy, are
you a contractor for building this road?' " If Joy had indeed enjoyed
such a secret interest in earlier contracts, that was hardly an excuse:
"Two or three or ten wrongs do not make one right." The expedient
plea of past success could not justify a lapse of integrity: "I regret,"
Forbes wrote, "to find you opposed to me, and to the general opinion
of business men." Forbes rallied his old-style friends to purge the
offenders from the Burlington board. Within a week he gathered his
proxies; then on February 24, 1875, he forced Joy out at the annual
meeting in Chicago. With three new directors Forbes gained a bare
majority and control of the company once more.[5]

It was Joy's open defense of opportunism as much as his specific
transgressions, that drove Forbes to such dramatic measures. Joy's
management of the River Roads symbolized the reckless practices
and principles that had always threatened the peace for Forbes's
"gentleman–entrepreneurs." A year earlier Forbes had blamed the
late panic and depression on just such "extravagance" in business.
Paper currency led to "borrowing in all directions" by "speculators"
who became overloaded with an "immense debt" based on railroad
securities of "doubtful value." Capital was everywhere tied up in
these worthless railroads: Credit collapsed and "legitimate borrow-
ers, the business men of the country . . . were made the victims." The

argument was cast in the language of ethics; his analysis of the panic was a critique of every loose practice that had grown up in the system of American enterprise. Now Forbes's own organization stood guilty of those very crimes. His indignation was more than personal. The behavior of Joy and the others was an affront to decency and a violation of public trust. Charles Perkins summarized the point: "We Railroad men had eno. bad reputation to stagger under before, but the Boston management had been considered above suspicion[;] now the public thinks we are all thieves!"[6]

If the dramatic confrontation at the Burlington annual meeting restored Forbes's image of the model entrepreneur for the moment, it solved very little. Joy's strategies and methods stood renounced, but alternatives for running an interstate railroad were not readily at hand. Conditions were radically different in 1875 from the days when Forbes and Brooks were learning the business in Michigan. Forbes was now unsure how to proceed. Citing "flagrant . . . misuse of power" by the current generation of railroad leaders, he wondered if large railroads had become unmanageable. Having broken with the empire builder, Forbes questioned the wisdom of great systems themselves: "In general principles the larger the body managed—the less economy." His own career notwithstanding, Forbes now concluded that one-man power "managing other people's property" was not generally "in the long run successful."[7]

The erosion of virtue among businessmen since the glorious days of the Civil War had left genteel paternalists like John Murray Forbes alone and embittered. His closest friends were falling from grace, and now Forbes himself was trying bureaucratic solutions to his leadership problems. "As business is business and not guessing," he snarled, he wanted dozens of facts and statistical series sent on to Boston to serve as a basis for policy. The "great fault" of past administrations, he concluded, was this: "We have not been training Lieutenants." Here was the old maverick who cherished his freedom from red tape calling for systematic planning, succession, and hierarchy. Within a few months of the February "revolution" Forbes installed Charles Perkins on the board of directors and solidified his control of the CB&Q. Still he lamented the lack of experience in Boston: "We have plenty of law, finance etc. but no R Road skill whatever." Forbes found it was "work enough to carry on the machine *peacefully*," and he eventually abandoned his efforts to recover damages from the River Roads schemers. His righteous assault on unfaithful colleagues had uncovered a more pressing need: the complete reorganization of the sprawling Burlington road.[8]

PRACTICAL POLITICS

All the while Forbes wrestled with Joy and Brooks and the River Roads scandal, the trouble in Iowa deepened. The Granger Law took effect in July 1874, fixing schedules of maximum rates for freight and passengers across the state. Forbes expected "a long fight" against those political "rascals" and "fools" he thought were responsible for regulation. He traced the Grangers' hostilities to wicked leadership—the same weakness of public morals that had fostered James F. Joy's loose notions of business.[9] Public ignorance, the excessive influence of party machines, and the popularity of demagogues had demoralized government and business at every level. Virtue was gone from public life. The task, as Forbes saw it, was to rescue the true principles of political economy from the grasp of licentious democracy.

With so much at stake the Burlington chose to stand on principle. Iowa had gone "about as far as it can go in hostile legislation," concluded CB&Q President James M. Walker in 1874, and there was little to be gained "from any attempt to conciliate voters and politicians in this regard." Walker recommended proceeding "as though no such law had been passed." No corporate response was more arrogant or inflammatory than this refusal to acknowledge the rule of law. When the new law took effect in July, the company ignored it. The opposition cried out against this insult to the sovereignty of the people. Even the usually supportive Burlington *Hawk-Eye* called for the "strong arm of public will" to reduce the railroad "to serfdom, if necessary." The company was undaunted. Walker chose to make a symbolic issue of the statutory passage fares. Stubborn Iowans began boarding trains without tickets and then offering the legally prescribed three cents per mile. Walker ordered conductors to accept no payments aboard the cars, forcing passengers to pay higher company fares at the stations. The confrontation created more ill will than real hardship. By autumn, CB&Q revenues had reached record proportions, but the lawsuits were piling up. Should the Iowa attorney general ever move against the Burlington, the defense might go badly. On January 5, 1875, to forestall that possibility, the company sought an injunction in United States court, barring prosecutions under the Iowa tariff law.[10]

The managers of all the Iowa roads were shocked and disappointed in May when the federal courts rejected the Burlington's plea. Reporting the decision to Forbes, Charles Perkins expressed his fear that the lower court's opinion might be shared by some Supreme Court Justices as well. Furthermore the ruling stirred up the people again. The Burlington *Hawk-Eye,* recently enlightened by an infusion of five thousand dollars of Forbes's money, pronounced the decision good law but bad policy. The "calm" that had settled in should not be disturbed. Such peace might have been a popular wish, but neglect would not resolve the issues raised by the Granger Law. The repeated vindication by the courts of rate regulations forced railroad leaders in the Burlington organization and across the nation to reexamine their positions.[11]

James M. Walker met the circuit court's ruling with carefully guarded concessions. He outlined a strategy that would minimize public conflict without jeopardizing the company's legal position as long as appeals were pending. Passenger fares were quietly reduced to the legal limit "to avoid personal collisions and difficulties on the trains and at stations." Freight rates were left in place, however, until such time as "action of the state authorities" or "trouble along the line" should force them down. Considering the $500 penalties for each violation, payable to the state school fund, Walker stressed to his directors the risk in their position. As the legal battles continued he hoped to avoid confrontations and continue the present rates through the year. Next winter the company might better influence "the repeal of this most disastrous legislation."[12]

Walker's approach touched all fronts at once, blending principle and expediency without real focus. Charles Perkins, on the other hand, chose to select certain principles and stand by them. Furious at Walker's reduction of passenger fares, Perkins poured out his anger to John Murray Forbes. "We made a mistake," he complained, "in not paying $10,000 to defeat the law originally." Reducing passenger fares was another blunder; Perkins thought it indefensible to reduce fares and not freights, and he warned of more trouble with angry shippers than had been seen as yet. In a long essay in June Perkins explained his general theory of regulation more fully. "Communism in any form" was "dishonest and unwise and utterly inconsistent with civilized progress." Because the "regulation of Railroad rates by the public" amounted to confiscation of property—communism—there were but two ways to solve the railroad question: "Either the Government must buy[,] own & operate the Railroads or the laws of competition, of supply and demand, must solve the problem. The latter, in my judgment is the true & safe course." Government ownership was theoretically harmful to private enterprise, and it also gave the federal executive "a patronage which would practically make him dictator." Therefore, state enterprise was in conflict with republicanism. Perkins warned Iowans that their railroad laws were not only ill-advised, but "bad." Capitalists would shun their state. "The right of property," he lectured, "is at the bottom of all stable Government."[13]

John Murray Forbes agreed with Perkins's arguments, but he knew the matter was not so simple. The right of property claimed by Perkins was not unusual; the novelty lay in allowing chartered corporations to pursue their rights to the injury of individual private interests. In the popular mind, corporations enjoyed a legal, but not a moral, identity as individuals. Therefore justice must somehow work in favor of the "true" individuals against these legal fictions. Public regulation of railroad rates tended to skew the conflict of rights in favor of the individual shipper, which Perkins saw as an assault on the rights of the corporations. The occasions for conflict and injury were legion. There were literally millions of transactions in which freight rates were quoted, and the sheer volume of trade insured that extraordinary examples of discrimination would occur.

One such case of discrimination on the Burlington line reached E. L. Godkin's desk at *The Nation,* illustrating the root of hostility between the carriers and the shippers. A merchant in Glenwood, Iowa, reported "great hardships" that were caused by a rate structure that favored Chicago and New York. Local freights near Glenwood moved cheaper on wagons, and coal from nearby Iowa mines cost no less than Pennsylvania fuel on the retail market. The Burlington's rates rendered competition "between the great marts of the country impossible." Even Perkins was surprised to learn that the facts of the case were true, but he agreed with General Superintendent Robert Harris's explanation: "It is not the business of Railroads to open up 'competition between the great marts of the country.' " The people expected their railroads to be neutral servants in the contest between individual buyers and sellers, but the railroads had become contestants themselves in a national market that scarcely felt Glenwood's pain.[14]

Here was the basic ambiguity that plagued the railroad question for a generation: Cheap transportation cut two ways. Railroads could not erase distance for Iowa corn without erasing distance for

Pennsylvania coal. The hopes of the first generation of Iowa railroad promoters, that their natural advantages would be preserved while their geographic barriers were removed, had been vain from the start. Charles Francis Adams, Jr., a Massachusetts railroad commissioner and an early student of rate regulation, was among the first to articulate the connection between economic aspirations and cultural attitudes in a "history" of the recent Granger Movement. The absentee owners of western railroads, he argued, had been imperialistic in their demands; but western people in turn had expected too much. The people, Adams explained, had assumed that railroad transportation was "subject to a law of supply and demand exactly in the same degree as factories and mills in the production of cotton cloth or flour." Adams was convinced that such competition was "simply impossible." Frustrated by the imperfect results of railway competition, western people were then infuriated by the arrogance and bad manners of railway officials from directors to baggage handlers. It came as no surprise to Adams that these farmers applied their exaggerated faith in popular legislation to the elimination of injustice at the hands of rude servants of these foreign masters.[15]

The solution, thought Adams, lay in getting farmers and railroad managers alike to forget about free competition. In his critique of the Granger Movement he brought into focus the structural novelties of railway economics and the cultural assumptions that obscured the vision of all parties concerned. This highborn Bostonian could hardly approve the tantrums of western democracy, but he did recognize that the axioms of political economy so dear to his own class of businessmen did not square with reality. Railroads could not compete at every shipping point, nor could they withdraw from the market once built. Discrimination, combination, and monopoly were the natural consequences of competition under those conditions. Men like Forbes and Perkins and the western shippers all failed to understand that, and their grievances could be traced to this interpretive failure. Adams hoped to steer debates toward the practical issues of railroad policy, but neither the railroad men nor the shippers were prepared to abandon the language of free competition.

Theoretical arguments, especially if they contradicted treasured notions about the laws of trade, could not easily replace experience as the source of truth about railways. John Murray Forbes admitted that young Adams was "smart, but he is totally inexperienced." Charles Perkins, who was something of a theorizer himself, reprimanded Adams for handing the Grangers "more ammunition" with which to attack business interests. Neither man could agree with Adams that there was something wrong with the commercial system. Forbes suspected instead that there were "dishonest politicians working upon" the people. When Adams criticized the railroads for subverting the regulatory force of public opinion, Forbes could not even see that this was possible.[16]

It may have been impossible for business to ignore public opinion, as John Murray Forbes believed, but it was very much within the power of business to affect public opinion and materially improve the climate of politics. In the case of the Iowa Granger Law, it was clear that the people must be shown the error of their legislation and brought back into sympathy with their railroads. Burlington strategy was drawn accordingly. In mock compliance with the Iowa law the Burlington raised all through rates to the level of local tariffs. Then the company terminated all special concessions to favored shippers. This application of the antidiscrimination guidelines of the law, without the overall reductions in charges, worked an immediate hardship on those shippers most eager for relief. Exploiting the uproar, the railroads blamed every increased cost, each curtailment of services, or individual hardship on the "hostile" statute. Emphasizing the radical image of antirailroad agrarianism, the companies launched a propaganda campaign against the Grange itself to discredit the regulatory movement. "The howling has been as hideous as it has been untruthful," wrote Coker F. Clarkson, leading Granger and farm editor of the *Iowa State Register*. The rate law that the Grange had actually opposed in 1874 was now being used to ruin their order, while the merchants who had drafted the bill pledged their timeless allegiance to "free capital, free competition, and free commerce."[17]

Charles Perkins was in charge of Iowa politics, and he pinned his hopes on repealing the rate law in the General Assembly. As the Iowa lawmakers gathered in February 1876, Perkins tried once more to explain the railroads' discomfort with the ironclad tariff in 1874. It was true that some roads earned record profits in 1875, but this was entirely the result of unusually *high* rates mandated by the law. Why then were the railroads seeking repeal? Because "the rates which they are charging to Chicago are higher than the products can bear and at the same time bring in enough return to the producer to encourage & stimulate industry to its utmost." Perkins's sudden interest in producer welfare was perfectly "logical" and should be evident to "every farmer in Iowa": The railroads were fixtures that could not be moved, so they were "directly interested in developing the country" they occupied. In short, the railroad managers were concerned that dangerously high rates would stifle the enterprise of Iowa. Perkins overlooked the fact that his entire schedule of rates violated Iowa law.[18]

Heroic arguments notwithstanding, the Iowa lawmakers were not ready to repeal their statute. Instead they adopted an amnesty measure forgiving past violations in return for immediate compliance. Perkins feared that the session had done nothing more than "call attention to the fact that we are not obeying the law." With the benefit of hindsight he now believed that the Burlington "ought to have complied" with the law from the start, and then "in combination with the other Roads" it should have put up through rates "even higher than they have been—but that is a vain regret." Discussing the problem with Robert Harris, now president of the CB&Q, Perkins acknowledged that acceptance of the amnesty was the best course. Only a Supreme Court ruling against the Granger Laws would materially alter the situation, and he did not expect one that spring. The Burlington directors stalled and studied as long as possible, then on May 10, 1876, they accepted the terms of the amnesty. The Iowa rates were law.[19]

SELECTING AN HEIR

Since the end of the Civil War John Murray Forbes had tried to distance himself from the Burlington railroad and focus his eyes on the larger scene. Preoccupied with Republican politics, Reconstruction in the South, and the funding of the national debt, Forbes fancied himself more of a consultant to power than an active businessman. With trading interests continuing in Europe and China, with land speculations across the United States, with politics, finance, and, of course, railroads to watch, his attention was spread pretty thin. Then James F. Joy's empire began to collapse, and the panic of 1873 brought business up short. The sting of scandal touched Forbes directly in the River Roads incident, while Grangers, inflationists, and silver heretics flourished throughout the West. The men in the field— Charles Perkins, Robert Harris, James M. Walker—were perhaps coping well enough with immediate problems, but the complexities of strategy and politics in the middle 1870s brought home to Forbes and the Burlington's Boston directors how badly they needed better command in the West.

The first signs of recovery from the depression, and the certainty of a railroad boom to follow, spurred Forbes and his colleagues to action. On March 2, 1876, they named longtime General Superintendent Robert Harris president. Former chief James M. Walker became general counsel, and Perkins, who had been running the B&MR Nebraska since 1872, was made vice-president of the CB&Q as well. These three made up the western executive committee which tried to administer company business for the next two years. The arrangement was really an experiment: No single man seemed right for the role vacated by James F. Joy. Walker had always enjoyed Forbes's confidence as a lawyer but not as a railroad manager. Harris was the most experienced railroad man in the Burlington family; he represented that close knowledge of technical detail that Forbes thought was missing from policy decisions. Charles Perkins, ten years younger than Harris, was Forbes's own protégé. Brilliant in his management of the western feeders, Perkins had an independent temper that endeared him to few of the directors. Forbes hoped that, in harness with Robert Harris, Perkins might win the board's confidence.[20]

In more than a decade of service as the general superintendent of the CB&Q Robert Harris had proved himself an operating technician of unmatched skill. Men with similar backgrounds were rising to executive positions in other large systems, and some of the Burlington's directors felt Harris was the man to run their railroad. He was conservative and pragmatic, tending always toward achievable goals and minimal risks. Harris denounced the whole system of rebates and concessions, made in the scramble for competitive business, as a "passion among RR managers" to give the service away. In his caution and his dedication to the transportation business "strictly defined," Robert Harris should have impressed John Murray Forbes as the ideal president for his railroad system. But Harris lacked those personal qualities that Forbes equated with entrepreneurship. Harris became president in 1876 because Forbes's own man was not ready to lead.[21]

During his profitable command of the western lines Charles Perkins had clearly demonstrated—perhaps too freely—both the intellectual vigor and the personal drive of an old-fashioned entrepreneur. Brought up through the ranks of railroad hierarchy, he was more of a company man than Forbes; but Perkins played his part with an entrepreneurial flare. His mind was never at rest. Regularly he sent pages of lucid commentary on railroad problems to John Murray

Forbes. He tirelessly pursued an ideal political economy—sometimes in the face of practical evidence. Perkins tolerated no suggestion that railroads were exceptional or that the laws of trade were not universal. Shrewd and expedient in practice, he still never compromised his principles to explain his behavior. Perkins showed the spirit and the integrity that John Murray Forbes demanded in a successor, but his headstrong temper worried the other Burlington directors.[22]

The choice between Robert Harris and Charles Perkins mirrored an ambiguity in the railroad business itself. The railroad was at once a *network* of trade and a *participant* in commerce. It could be managed for equilibrium as a servant of business, or it could be pursued as a dynamic growth industry. The tension between those objectives could not be resolved. By the 1870s good railroad managers were constantly balancing the security of pools against the ravages of speculation, rate-cuttings, and competitive construction. Retreating from James F. Joy's aggressive methods, John Murray Forbes had embraced pools and alliances; but the price of security was withdrawal from aggressive development. Among Forbes's executives, Harris was the stabilizer, Perkins the builder. As recovery from depression brought signs of a new wave of expansion, Forbes could not honor his peaceful principles. If Robert Harris was the technician Forbes claimed to respect, Charles Perkins was the man he admired.

The issue first came to a head in early 1877 over transcontinental interchange. During the recent depression Jay Gould, a hard-driving speculator whom Forbes and Perkins despised, had gained control of the Union Pacific and started threatening the harmony of the Iowa Pool. On behalf of the B&MR Nebraska, Perkins once more demanded free interchange at the far western gateway of Fort Kearney—as required by the Pacific Railroad Act of 1864. Perkins's move drew retaliations from Gould. Forbes warned Perkins not to press too firmly. Reports in Gould's New York *Tribune,* that the "pugnatious [sic] Perkins might be dropped from the CB&Q," indicated to Forbes that "some folks" saw Perkins as the aggressor. "Extension is unpopular," Forbes concluded. "I don't want you to be its champion nor Harris its opponent."[23]

Forbes's wishes could not prevent that distinction. CB&Q President Harris and a majority of the directors saw peaceful accommodation as the only true course for the Burlington road. From their point of view the Nebraska line was an expendable feeder. When Gould offered peace in Iowa at the expense of Perkins's Nebraska demands, Harris was eager to accept. But Perkins saw Nebraska as his personal domain and the instrument of the Burlington's westward growth. He would not surrender his right to own that territory for a doubtful promise to share the business between Omaha and Chicago. Forbes held the balance; and while he agreed with Harris in principle, he distrusted Jay Gould too much to give up his future outlet. Forbes privately advised Perkins to "show no more white feather" and continue to plan toward a westward extension. Charles Perkins took this as a signal to fight; in May of 1877 he buried Gould's Iowa contract in intransigent, detailed demands.[24]

It was already clear that Perkins and Harris did not work well together. After the bitter encounter over Nebraska, Perkins tendered his resignation, wanting no part in a railroad that was managed by Harris. His letter was set aside, but a sudden nationwide railroad strike finally destroyed any working relationship between the two men.

Because of the lingering effects of the panic and depression, several eastern United States trunk lines posted wage reductions in May and June of 1877. Other lines soon followed. Already worried because the Burlington's engineers earned less than those on the other Chicago roads, President Robert Harris warned the directors against "pauperizing" the work force. Still the CB&Q cut wages. Strikes broke out on the Baltimore & Ohio line on July 16, 1877, and spread quickly across the nation. When Chicago railroaders went out on July 24, Harris kept his trains running and invited the men to present their grievances. Impatient with the very idea of labor unions, Charles Perkins urged a lockout along the entire road. When Harris refused, Perkins shut down the Iowa lines on his own. The strike collapsed in Iowa, while federal troops were required to restore order in Chicago. The comparison was unfair, but to Perkins the lesson was clear: "Vacillation and unsteadiness, in dealing with these men, is fatal."[25]

If Forbes ever had doubts that Perkins should succeed him, none remained by the end of 1877. As he turned once more to the business of executive reorganization, Forbes now openly conspired to install his younger cousin as chief executive. Perkins's aggressive temperament continued to trouble many directors; Forbes worried that "judging from my own timidity there will be grave doubts as to your carrying the Board as Brooks & Joy & Thayer used to do." Summing up the year just past, he lectured young Perkins on the virtues of restraint: "Cannot you see your way clear when the responsibility is

on you, of advocating a policy of perfecting the close business management of . . . our existing line with little construction and only such
productive extension of inevitable Iowa branches as are clearly occu-
pying our own territory in a nearly direct line West?" Forbes looked
to "having a compact well managed rich well equipped Road" for
his protection against competition—a position he had advocated for
thirty years. "We cannot grasp *every thing*," he continued, "unless we
take the Joy policy back." Instead of wasting strength on all fronts,
Forbes wanted to concentrate his effort again in "stepping out in the
line of migration." Toward that objective, he urged the younger man
to take "a conservative policy as to CB&Q—at least until we have
perfected its business management in details & thus win to you the
confidence of the owners."[26]

Here, after three decades of railroad development, was the original Forbes model still intact. Whenever he looked to the West Forbes
could not help feeling that the work was unfinished. But he was not
blind to the changes that had come, and he ended his lecture to
Perkins with a plaintive question: "Must we grow in branches &
feeders as the Devil fish grows & as Joy believed in growing or can
we take a breathing spell and perfect our own line?" Was Perkins
convinced that widespread extensions were needed "to live"? Or
could they aim for "safe and sturdy management" and an 8 percent
stock "growing stronger" by cutting expenses and avoiding debt?
Whichever proved better, Forbes now felt himself so thoroughly committed to the CB&Q that "unless the united Board which I have now
got built up, disappoints me & quits me—I cannot quit them until
health takes me out or *off* altogether."[27]

RAPPROCHEMENT IN IOWA

In March 1877 the United States Supreme Court upheld the so-
called Granger Laws in the upper Midwest. This perpetuation of
local prerogative was a blow to the railroads, to be sure; but recovery
from the long depression was well under way and most Iowa railroad
leaders were now focusing on extensions more than rates. Renewed
competition promised to soften up the political opposition as poorly
served communities clamored for rails. "If the legislature will give
proof," explained Robert Harris to an Iowa correspondent, "that the
property of those who live out of State . . . shall have the considerate
protection of the people . . . I think there will be no difficulty in

getting the means of developing Railroads in . . . the rich valleys of the Western slope." For a majority of Iowans the threat of being left behind now outweighed the benefits of rate regulation. Other Granger states had already revised their regulations, and most Iowans agreed that the time had come for modification of the original tariff law.[28]

The repeal effort centered this time on the establishment of an advisory commission with investigatory powers. Of the various proposals introduced in the 1878 session, the most popular called for railroad commissioners, appointed by the governor, who were authorized to investigate complaints and to examine the books of the companies, reporting their findings to the legislature each year. If the circumstances warranted, the commissioners might recommend prosecution in the civil courts. Substantially the same bill that the Grangers had favored four years before, this commission system was now the more popular alternative to ironclad tariffs.[29]

It seemed that everyone except the river town shippers was willing to try the commission system. With a patience born of desperate self-interest, the wholesalers of Dubuque, Davenport, and Clinton tried once again to explain events since 1874 in a favorable light. They pointed out that the hardships endured by Iowa shippers were due to railroad retaliation, not to Granger tariffs. They argued that the roads had prospered and continued to build in Iowa in spite of themselves. The merchants of Clinton ended their memorial with an impassioned plea for increased, not diminished, protection:

> It is the same spirit of extortion, discrimination, defiance of public opinion, and disregard of the interests of the State, which forced the people of Iowa to the adoption of the Iowa Tariff Law as a measure of protection against its rapacity, and which should be checked and bridled not alone by State but by National control. The Tariff Law is in no wise responsible for these extortions—it had cured the evil within the borders of the State, and it should be the effort of the people of Iowa . . . to secure Congressional regulation of railroad traffic between the States.[30]

Time and again the river towns had promised to forward the surplus of Iowa to the markets of the world, but their consistent failure to perform told the tale. Some stalwarts argued that the railroad lobby simply overpowered the Iowa legislature in 1878, but the establishment of a board of commissioners was truly a popular reform. Western Iowans, interior businessmen, and agriculturists all favored the more flexible arrangement. The commission system promised relative market advantages for shippers without driving investors from the state. Unwilling to enthrone the river merchants as permanent masters of their trade, most Iowans in 1878 sought a solution that could grow with the territory. The advisory commission was their answer.[31]

John Murray Forbes left this political matter in the hands of his Iowa specialist, Charles Perkins. Perkins made it clear that he too wanted the commissioner bill; he instructed his "friends" in the legislature to see to it. Governor John H. Gear's nominations for the three new commissioners received quick public acclaim from the major corporations. Peter A. Dey was a civil engineer with railroad experience. James W. McDill was a lawyer, a former district judge and congressman. Cyrus C. Carpenter was the former governor whose administration had inaugurated railroad regulation in Iowa. CB&Q President Robert Harris was confident that these men would "seek to consider the general interest of the State rather than that of particular localities or particular interests." He greeted their appointment with this word of advice: Seek a resolution to the complex "Railroad problem" through "patient and disinterested study."[32]

Harris's injunction was laudable, but the new Iowa commissioners lacked both the tools of analysis and the disinterested perspective that were needed to assess the railroad question. Adequate series of statistics, on which quantitative studies might have been based, did not exist. The best figures—those compiled by the railroads—were hardly credible in the public's eye. Neither was the issue perceived as simply a matter of lowering rates. Arbitrariness and inconsistency were condemned at the same time that mechanical equity in the form of pro rata pricing was almost universally rejected. The resolution of conflicting interests would be complicated at best. Finally, in light of the four years just past, the Iowa commissioners were charged with harmonizing relations between shippers and carriers—an objective that brought them inexorably back to politics. In the coming 1880s the railroad commissioners would be hard put to serve the "general interest of the state" while being fair to the owners of invested capital, regardless of the principles applied.

Even the condition of midwestern agriculture was difficult to measure. Objective judgments about the agricultural sector in the generation after the Civil War eluded farmers, carriers, and commissioners alike, and a century later the evidence is still ambiguous.

Overall, farming expanded enormously in Iowa from 1850 through the end of the century. The number of farms nearly doubled between 1860 and 1870, from 61,000 to 116,000; another 69,000 units were created in the 1870s before the last of Iowa's virgin land was sold. After that date expansion slowed but did not stop until the turn of the century. By 1880 Iowa boasted almost 25 million acres under the plow, and the value of land was rising steadily. The average value of an Iowa farm rose from not quite $2,000 before the war to $2,700 in 1870, $3,061 in 1880 and $4,247 in 1890. The increase, amounting to roughly 4 percent per annum, represented additional capital stocks of machinery, livestock, fences, and buildings, as well as the accumulated "rent" on the land itself. This was perhaps not a windfall, but the successful Iowa farmer at the end of the nineteenth century was often a prosperous man of considerable wealth.[33]

Rising farm values alone do not tell the whole truth. For the great majority of the state's agriculturists, who were making new farms in this period, rising values called for ever-greater inputs of capital. Farm-making costs are difficult to determine because they were often deferred by mortgage debt, concealed by unpaid labor of the farm family, or charged off to the increased value of the improved acreage. In the short run, however, the yearly cash balance of each man's operation meant more to him than his final, theoretical worth. Even if he purchased his land for cash, many an Iowa farmer mortgaged his holdings to raise working capital. Machinery and livestock investments per farm rose steadily from 1860 to 1890, doubling in the case of implements and more than tripling for animals. These investments represented relatively smaller proportions of total farm value, but they stood for immediate cash outlays at a time when farm prices and rates of return were both falling. In other words, the successful farmer was investing more to earn the same profit, while his less astute neighbors worked hard to get into debt. Farm tenancy increased during the period precisely because the rising costs of owning a farm, coupled with the diminishing return to the owner-operator, either compelled or persuaded many farmers to rent. According to the most recent study of Iowa tenancy, the rate of return to Iowa land fell steadily after 1870, falling below prevailing mortgage interest rates by 1900. Prosperity in Iowa was real, but it was not evenly distributed and it was becoming less so.[34]

On the farm, the most immediate measure of prosperity was the price of corn or wheat or hogs multiplied by the surplus for sale, all less the cost of transportation to a paying market. Here aggregates break down more severely. Farm prices fell generally between 1865 and 1890, but they fluctuated wildly between the endpoints and from one commodity to the next. Wheat fell relatively faster than other midwestern staples, but corn, hogs, oats, and cattle all had good and bad years. A diversified farmer with good information and a trader's luck might profit by adjusting his product to suit the market, but another man might produce the wrong crop every time. Drought, frost, and visitations of locusts heightened the farmer's uncertainty. Against this capricious prospect the farmer perceived much steadier (if declining) prices for the items he purchased. Finally, the railroads figured into this treacherous game as a third party at the table—and frequently the player with trump. Freight rates declined for the period, but whether they fell faster than farm prices depended on whether or not one paid the published rate. The regional terms of trade may have improved slightly before 1880, but after that time the most generous calculations show a deterioration of the farmers' position. This aggregate trend says nothing at all about the producers who paid disproportionately high rates at rural waypoints and non-competing centers, effectively subsidizing their more privileged neighbors and helping to "cause" the decline of railroad ton-mile revenues. If the nation and the region profited from increased productivity and improved transportation, hundreds of thousands of individual husbandmen had precious little reason to celebrate the progress of the age.[35]

Popular faith in the doctrine of economic progress had carried a revolution in trade and commerce for nearly two generations in America, yet at the bottom of the postwar regulation question lay a nagging fear in the popular mind that this progress was illusory. Rhetoricians like E. L. Godkin might easily attribute the whole progress of the nation to the blessings of organized capital and railroads, but most Iowa farmers had worked too hard to believe that. They piled up record harvests, yet they watched friends and neighbors brought to despair. They borrowed money and reinvested earnings in more land and equipment just to keep even with falling prices. Good harvests and profitable years understandably slipped from memory when crop failures—or worse, record yields—ruined farm incomes and jeopardized mortgaged homesteads. Aggregates meant little as each man approached reality in person; the popular mind in the Gilded Age was formed out of hundreds of private views.

"STEPPING OUT" ANEW

The repeal of the Granger Law and the establishment of a rail-road commission in Iowa placed the regulation question on the most reasonable footing since the last years of the 1860s. It remained for the CB&Q to find as hopeful a solution to its leadership crisis. By February 1878 John Murray Forbes was impatient with his chief executive, Robert Harris, and he was actively pressing for another change. Forbes hoped to "let him down easy," but Harris rallied his own friends on the board and refused to step aside. Frustrated, Forbes redoubled his efforts to gain control. "If I were reasonably sure that you could organize the C.B. & Q. so that you could run it after a year," he wrote to Perkins, "there would be less worry in [my] taking the place of either Chairman or President for a year than in running the concern to the extent I now do—& having to work through others." Some directors urged Forbes to hire professional managers to lighten his load, but he balked at the prospect of "employees" doing the work of the owners.[36]

Owner control was at the heart of the leadership problem for John Murray Forbes. The tradition of personal enterprise taught that it was irresponsible to surrender the business management of the stockholders' property to hired technicians like Robert Harris. If Forbes's assessment of Harris was unfair, his concern for the future of owner control was not far from the mark. But age was beginning to show on Forbes; he would soon be unable to mold the policies of the railroad he had nurtured for thirty years. "I am too old & too timid to keep up with such a Hydra as the C.B. & Q. has got to be," he complained. Even though he knew it could never stand still, he yearned for a policy of "perfecting its present line instead of reaching out new feeders." Only Charles Perkins, in Forbes's eyes, had the vigor *and* the conservative sense to steer a course between stagnation and disintegration. True, the younger man bombarded his conservative board with demands and projects and orders for funds, seldom taking the time to persuade them of his purposes. Still Forbes believed in Perkins, and he threw his whole weight against the resistance of more timid directors. In May 1878 Forbes assumed the presidency with a mandate to reorganize the company and name a new chief of western operations. Perkins was the man. The manuever had not been subtle, and within a month Sidney Bartlett was charging Forbes and Perkins with "turning the great Co [sic] over to a family concern."[37]

Behind this personal struggle in the Burlington board of directors lay an old division of interest between those who viewed the CB&Q as a regional unit and those who still saw it as the driving force in a westward development. For all his conservative talk, Forbes was the clear leader of the latter group, and his victory in May of 1878 guaranteed Burlington participation in the new wave of competitive construction. Forbes had resigned from the board of the B&MR Nebraska as a gesture of singular devotion to the CB&Q, but Perkins's stubborn refusal to do the same was the real indicator.

John Murray Forbes had felt worn out in March of 1878, but his return to active command in the field of western railroads restored his vigor. This time his adversary was that "low" speculator and longtime enemy, Jay Gould. Unlike fighting with friends, which wounded the spirit, this virtuous combat was a tonic to Forbes. He despised Gould, his methods, and all he stood for. His hostility was "chiefly personal," he admitted, but it turned on a "deeper" resentment of Gould's "Raider" tactics. "I don't care 2 cents what the outside public says," Forbes stormed when he was criticized for appearing aggressive. "Jay Gould will be peaceful to the *strong*, not the weak—Perkins & I are not pugnacious—we mean peace." Between June 1878 and October 1881, Forbes's pursuit of "peace" more than doubled the overall size of the CB&Q and stretched its western terminus to Denver. Through it all Forbes repeated his cautious intentions: "Take a good deal of risk rather than push into Joy-like Road building."[38]

What distinguished Forbes's and Perkins's expansionist impulse from Joy's sprawling ambition was their concentration on an integrated, not a comprehensive, network. Perkins had learned to understand the difference well: "If we make everything we do pay into our system we shall not strike on the Joy rocks." The existence of a comprehensive regional monopoly, however, allowing the manipulation of traffic over one line or another, contradicted the workings of an integrated service. Joy and Perkins had clashed over this in the early 1870s, and now Perkins faced the same kind of threat from Jay Gould's Union Pacific. As Gould gathered up control of the far western lines, other Iowa roads hoped to pool the business and survive. But John Murray Forbes would not countenance an alliance with Jay Gould. Thus his peaceful intentions bred warlike results.[39]

The "crime" of the Union Pacific was its longstanding refusal to interchange with independent branches on equal terms. Forbes's analysis of this old problem was now steeped in vitriol. "Your quick

eye will see," he wrote to a Nebraska editor, "the absurdity of allowing the monopolists who got hold of the great Stem lines of the Union
Pacific to shaft off [sic] the Branch lines & the people depending on
them." Built originally "at the public expense," the Union Pacific
was now in the hands of "the Ring" who "squeezed" large profits
from it while "sucking the branches dry." Gould and his friends were
simply "monopolists pampered by the public subsidies now turning
to eat up their benefactors." In plain language, this meant that
Gould was moving to acquire control of the Kansas Pacific (KP) and
the other independent branches that competed for Union Pacific
traffic. By late summer of 1878, he had captured the KP and started
building feeders into the whole length of the B&MR Nebraska's local
territory. Moving more quickly and recklessly than Forbes, Gould
could not be restrained by ordinary methods.[40]

By the New Year 1879, Forbes and Perkins were devising a
grand plan of defense for the CB&Q. First merge the parent with its
Nebraska affiliate to prevent any conflicts within the "family." Then
secure a permanent affiliation with the Rock Island Railroad, re-
moving that line as an instrument of aggression. Finally, form a
binding relationship with some eastern line—perhaps the Pennsylvania—to complete an interregional system. With excessive caution (he
accused himself of "indecision") Forbes spent more than a year react-
ing to pressures and laying the groundwork for the Burlington's response. Perkins was out of patience more than once. Gould's campaign of acquisitions required strong action. Perkins suggested that
perhaps the Burlington ought to "go through to the mountains." The
railroads, he argued, would one day "group themselves" into "self-
sustaining" systems. "Each line must own its feeders," was the inevitable conclusion. "This law, like other natural laws, may work
slowly, but it is the law nevertheless." If Gould and others formed
huge combinations against the Burlington, then there "ought to be a
counter-combination . . . for the good of the country and the Railroads." Perkins's ideal was a union of Pennsylvania Railroad, Rock
Island, CB&Q, B&MR Nebraska, and the Atchison, Topeka &
Sante Fe. "I don't know who can form it or lead it," he pleaded to
Forbes, "but yourself."[41]

Possibilities for such extraordinary system building seemed inexhaustible in 1879. It fell to Forbes to discover by what means a
plan could be implemented that was both strategically effective and
financially sound. He sifted the "formidable array of new work,"
instinctively looking first for that which could be "averted." He pre-

ferred alliances in the East and acquisitions in the West; but either way the scale of management and finance worried him. The "carnival of bankrupt Roads" that prevailed in the summer of 1879 did not present a legitimate market. Forbes resisted all efforts to buy or build defensive lines, expecting that peace would elude him once more. Good arguments abounded, especially for expansion into the Southwest, but Forbes wanted to "see our main line through and local lines strengthened—rather than exhaust ourselves too much in the S. West." In truth he withheld his assent from everything until the CB&Q directors agreed to consolidate with the B&MR Nebraska. Resisted in this, his first objective, Forbes put off all new propositions with a shrug: 'The CB&Q is an old fogey concern with a Fossil President, a Sick Auditor, and practically no financial wit or wisdom."[42]

The major obstacle to a merger with the Nebraska line was a pending alliance with the Rock Island Railroad. Here the strategies of parallel and sequential consolidation came face to face. Several directors in each company thought that Nebraska consolidation positively precluded any balanced arrangement with the Rock Island, but Forbes refused to see one as excluding the other. His ideal was to unite Burlington and Rock Island in a "local" network "indifferent to the long lines . . . to the Pacific." Although such a broad system would naturally benefit from whatever traffic its far western feeders could bring, it would not *depend* on the fluctuations of the transcontinental business. Here was Forbes's original conception of self-sufficiency expanded on a grand scale; still he was not sanguine about its success. He was leery of the "unlimited consolidation, which seems to be taking the public by storm," and he worried about administrative efficiency, economy, and the appearance of monopoly. "Permanency and other things being equal," he preferred not a merger but an "alliance" with the Rock Island.[43]

The Rock Island union never materialized, but consolidation of the CB&Q and the Nebraska line was accomplished in February 1880. New shares of Burlington stock were exchanged for the stock of the Nebraska companies. An additional issue was distributed as "surplus earnings" to the old stockholders on the CB&Q. Another great step secured, Forbes once more backed away from useless competition. Perkins approached him in May to buy into the Wabash, and again in August to buy back the Hannibal & St. Joseph, but Forbes refused. "If the young and vigorous leaders in R. Roads do not take a lesson from 1870," he thundered, not at Perkins so much as youngsters in general, "we are in danger of another era of R. Road building and another break down." Contractors and "too enterprising Railroad projectors and raiders" were worse than Grangers: "In fact we may again welcome Granger legislation as a check to over production of roads."[44]

The warnings went unheeded. Charles Perkins's efforts to contain Jay Gould's western designs placed repeated calls on the Burlington treasury. Money itself was not scarce; Forbes was plagued with buyers at each new issue. The problem was an overheated speculators' market in which real investors were hard to find. By November 1880, the financial pressures of competitive construction and consolidation forced the Burlington to free some of its assets. The only way was to "water the stock." It was painful for John Murray Forbes to dilute the investment value of his proudest stock ("pure milk") in order to save the earning power of the road; but the youngsters said it must be done. Forbes believed that the proposed two-thirds inflation was the "first real water" that must be charged against profits and the enhanced value of the road. Perkins's shopping list was staggering: "Atchison & Topeka 40 or 50 millions, H. & St. Jo. 10 to 20, Stones Road ?, etc., etc." Hoping the cup might pass, Forbes offered to retire on grounds of health and let Perkins "take up . . . the water spout." Still, if he had to order this "leap into the flood," it had better be done quickly "while the fashion lasts!"[45]

The purposeful inflation of the Burlington stock was a psychological blow to the aging Forbes. He fretted through the remainder of the winter, reassessing his decision. Finally his health and spirit broke. He was unable to decide the simplest of questions, and he worried interminably about great problems and small details alike. The only thing he still was certain of was the folly of trusting Jay Gould. Pestered even in retreat by endless negotiations with the western roads, Forbes exploded. It was the "honest purpose" of the participants, he scolded William H. Vanderbilt of the New York Central, not the "legal or technical validity" that made agreements work. For that reason he could make none with Jay Gould. At an impasse, Gould invaded Perkins's Nebraska territory once more, and the Burlington struck out for Denver. By September 1881, the last major phase of the Burlington's long westward trek was under way. One month later an exhausted John Murray Forbes stepped down for good, and Charles Elliott Perkins took hold of the sprawling Chicago, Burlington & Quincy Railroad.[46]

John Murray Forbes had kept pace with the hectic development of America's railroad industry for more than three decades. The CB&Q, his proudest creation, now spanned four western states and operated 2,924 miles of railroad. The Burlington took in over $21 million in revenues in 1881—nearly three times the sum of a decade before—and it continued to pay with monotony a dividend of 8 percent. That a railroad with a capital stock of over $55 million finally outgrew Forbes's energy and talents was itself a tribute to a brilliant career.[47]

Since leaving the backward mercantilism of old Canton Forbes had played his part in the transformation of American enterprise. He set a conservative style and ethical standard by which progress might well have been measured. He generated a model for developing the vast interior of the United States, and he adapted or invented many of those instruments of corporate enterprise with which industrialists and financiers revolutionized American life. By 1881 his ideal railroad designs had been battered and distorted by decades of ruthless competition and reckless economic growth, but his ideas formed the stable core around which Burlington policies continued to be built. His shamefully irregular work habits had been replaced by bureaucratic methods, and his hard-money stocks had been diluted by more fashionable securities, but the CB&Q remained essentially the developmental railroad Forbes had meant it to be. Charles Perkins would perpetuate as the next president something of the "model entrepreneur" that had enchanted his mentor. It was a good time to rest.

By the time of Forbes's retirement the outlines of industrial America were evident on the face of the nation. Systems of transport and commerce were in place over much of the continent. Big business was spreading into industry, and the consolidations and combinations that would mark twentieth-century enterprise had already begun. Most important, the process of change—the idea of progress itself—was almost universally embraced by the coming generation. Outside the rural South and the newest regions of the agricultural West, the period of initial adjustment was past. Centralization, consolidation, speed, and power, if not uniformly appreciated, were widely enough accepted that no generation to follow could realistically reject them as features of modern life. It now remained for elements within American society to redefine their political and cultural relations with their instruments of progress.

7

The Ordeal of Regulation

POPULAR AGITATION for railroad control began with the earliest railroads. Pioneers like John Murray Forbes promised harmony and benevolence from the revolution in transport, but the rapport they hoped for never came. Each time railroads penetrated new territory, bringing fresh competition to regions that had once enjoyed geographical immunity, local interests raised an injured cry. In the new world brought by the railroads, local businessmen and local governments found themselves increasingly powerless to stay the advancing centralized systems. Even when people accepted the economic consequences of centralization, they viewed with alarm the accumulations of power that followed trade. Bureaucracy and professional management further removed the exercise of power from the realm of ordinary people. National institutions of business—which the great interstate railroads had become—disoriented citizens of the republic who still thought of themselves as sovereigns. Americans might accept the natural laws of supply and demand, but they saw manipulations by powerful new men and corporations as illegitimate perversions of American political traditions.[1]

For the most part the motivation for railroad reform came from displaced local interests. Little governments close to home were the favorites of American political culture, and even though governments had played an active and complex role in developing the integrated market, the new larger structures remained objects of suspicion. John Murray Forbes and his generation had used the power of government to break down local prerogatives that restrained trade. By the time of the Civil War, their progress had seriously undermined local authority in questions of enterprise. The war itself had irreversibly advanced the status of federal authority over the multiplicity of state jurisdictions. The generation that managed business after the war followed national priorities, and they condemned as nostalgia the

complaints of local industries and country towns. Forgetting (or perhaps remembering too well) the role of government in their own
liberation, Gilded Age businessmen called for unqualified freedom
from government interference in business, especially at the local
level. Railroads dominated this subjugation of political tradition to
higher laws of laissez-faire theory. Even the unavoidable injury to
some kinds of business that resulted from rail transportation offended
the guardians of local power, and community leaders as well as injured shippers found it easy to point to the railroads as enemies of
freedom and hometown growth.[2]

The ordeal of regulation grew out of hundreds of clashes between local commercial and political interests and the advancing
national railroad systems. It was a recurrent problem from the Great
Rebellion to the First World War. It was a swamp of economic confusion and popular hostility apparently without bottom. First the pro
rata movements of the East, then the Granger outbreak in the Middle West reflected local outrage at the introduction of new competition that was favored by long-distance railroad rates. But local efforts
like the Granger laws always failed to solve the basic problems, because reform agitation derived from a multitude of technical complaints that varied from town to town throughout the railroad network. The sum of these complaints was an incoherent tangle that
could only be adjudicated by the operation of the market (however
clumsy) or by legislative fiat. Neither option appealed to a free capi-
talistic people.[3]

By the last third of the nineteenth century the railroads had
outgrown the structures of local government. As corporations combined into large interstate systems, local reformers turned to the federal government for instruments of protection. Such an exercise of
federal power was condemned by Perkins and Forbes as dangerous
innovation, but the business structures themselves were just as new.
Congressional action opened a new era in commercial regulation, but
the Interstate Commerce Act of 1887 did not supplant state and local
control. Local tempers continued to flare. State legislatures like
Iowa's struggled to perfect a system of railroad regulation that guaranteed the public interest. Each time the agitation necessarily focused
on corporate power, not the technical complaints of one shipper
against the next. Not surprisingly, the resulting regulations often
failed to improve the transport market, and they sometimes made it
worse. Nevertheless, the ordeal of regulation was a necessary step in
the passage of Americans through the railway age. It set aside forever

the unchallenged liberalism of John Murray Forbes's generation and ushered in a new age of business, philosophy, and social science.[4]

RETURN TO RAPID EXPANSION

Competitive construction and endless cycles of competition and combination were the chronic causes of rate discrimination in Gilded Age America. Discrimination in turn was by now the prime cause of agitation for railroad control. Struggling like Sisyphus against the "monopolies," shippers encouraged the construction of parallel lines while the carriers tried vainly to police themselves with pools and promises. Long-distance rates fell to the margin and below, while local freights staggered under recuperative charges. Public demands for regulation seemed to alternate with the outbreak of warfare among the roads themselves. That is why, as Charles Perkins explained to John Murray Forbes, a new boom would surely follow the period of recovery from the panic of 1873. By the time Forbes retired in 1881, that boom was under way.

The accession of Charles Perkins to the presidency brought aggressiveness once more to the head of the Burlington railroad. Shy, reflective, and totally sincere, Perkins nevertheless had a way of achieving his objectives that appeared to others belligerent. He was a big, barrel-shaped man with a small face and a great mustache that concealed his mouth altogether. Dressed for business in his suit, waistcoat, gold chain, hat, and walking stick, he cut a commanding figure. Charles Francis Adams, Jr., a longtime friend and professional adversary of Perkins, found him no less exasperating than the "typical head of a small independent state." According to Adams, Perkins jealously guarded his "petty independence," always begging for "peace and two-thirds of the traffic." But Adams was a patrician reformer at heart, and he never understood Charles Perkins's corporate perspective on the railroad market and business in general.[5]

John Murray Forbes did understand Charles Perkins, and he was sure that his younger cousin was the right man to lead the Burlington railroad into the coming age. Perkins was family, which still counted heavily with the older man. More importantly, Perkins was a company man whose loyalty could not be doubted. He passed his whole career on the Burlington Route. Finally, Charles Perkins was a systematic manager, which Forbes was not, and this is what made him modern. During Forbes's presidency, Perkins had restructured the internal operations of the Burlington. In the two decades of his own administration, Perkins wrote hundreds of pages in letters and memoranda detailing his theories of organization, administration, and human relations—some passages of which are classic statements of management science. Ironically for Forbes, Perkins despised paternalism as a dangerous intrusion in a scientific world. He was recognized as a teacher of railroad men. Perkins established lines of authority and communication and enforced them strictly. His hierarchy was both elegant and symmetrical. Atop the whole structure sat John Murray Forbes, chairman of the board, elder statesman, and founder of the firm. Perkins could not describe Forbes's actual duties, but "in our case," he concluded, "he is the head man."[6]

Returned once more to the position of overseer he had enjoyed in the 1850s when John W. Brooks ran the Michigan Central, Forbes watched with pleasure and enthusiasm as Perkins took up the load of running the CB&Q. Styles of business were changing, and Forbes would learn from a distance now. For example, public relations and corporate image were important new elements in Perkins's science of management. Early in his administration he launched an advertising campaign to divert public attention from the problem of rates. Calendars, maps, and even playing cards emblazoned with the Burlington name were kept constantly before the traveler's eye, emphasizing service and convenience. Ignorance and misinformation, according to Perkins, were the chief causes of public hostility, and he strove tirelessly to enlighten the people on the principles of political economy. Even when the tone of the local press was enough "to discourage almost anybody," he refused to be demoralized. "[W]e must keep at it," he wrote in 1885, "and do the best we can to educate honest people, who are greatly in the majority." The remainder were "dishonest" and could not be reached "except through their pockets."[7]

Perkins's image campaign was premature because politics, not public relations, still structured life in the 1880s. But Charles Perkins was also a skilled influence broker; he and his lieutenants maintained powerful political connections in Iowa and Nebraska. Often calling on Forbes to feed money or doctrine into local campaigns, Perkins manipulated candidates and officials from either party with no concern for impropriety. He paid $1,900, for example, "nominally for advertising," to the Burlington *Gazette* because it was "for our own interest . . . that the Democratic paper here shd [sic] not be run as a Communistic sheet." This was only one of many "investments" made by Perkins and his staff to further the interests of the company.

Should a "friend" thus won subsequently desert him, Perkins thought nothing of having him exposed as a paid lackey of business corporations.[8]

With his strong intellect matched by administrative and political skills, Charles Perkins was a formidable new chief for the Burlington Route. More confident than Forbes in this fast-changing world, he stepped in just as another wave of railroad expansion was cresting. Before the decade was out he had finished the Denver line, bought back the Hannibal & St. Joseph, built an entirely new line to St. Paul, accumulated hundreds of miles of branches within the original Burlington network, and opened negotiations for a route to the Pacific Ocean. In seven years Perkins doubled the size of the Burlington system. His ideal goal was inherited from Forbes: A "theoretically perfect Railroad system would be long and not very wide," holding to itself "a belt of country perhaps 50 miles wide—with arms here & there reaching to great centers not within the system." But the ability of any man to impress order upon the structure of railroad markets was being destroyed by easy money and cutthroat competition. Consolidations were now taking place on a scale never imagined, and the resulting giant systems seemed ever more vulnerable. Strategies were determined by the growth of the systems themselves. Equilibrium proved elusive.[9]

The Denver line was already under construction when Perkins took office in October 1881. In contrast to the long years spent building across Iowa, this railroad to the mile-high city was opened in 229 working days—a rate just under one mile per day! Before the end of 1883 Perkins had outlined a dizzying array of projects for the years ahead: Kansas City to the southwest, St. Paul and Minneapolis to the north, and the wilds of the Pacific Northwest. Forbes worried that the younger man's construction plans looked warlike. Were they prepared, he queried Perkins, to extend the Burlington to the Pacific? Or would they "creep back" into their "conservative niche," building only such feeders "as may be considered legitimate children"? In an overheated securities market small choices had transcontinental consequences. It was a speculator's environment. Forbes cautioned: "I shall not be surprised to see a boom."[10]

In reality the market had been rapidly accelerating for several years already. Under such conditions it was the task of management to steer between the twin perils of government regulation and Wall Street speculation. Perkins charted the course while Forbes played the part of foreign secretary. In his best personal style Forbes assured his nervous competitors that the Burlington's ambitions were honorable. He only wanted to keep any strategic property from becoming "a foot ball in the game of Bears & Bulls—in which an old fashioned slow concern like CB&Q can take no part." Diplomatic language notwithstanding, the CB&Q was neither old-fashioned nor toothless. By the summer of 1885 a new Minnesota line—the Chicago, Burlington & Northern—was building toward a junction with James J. Hill's St. Paul, Minneapolis & Manitoba Railroad at St. Paul. America's railroad systems were taking on a new dimension, claiming whole quadrants of the continent instead of long strips of territory. Through subsidiaries and alliances, if not direct expansion, the Burlington was following suit.[11]

Perkins's northwestern strategy was truly a new departure for the Burlington, and it caused John Murray Forbes a dilemma. Forbes fretted that the new securities were "too highly charged with colored water," but the enthusiasm of the youngsters and the "*electric atmosphere*" around his Boston office carried him along. The CB&Q was not attacking anyone, he tried to argue. Like "the rest of the world" it was simply "browsing into legitimate pastures." Of course, playing host to similar browsers was another matter. When the Atchison, Topeka & Santa Fe proposed a new route between Kansas City and Chicago—through the heart of the Burlington's territory— Forbes and Perkins raised a bitter resistance.[12]

For all their conservative pleading, Forbes and Perkins did as much to stimulate the boom as to curtail it, and they kept ahead of the game. By April 1887, Perkins began to relax. His position was secure in the Mississippi Valley—"the Seat of Empire, & trade"— and he was comfortably allied with James J. Hill, who was opening a path through the northern Rockies. The construction boom, nearly a decade old, was now expiring. The time had come to economize the Burlington's operations and recover the costs of rapid construction. To John Murray Forbes the pause was a blessed relief. Competition was his tonic, but the strain of prolonged war was too much for the old man. "I am old, timid, crooked, tired, sceptical," he wrote to one of his young brokers, "and I should wish you to the Old Harry if you led my crutches into any hobbly places." Forbes and Perkins now hoped for a period of "*peace and pools,*" but popular demands for government regulation would deny them both.[13]

John Murray Forbes's original design for the synchronized development of settlement and transportation was ideally intended to avoid the contradictions and conflicts of interest that had grown up with America's railroads. But railroading had not followed Forbes's plan, and by the 1880s it was evident to everybody that order must be introduced after the fact. Who would impose such order? The corporations assumed that they could police themselves, but the people whose communities the railroads served felt a continuing right to interfere. Here was the heart of the regulation question, and the pressures of the recent boom brought the problem to the fore once again.

The fact that the focus of regulation in the 1880s was on the federal government was a natural outgrowth of frustrations at lower levels of government. Local efforts to restrain the carriers in earlier years had always been blunted by the limits of state jurisdiction. The railroad network was oblivious to state boundaries, and most corporations now operated interstate roads as single units of enterprise. The rate structure devised by these roads conformed to the interstate market for transportation, and this frequently compromised local ambitions. Furthermore, interstate roads could ignore state regulations or exploit the local application of laws to their systemwide advantage—the Burlington had tried both recently in Iowa. If there was to be effective regulation of these growing railroads, it would have to come from an authority more comprehensive than the state.[14]

During the Granger years, and certainly in the decade that followed, it was rate discrimination rather than high rates per se that irritated most consumers. Railroad charges had fallen steadily and dramatically since the Civil War decade, with the most impressive advantage going to interregional exchange.[15] This aggregate improvement, however, had not come evenly; it did not reflect the rational distribution of savings by increasingly efficient carriers. Rather, the decline in rates was the result of unrestrained competition in a rough-and-tumble market that saturated competing points with services while straining the revenues of the companies and sacrificing marginal territory along the way. Waves of competitive construction, like the one under way in the West in the 1880s, exacerbated the problem. Excess capacity yielded cutthroat competition that drove down through rates and exaggerated the high freights paid by captive shippers. When the carriers tried to curtail competition—as in the Iowa Pool, where the Chicago roads divided the transcontinental business at Omaha—consumers stepped up demands for competing services on the classical assumption that competition prevented monopoly.[16] If competition succeeded in reducing the freights paid by some shippers, or by the region as a whole, this was usually accomplished at the expense of those who paid much higher rates on noncompeting business.

Classical theory failed to resolve the issue of rate discrimination. Discrimination was inherent in any national transport system that imposed hierarchical order on a series of local markets. Most shippers and carriers now knew that this was true. It was "unfair" discrimination that sparked their complaint, and here the emotional component took hold once more. One veteran of the Iowa struggle concluded that the railroads "assumed greater powers than those of Deity": "They abrogated time and space; they changed the geography of the country. If rates were a guide, Omaha was situated between Chicago and Iowa, Denver was on the Mississippi, and San Francisco on the Missouri, while the interior towns of Iowa and Nebraska were located on Behring Strait."[17] The fact that railroads had been built for the express purpose of abrogating time and space did not make the complaint less bitter.

It never occurred to John Murray Forbes to deny that railroads could change the natural markets. Perhaps because he had always envisioned a comprehensive system of developmental roads governed from above, Forbes acknowledged the power and the possibility of abuse. In a dialogue that began in July 1879 and continued for many years, Forbes separated the regulation problem into business questions and politics, while Perkins saw the whole issue as a single threat to the corporate system. "Whether and how far to foster large dealers by rebates and thus run the risk of enlisting small dealers and farmers against us," Forbes posited, was a pressing question of "internal administration." A second was this: "How far is it wise to hire large dealers to go into our neighbor's territory to get business by rebates— which is merely one form of cutting rates?" To Forbes these were simply matters of policy. They could be continued or not at the company's pleasure, unless politics made them inexpedient. In 1879 it was becoming a "big question," he advised Charles Perkins, "and I hand you some comments from Tuesday and Wednesday New York Graphic, which show what a field there is for the Grangers to work in case our system gets an overhauling before any legislature."[18]

For Charles Perkins the problem of regulation was an intellectual challenge that transcended the expedient matters of company policy and business practice. Responding to Forbes's clippings about the New York rebating hearings, Perkins refused to be frightened by adverse exposure. The stories were simply untrue! The "Commercial life of towns and communities" was not left "in the hands of a few irresponsible Railroad employes [sic]," regardless of what New York witnesses might say. "It would puzzle wiser men than Railroad freight agents," he explained, "to state upon the witness stand . . . all of the considerations and influences which make the basis of the rates for transportation by rail." For Perkins, rate making was a "contest" between the agent and the shipper, and the shipper "usually" got the "benefit of any doubt." Perkins believed that the "evil" of oppression by railroad pricing was "theoretical and imaginary, not real." To remedy the trouble "you *may* make" state or federal tariffs, but they would have to be "fixed and inelastic." Given such a fixed price, no businessman could undersell his neighbor; "you take out of business the 'root hog or die' principle."[19]

Perkins was worried about the vitality of the competitive system as a whole. He could not imagine enterprise with a transportation system that was neutral to all. Forbes accepted Perkins's theories as truth, but he knew they failed to address the real, *political* problem of rate discrimination. "The question of discrimination seems to me to be the most difficult one," Forbes counseled some time later; "you have got to dodge it or make a better answer than has yet been given to justify discrimination." By focusing on railway economics, Perkins was perhaps close to the theoretical issue at hand, but he was missing the essence of the regulation movement itself. Forbes's approach was that of an old merchant: Whether or not the people are attacking the right quarter, take in sail. He would abandon such rebates and discriminations as were causing him grief. Perkins responded tirelessly with another lecture. Railroad transportation was "commerce," he argued, "not a tax or a toll." The ordinary laws of wholesale and retail trade therefore governed transport services as well, and if commercial practices worked occasional hardships on individuals, they were on the whole "beneficial to mankind."[20]

Of this benefit the public was not persuaded. Individual cases of abuse seemed to outweigh the evidence of overall gain, and by the middle of the 1880s a popular clamor for federal regulation could no longer be ignored. The statutory prohibitions of pools and discriminations—especially in the punitive terms of bills sponsored by Texas Congressman John H. Reagan—were increasingly attractive to angry and frustrated interest groups across the nation. In the popular mind, discrimination was the evil that united consumers of railroad services. Pools worked to minimize competition; and since competition was considered a cure for discrimination, then pools must be banned as well. This tandem barrier to pools and discrimination was the logical product of popular, though misguided, assumptions. Under pressure from the streets once more, Forbes and Perkins stiffened their resistance.[21]

In 1885 the United States Senate established a select committee to investigate the whole problem of interstate commerce. Headed by Shelby M. Cullom of Illinois, this agency collected testimony from shippers and railroad officials across the nation. Its first act was to circulate a questionnaire among railroad executives, asking for their views on the nature of the problem and the various alternatives. Perkins responded for the Burlington, and once more he took the high road of theory. He dismissed as "trifling" those instances of inequality that inevitably occurred in a free market. No country so prosperous as the United States could possibly be suffering from burdensome railroad rates. If certain centers of trade enjoyed better service and cheaper rates, this was hardly the fault of the railroads. With this last assertion Perkins shed the whole weight of historical reality in American railroad development. From that point forward his argument flowed with clarity and force. He was correct, of course, that arbitrary discriminations and ruthless competition did not *necessarily* accompany railroad development. Unfortunately, in this country they did.[22]

Perkins was especially eager to shift attention away from the moral emphasis of public rhetoric, toward the cooler logic of abstract market systems. "Justice" played no part in the laws of trade, he argued, and it should not be interjected by force. In context, the railroad question was incredibly complex and riddled with traditional notions and conventions. Perkins wished to rise above the history. The bare "right to regulate the charges of railroads" was "no longer disputed," he admitted. At issue now was the wisdom of public interference. Society might take hold of the business either by regulating rates or by limiting the construction of new lines. He warned against both:

> If you limit construction, it will be more or less necessary for society to interfere directly with the price of transportation, which, on the whole, it is not best to attempt, because reasonable prices can only be produced by natural adjustment; while, on the other hand, if you attempt to fix prices by law, without limiting construction, it will not be regarded as reasonable by private investors; and the tendency will be to drive railroad property into the hands of speculators, and to impair its efficiency and usefulness. Let competition and the fear of competition, direct and indirect, regulate the prices.

In sum, the transportation problem "was working itself out more rapidly than could have been thought possible twenty years ago." For Perkins, the "real Railroad Question" was no longer how to secure cheap transportation, but how to preserve free enterprise in America.[23]

Perkins's essay was well crafted and powerful, but he had missed the point. Even John Murray Forbes found his analysis naive in places. Free trade in railroad construction, Forbes sputtered, only loaded up the "solid Roads with cats (something as the early surveyors boots used to be weighted with rattlesnakes hanging on to them . . .)." When Perkins tried to deny that watered stock influenced the price of transportation, Forbes balked again. "Fraudulent value," Forbes reminded his cousin, was "often interjected in order to deceive" the public. It might be "inexpedient" to legislate against watered stocks, "but it is not unjust." Forbes knew that Perkins's argument was abstract, his analysis out of context; still he found the whole compelling. He was ready to endorse it "even if you don't care to alter a word of it." Unnerved by the starkness of Perkins's warnings, Forbes recoiled at the prospect of government control as "a step backwards toward the dark ages."[24]

By the summer of 1885 both Perkins and Forbes had begun to see federal railroad regulation as a form of civil disintegration. They were responding to an inflated menace. Sweeping away the record of failures in private enterprise in the last several decades, Forbes traced the industry back to his early days when the country was "*strewed* with the wrecks of State Rail Roads from Michigan to Pennsylvania." What the states had failed to do "would be ten times worse under U.S. management involving an enormous patronage & in short almost a revolution." Forbes could not overstate the danger from such "*centralization*,"—the "Sum of all folly not to say wickedness." Once an avid proponent of central control, the old nationalist Forbes now cringed at the prospect of using government power to restrain the systems he had created. Why? Because politicians, not entrepreneurs, had gained control of government after the Civil War. Forbes had welcomed politics when it fostered his image of national unity and enterprise, but now he withdrew. He feared the national party machinery, even more than the old state democracies. In Europe, nationalism was leading to socialism by "pampering the unwashed classes." Such a drift was apparent at home as well, where Forbes thought it could run "*right up to* communism." It was Perkins who put the finest point on the matter: "In a republic where every man votes you are lost if you don't insist upon and rigidly adhere to the principle that Government is merely to protect life and property."[25]

Here was the bedrock of Jacksonian Democracy rediscovered in conservative Republican thought. The adoption of laissez-faire by Republican business interests after the Civil War marked the beginning of a long retreat from the centralizing, interventionist posture of the wartime "Liberty" party. The new spirit and purpose for government that had propelled James W. Grimes and his Republicans to leadership in Iowa in 1856 now stood repudiated by the beneficiaries of Grimes's reforms. In language startling in its similarity, Perkins claimed for government exactly that Jacksonian role that Grimes had defeated. The circle was closing. Sensing his awkward stance, Perkins hurried to explain. Education had developed "the sympathetic side of human nature more rapidly than . . . the *science* of political economy—or of life." The result, for Perkins, was a tendency of "sympathetic people to take the side of all who are either bad, lazy, or unfortunate and to lean towards Socialism."[26] Inexorably the problems of rebates, pooling, and long–short discrimination had been transformed into a struggle to save a softhearted people from unscientific paternalism or the tyranny of the masses. Charles Perkins was an admirer of William Graham Sumner's Darwinian sociology, and he arrived at this position easily. For an old paternalist like Forbes, however, it was agony.

LOCALISM REVITALIZED

For John Murray Forbes the passage of the Interstate Commerce Act in February 1887 marked the end of true liberalism in America. But for people like the Iowa shippers along the CB&Q it was a sign of new hope. The country's first effort at federal railroad regulation laid down broad antidiscrimination principles and established a permanent board of commissioners to administer its provisions. The new law prohibited pooling, by which the railroads had hoped to achieve a measure of stability through self-regulation. On the more difficult question of long- and short-haul discrimination, the lawmakers hedged: Greater charges for the shorter haul were prohibited only if the services were performed under "substantially similar circumstances." The mandate was vague, the implied challenge broad. However, the mere passage of a national law, embodying tough antirailroad language and establishing continuous oversight of the railroad industry, made a favorable popular impression. Here was proof after all that the railroads were not beyond the reach of popular government. With renewed zeal, the Iowans turned their attention once more to the problem of state railroad control.[27]

Since 1878, when the Iowa General Assembly repealed the maximum rate law, the Board of Railroad Commissioners had been responsible for supervising Iowa's railroads. Their role was strictly advisory, and the commissioners enjoyed limited powers. They could only investigate complaints that were brought to them by an injured party, and their recommendations were unenforceable. Their first purpose was to reduce the hostility between the people and the carriers; "adjustment and harmony" were their primary goals. Measured against these modest objectives, the advisory commission was reasonably successful. The commissioners maintained communication with the railroad companies, securing their cooperation in some rate adjustments and mollifying the shippers in other cases. Some members of the board were perhaps too intimate with railroad executives, like Judge J. W. McDill with Charles Perkins, but on the whole the Iowa board was no mere instrument of corporate whimsy. The commission had not wrestled the railroads into submission, but that was never its stated goal. The commissioners would be attacked in time for cowardice, but the charge was unfair.[28]

The Iowa commissioner law of 1878 was the product of chastened optimism that followed the depression of the 1870s and the ill-fated Granger law. Its limited objectives reflected the mood of a people whose anger was vented and whose future looked momentarily bright. The illusion of harmony, however, peaked with the farm price index in the early 1880s, and the popular mood turned angry once more. By 1884 overproduction was forcing down farm prices, and rural communities felt the familiar squeeze of reduced income and steady, high local charges for transportation. Even Perkins admitted that some reductions were probably in order, but he would not act for fear that the regulatory commission would hold him to the lower rate forever. Six years of "harmony and adjustment" had gained little real compromise from the railroads serving Iowa.[29]

The inadequacy of the Iowa system in the face of changing popular feelings came to light in June 1885 at the interstate commerce hearings in Des Moines. Senator Shelby M. Cullom's committee listened intently to the commissioners' accounts of the general progress they felt had been made toward lasting harmony between carrier and shipper. Then countless merchants, farmers, and whole-salers paraded through the hearings telling tales of hardship, injury, and ruin which the embarrassed commissioners were powerless to address. Many shippers proved by their testimony that they only wanted lower rates for themselves, or higher rates for their competi-tion, but the overall pattern of arbitrariness and inequity could not be dismissed. Animosities spread across the state as farm prices and local business continued to slide. By early 1886 Iowans had grown tired of "charming" theories about natural laws and railroad charges. Even Perkins's confidant on the Iowa board, Commissioner J. W. McDill, had reached his limit: "The man who goes down under the doctrine of the survival of the fittest can never be satisfied with his downfall because it is the result of a law which may be shown to serve the universe so well."[30]

McDill's defection came too late to alter the moods of Forbes and Perkins. By March 1886 neither man was receptive to the "omi-nous warnings" passed on to them by the Iowa railroad commission-ers. The "misunderstanding and jealousy" that prevailed between shippers and carriers was truly deplorable, the situation dangerous. The merchants were especially restless, and the commissioners feared that without relief, the "wholesale and manufacturing interests" of Iowa would be "more or less crippled." Perkins replied with a stone. "I have never known of a single case," he wrote, "of failure because of rates charged by a Railroad." More often it was the corporations who were "preyed upon by interested and designing persons, who misrepresented or distorted the facts in order to benefit themselves." State regulation had reached a stalemate just at the time that Con-gress was debating a federal bill. Both shippers and carriers watched in suspense for an interstate railroad law.[31]

When the new law came, early in 1887, it was hailed in Iowa as a triumph of popular government at the highest level. The Iowa railroad commissioners were personally excited by the prospects of bringing state regulation into "perfect harmony" with the federal Interstate Commerce Act. To these professional servants of a trou-bled industry, here was a chance to approach the problem with unity and system.[32] In the popular mind, however, a power struggle had been renewed. Now totally dependent on railroads for their business, but encouraged at last by the promise of federal control, Iowa's ship-pers struck back at the carriers to recover some of the power that their state of economic dependence had cost them. This new outburst of local temper was brought into focus by a businessman-turned-reformer, Governor William Larrabee.

TO ADVOCATE THE PEOPLE'S RIGHTS

William Larrabee was a Connecticut Yankee who had come to Iowa in 1853—the same year John Murray Forbes took an interest in the Burlington railroad. Larrabee eventually settled in the village of Clermont, in northeastern Iowa, where he prospered as a flour miller, farmer, banker, and land speculator. In 1867, after a brief experiment in railroad construction, he was elected to the Iowa Senate. Nearly twenty years' loyal service to the state and the Republican party placed Larrabee in the running for governor in 1885. Endorsed by the leading papers, he won easily. A stately, prosperous-looking man, the new governor's visage was overwhelmed by a mustache more luxuriant than even Charles Perkins's. Vigorous and energetic at the age of fifty-four, he took office in January 1886, pledging to stop the flow of whiskey and to reform the public finances in the state of Iowa.[33]

What brought Larrabee into conflict with Forbes, Perkins, and the Burlington railroad was a little incidence of economic injustice that perfectly illustrates the escalation of tempers in the railroad question. Nothing in Larrabee's past record suggested radical views on railroad reform; also, there had been no general outcry in the state campaign that year. Prohibition and fiscal responsibility—both solid Republican issues—had given the governor his majority, and it was during a subsequent audit of the public books that a problem arose concerning the CB&Q. The issue sparked an attack on the railroads that astonished Larrabee's friends and his party. It seems that the CB&Q was charging the state more to transport coal to the Feeble Minded Institution at Glenwood than to transport the same commodity to a site in Council Bluffs. Since the same train serviced both towns, and since Glenwood was nearer the mines, Larrabee thought that the charge was unfair. He asked the railroad commissioners to investigate.

In December 1886, the Iowa board asked the Burlington for an explanation of the Glenwood rate. Perkins responded that competition at Council Bluffs forced a low rate there, but that it should not be construed as a paying rate for a local point like Glenwood. This seemed reasonable to the commissioners, who were familiar with the distortions caused by competition, but Larrabee was not satisfied. He demanded a thorough investigation. While the board was reviewing the case the Interstate Commerce Act was passed, outlawing such discriminations in interstate service and strengthening Larrabee's argument. On February 10, 1887, the commissioners asked the Burlington to end discrimination at Glenwood. Perkins chose not to lower the Glenwood tariff, but to raise Council Bluffs to the higher rate. Larrabee's response was explosive. He refiled the case on March 7, damning railroad company and railroad commissioners alike for ignoring the law and violating the public trust.[34]

Discrimination like that at Glenwood typified differential pricing throughout the railroad system. With the practice now banned in interstate commerce, the whole burden of noncompeting charges was likely to fall on intrastate traffic. This gave Larrabee the opening he needed to introduce new, aggressive principles of regulation. With all the fervor of the newly converted, he swept away fine arguments and demanded that the railroads *prove* that they had not injured the complaining shipper. When the CB&Q argued that their competing rate at Council Bluffs was ruinously low, Larrabee dismissed their plea as nonsense: Rational businessmen did not voluntarily set rates below the cost of service! Perkins's agents then replied that the rate-making process was too complicated for laymen like the governor to understand. Larrabee denounced this as obfuscation: "It is no use in permitting ourselves to be mystified by having the idea prevail that this is so complex a matter that a reasonable man cannot comprehend it."[35]

Larrabee's attack was novel and broad. It struck at the heart of a cherished conviction of Forbes and Perkins: that the layman just couldn't understand. Iowa's governor abandoned the intricate points of economic theory for the democratic values of utility and equity; he would stop the flow of power to the technicians. With a populism worthy of the original Jacksonians, he set about debunking railroad managers and commissioners alike. Larrabee thought the commission had become dependent on railroad favor (McDill, he believed, was employed by the Burlington). He denounced their delicate procedures and the "trifling character" of their work. Despite the clear limitations of their powers, Larrabee condemned their inaction. "You should know," he thundered, when railroads break the law. "You should not wait to have the complaints brought before you." Before he was through, the governor had outlined nothing less than an advocate's role for the advisory commission that it never would have dared to fulfill.[36]

Embarrassed and resentful, the Iowa board of railroad commissioners finally ruled that the Glenwood rate should be lowered. Their orders came too late. For Governor Larrabee, the issue had outgrown the case at hand. He was dedicated to vigorous railroad control. Reporting to Perkins from the Des Moines hearings, CB&Q Vice President Thomas J. Potter recognized the seriousness of the matter. "We have got to decide whether we will fight or surrender," he concluded, "and I am afraid we will be beaten in either course we may pursue."[37]

Why had Larrabee taken so fierce a stand over the cost of shipping coal? Perkins believed it was demagoguery—partisan madness. But Larrabee was not a demagogue, and he would lose, not gain, a party. What bothered Larrabee was the willful subordination of what he considered to be true republicanism to the demands of "grasping" corporations. Like James W. Grimes, Iowa's original Republican, Larrabee conceived his government to be the protector of the community, the handmaiden of Iowa enterprise and welfare. Institutions of local government were under attack from businessmen and clerks who behaved as if they were above the law; it was the obligation of government to resist. The regulation campaign that followed was not an effort to refine the principles of railroad economics but a war against the arrogance of "experts" who scorned the authority of popular government.

Characteristically, Charles Perkins met Larrabee's challenge with direct correspondence aimed at educating this heretic in the science of trade. The extent of the heresy was made clear in August 1887, when Larrabee proclaimed the railroads to be public highways subject to the same restrictions imposed on banks, hacks, and ferries. The corporation, he argued, was a "mere agency" of society and should never be free to set rates primarily for private profits and stock dividends. Perkins was horrified. Railroads were clearly and undeniably private corporations, as much entitled to their profits as any merchant, farmer, or manufacturer. If the governor desired reasonable railroad rates, Perkins knew but one way to achieve them: "Leave the commercial, as distinguished from the police, management of railroads wholly in the hands of their owners." Iowa's future development would surely be retarded if Larrabee's views prevailed. The governor retorted that the people of Iowa had been fair and generous with the roads: "Do not fear but more railroads will be

built." If, as Perkins insisted, the railroads were strictly private businesses, then they were not gifts bestowed upon the people and they
deserved no special gratitude. As instruments of private profit, railroads yielded discrimination and injustice; the perpetuation of their
freedoms must bring more of the same. It would be folly to leave
them alone. "[W]hat do you think of any business man," scolded
Larrabee, "who adopts your rule of charging what you can get, one
price to one and another to another?" In ordinary trade such a merchant could only hold his patrons "by cunning divisions or some
underhanded methods." Nothing but "public sentiment against it"
would correct these abuses. Perkins could only deny that such customs existed. Larrabee laughed: Railroad managers always denied
these charges.[38]

Perkins's educational efforts were intended to prove the logic of
nature's laws of trade, but instead they fueled Larrabee's fire. For a
generation Perkins's theories had been promoted as prerequisites to
growth and riches. Regulation had always failed because interested
parties were persuaded that it was unwise for them. Larrabee challenged the voters of Iowa to compare that wisdom with their own
experience. He leveled his criticism at the whole rate-making mechanism, and the people responded. Iowa's Republican party regulars,
led by United States Senator William Boyd Allison, whose presidential aspirations hung in the balance, tried to silence the governor.
Nothing worked. Perkins's political manager, Joseph W. Blythe, reported that Iowa was "determined upon some anti-RR regulation."
He frankly concluded: "I don't believe Clarkson & Allison can stop
it." The politicians could only hope that, once elected, Larrabee
would settle down.[39]

That hope went unrewarded. Larrabee opened his second term
with an antirailroad blast that shocked the party regulars. On January 10, 1888, he outlined for the General Assembly a program of
railroad reform that was thorough and stern. Destroy the pass system
"root and branch," he began, and reduce the pernicious influence of
the railroads upon public officials. Set a maximum two cents per mile
passenger fare to minimize discrimination in personal travel between
cities and the countryside. Reinstitute maximum rates of freight "on
the principal commodities transported by rail," and authorize the
railroad commissioners "to reduce said rates at any time when, in
their judgment, they are too high." If the delegation of rate-making
powers to an administrative board was deemed unlawful, let the
commissioners' rates stand as *prima facie* evidence of reasonable rates.

Such a rule would throw the burden of proof onto the offending railroad, which could well afford to defend itself. Larrabee encouraged a bill making railroad commissioners elective, and he urged that they be paid from the state treasury, not from railroad assessments as was then being done.[40]

The governor's program rested on angry assumptions. The corporations had proved unwilling to serve the community fairly. Now they should be prepared to defend their practices against shippers armed with the legal advantage. This was a simplistic, dangerous view that overlooked the mischief that shippers worked in the railroad market. Still, it was no more than John Murray Forbes had predicted back in 1881, when he had called for a better justification for discriminatory rates. The railroads had failed to make their case with the people, and now Larrabee saw them as "public corporations" whose officers should be "required to take an oath to obey the constitution and laws" of the state and the nation. For the good of the commonwealth, "stringent means should be applied to strong corporations, [while] the weak ones should be protected, especially the new roads making efforts to do business at lower rates." The railroad commission should become "a committee of the people obligated to advocate their rights." Railroad commissioners should "exercise full and complete supervision over the railroads . . . compelling them to comply with the laws. . . . With less than this the people of Iowa will not and should not be satisfied."[41]

From this position there was no retreat. Larrabee's party deserted him; James S. Clarkson, Des Moines editor and party boss, declared war on the governor in the morning edition of the *Iowa State Register:*

> It is plain that the Governor intended to make it the most extreme official utterance which has ever been made as to railways, and it is equally plain that he has succeeded in his purpose. The whole color and tone of the message on this subject is intense and exceedingly radical, . . . and suggests a sense of personal animosity, based on fancied personal grievances.

The most "extraordinary" of Larrabee's positions was the "declaration that the Railroad Commission was not made to help establish and maintain justice alike to people and railways, but to deal with the railways without justice and let them take care of themselves as best they can." Clarkson doubted that he could find "a dozen fair-minded people in Iowa" who would endorse "this astounding utterance." In addition to his public attack, Clarkson sent Larrabee eight pages of scorching criticism in a private letter, demanding that the governor rescind his views. Larrabee would not repent; his railroad reforms would be won or lost on the floor of the General Assembly.[42]

To combat the reforms Charles Perkins approved "any plan" that his political agents might adopt. He hoped that the governor had "rather overshot his mark"; but CB&Q Solicitor J. W. Blythe in Iowa prepared for the worst, calling in favors and lining up support for a major legislative battle. No source of pressure was overlooked. The CB&Q and other companies even circulated petitions in their yards and shops, and out along the line of their roads, shipping pleas by the dozen to Des Moines begging the General Assembly to be fair with the roads. Using time-honored techniques, the railroads labored to divide the electorate along lines of conflicting business interests.[43]

The railroads' campaign was met by astute opposition. Governor Larrabee was a veteran of Iowa legislative politics, and he prepared his ground well. Wherever editor Clarkson turned with a word of advice he found the governor ahead of him, "interviewing members of both houses, urging immediate & radical action and saying that the arguments advanced by [Railroad Commissioner] McDill and others are based on fabricated & lying statements of fact." Larrabee controlled the leadership of both houses, and the inertia of his movement left members cautious about taking the railroads' bait. The governor treated senators to dinner in pairs (one solid and one wavering), where, according to Blythe, he set out his case and lay "down on his man." Gradually support coalesced both inside and outside the legislature. The two-cent fare and the abolition of passes were lost in committee, but the essential bill for a strong commission empowered to fix reasonable rates and enforce their application passed both houses and emerged from a conference committee by April 2, 1888. Signed by a triumphant Larrabee on April 10, the new law took effect in just thirty days.[44]

Chapter Twenty-Eight of the Acts of the Twenty-second General Assembly of Iowa imposed new rules on local transportation. To fix tariffs that were reasonable and just was the stated goal; rebates, drawbacks, pools, and discrimination between persons and places were all prohibited. Differential pricing, to be legal, must be justified by a real difference in the cost or character of service. No greater charge was allowed for short over long hauls whenever the short was contained within the long. Volume discriminations *were* allowed on car-load and hundred-pound lots, but no further distinctions were granted between one unit and many. Tariffs must be posted where all eligible shippers might read them. Finally, the board of railroad commissioners was instructed to prepare a schedule of maximum rates that would serve in a court of law as *prima facie* evidence of reasonable charges. The true radicalism of the act lay in its aggressive mandate: Larrabee's commissioners must advocate the people's cause.[45]

Despite its punitive rhetoric, Larrabee's campaign produced a law that was legally defensible. Of course implementation would be difficult and court challenges were sure to follow. The existing commissioners began at once carefully assembling a schedule of rates, choosing in most cases a published tariff somewhere between the highest and lowest freight currently charged for each class of service. In May, after being reviewed by the railroad freight agents, the commissioners' rates were published, to be effective in thirty days. The Chicago roads immediately cancelled all Iowa tariffs except the highest distance rate; they even broke interstate shipments at the borders, charging high local rates across Iowa. Joined together in a secret pact for mutual defense, the CB&Q and three other lines finally secured an order from the U. S. District Court, on June 27, 1888, restraining the Iowa board of railroad commissioners from enforcing their schedule of rates.[46]

The essential complaint of the railroads was simple: The Iowa rates were "ruinously" low. But this was hard for the railroads to prove. Reflecting the narrowest of views, Judge David J. Brewer continued his injunction one month later, carefully focusing on the level of the rates alone. Brewer thought that the Iowa rates were probably confiscatory, but only time would tell. He exacted a $50,000 bond from the railroad companies for damages in case this injunction were found to be wrongfully issued. Suddenly the high distance rates being charged in Iowa were a liability, and the CB&Q made its first reductions in August. Political negotiations were opened to arrange a compromise between commissioners and railroads, but despite efforts to "put a ring in" the governor's nose, Larrabee proved immovable. In November a newly elected board of commissioners issued another revised schedule, and the railroads returned to Judge Brewer. Both sides idled away the Christmas season waiting for the court's reply.[47]

The prospect of a defeat at the hands of a clamorous democracy depressed Charles Perkins. He complained to Forbes that the Republican party had "gone clear over to the Devil," and he agonized over the possible judicial sanction of more state interference in rate making. Perkins was beginning to think that his case was lost. Brewer believed "confiscation" resulted only when the state took "the LAST dollar" of railroad profit, but Perkins thought any compulsory rate "below what the owner of the Railroad might otherwise reasonably charge" was confiscation as well. If the public could claim *any* corporate profits, this was "just as true of the first and every other dollar" as it was of the last. Perkins's lawyers agreed, but they advised him that his position was a legal novelty. Strict vindication of laissez-faire principles might be logically preferable, but a clear victory was unlikely. Throughout January Forbes waited and Perkins fretted. On February 2, 1889, Judge Brewer lifted his original injunction, giving force at last to the Iowa rates. This time Brewer would not condemn the schedule in advance. Only experience would show if the rates were too low. Clearly beaten, Perkins notified the Iowa board that the CB&Q would comply with their ruling immediately.[48]

Charles Perkins was bitterly disappointed in the outcome of the Iowa fight. Despite the effects of a massive strike that had crippled the Burlington most of the year, Perkins blamed the company's losses in 1888 on the effects of hostile rate regulation.[49] Several Burlington directors shared Perkins's gloom, but John Murray Forbes was undaunted. He was sorry his friends took "so blue a view." Judge Brewer's injunction, Forbes always thought, "was a little too good to last." The matter was now securely in the hands of the federal courts, where the railroads would get their best hearing. Patience would be rewarded. Forbes had survived these struggles before—even the passage of federal railroad restraints—and he was not expecting to settle the issue once and for all. Now seventy-six years old and "twice that age if you measure by the strain," the old entrepreneur refused to become demoralized.[50]

With resilience that concealed his years, Forbes endured the ordeal of regulation. By 1890, the railways he built had cut deeper into the fabric of American culture than anyone could have imagined a half century before. The power of the railroad to facilitate communications had centralized the network beyond all expectations. The resulting mass markets diminished the influence of individual producers and consumers alike. Such a sequence of dramatic changes as the railroads produced necessarily required hundreds of adjustments by individuals, institutions, localities, and industries, and much of the dynamic tension of economic growth and social change in the nineteenth century can be traced back in some way to the influence of high-speed transportation. Dozens of writers, from the 1830s through the end of the age, had proclaimed the importance of steam transportation, but E. L. Godkin was one of the first, in 1873, to recognize that the railroad threatened the "framework" of America's institutions. It was a power relationship that Godkin saw, and this was the heart of the regulation struggles that persisted into the twentieth century.[51] In the process of debating railroad controls, Iowans and other Americans were coming to grips with the changes that reshaped their environment and altered their dreams. Because railroads were both instruments and symbols of industrial progress, they suffered as the focus of this cultural ordeal.

It was Forbes's age—his survival from the early republic—that tempered his reactions to the ordeal of regulation in the Gilded Age. Practically alone now among his colleagues, Forbes enjoyed a long view of the process of railroad development and industrialization. He had seen transportation and communication accelerated beyond imagination, and then accelerated again in a cumulative fashion that left men dizzy. In his youth Forbes had learned a style of business that was intensely personal, fragile as a man's word, and limited by the energies of the family firm. From that perspective, the current affairs of the CB&Q, carried on by a small army of clerks, agents, and officers, and fed by the industry of whole regions of the United States, seemed secure as the land itself. Of course business still wanted attention, and the years just past had seen angry and unpleasant moments. But Forbes had worked for more than half a century perfecting the systems of rail transportation, and he was not surprised to see that the government of such a network might be equally hard to assemble.

Forbes had spent his long life shunning theories, preferring to "do the needful" and plunge ahead. The complexity of the technical systems he constructed steadily deprived him of that direct personal influence he cherished. Politics had gone the same way. Corporations and political parties each channeled personal efforts into larger impersonal structures. Size alone shielded these institutions from sudden shocks while inertia kept them moving forward. As this new corporate world took shape, Forbes gradually embraced Charles Perkins's large theories of economics and sociology, not for their systematic logic but for their usefulness in explaining the order of things. Still he never abandoned his pragmatic sense, and he was not surprised by irrational turns in human events. That Governor Larrabee was mad and his law unfair, Forbes had no doubt; that he had not seen the last of regulation, he was even more sure. The ordeal was far from over, and the question would be resolved according to experience. This was fair enough, for to John Murray Forbes there was no higher form of truth.

Charles Perkins had a greater investment in the rules of political economy and the procedures by which American business might be controlled. He was a system manager from the start, and his intellectual approach to railroading required the frequent review of his operations in light of the principles of economy and science. Perkins was pragmatic, to be sure, in his role as a chief executive; and he seldom pursued an ideal position to the injury of the CB&Q. Still his experience provided him with hundreds of examples to illustrate the elegant laws of trade, the frailties of human nature, and the promise of a scientific view. It was at this abstract level that Perkins the strategist and tough politician allowed himself to contemplate a world advancing toward perfection, where rationality replaced the clamor of interests and scientific management eliminated the need for boisterous, visceral politics. Perkins knew full well that neither the Interstate Commerce Commission nor the reformed Iowa railroad commissioners would radically change the character of rail transportation. Complexity was on his side, and no amateur body could master the intricacies of rate making so thoroughly as to threaten the owners' prerogative. Existing regulations offended his theoretical sense, but they did not yet seriously impede the operations of his railroad. What Charles Perkins feared was that popular legislation, guided by the fierce, emotional logic that was recently demonstrated in Iowa, would one day ruin the railroads, whether from ignorance or from spite.

William Larrabee, ironically, was a voice from the past whose local perspective and strident moral quality foretold a new wave of indignant, popular reform. His attack on the power of chartered corporations was an early example of emotional outbursts that would rock city bosses, utility companies, and eventually the great trusts in the decades to come. If his moral view was naive, it nevertheless touched a popular nerve. America was still a democratic republic, where the people supposedly ruled and where the beneficiaries of government were expected to serve the common welfare. Corporations were created by legislators, who were elected by a people whose will they should reflect. It was inconceivable to Larrabee, as it had been to James W. Grimes thirty years before, that a chartered corporation could be forever above the power of the assembly that gave it life. Therefore, it was no crime for the people to reclaim what they had granted. Larrabee's radicalism was a part of that populism that was central to the American political tradition. His "novelty" was merely a reflection of the changes that had ravaged the nineteenth-century world.

Epilogue

NEARLY A CENTURY has passed since the climax of this story of Forbes and the Burlington and the people of Iowa. In the intervening years communications in America have been revolutionized again and again until the acceleration has become monotonous. Business systems have expanded and become so complex that the nineteenth-century railroads look quaint to modern system managers. We take for granted the intricacies of modern business systems in a computerized world where calculations are performed with inconceivable speed. Viewed from the present day, the struggles of John Murray Forbes and his contemporaries seem almost naive; their partial understanding of complex systems is easily faulted. Yet in many ways our own understanding of American enterprise continues to reflect the limitations and the inadequate compromises first seen in the days of Forbes, Larrabee, and Perkins. A vocabulary of "free enterprise" and "socialism" that was more rhetorical than descriptive, even in the Gilded Age, still dominates all but the most specialized discussions of business and government regulation. Popular opinion sees conspiracy looming behind corporate and public actions. We have learned less than we might from an earlier time.

Guided by the evident failures of regulation in our own day, historians have frequently sought explanations for the nineteenth-century railroad question in the arguments of one combatant or another. Like the Gilded Age business leaders themselves, we sometimes forget that free popular government and free capitalist enterprise enjoyed a symbiotic closeness in the early United States. It was appropriate that dislocations in one sphere would alter the other. Our very notion of a contest between government and business is a product of the railway age: It was an unfortunate, imperfect view that grew out of the efforts of men like Forbes and Perkins and their customers to understand change and at the same time advance their own interests by it. Contemporary analysis was necessarily flawed by opportunism, and when we borrow the framework of their debates we

197

limit our own understanding. In the same way that Forbes's long career bestowed upon him a certain perspective in the face of events, so does the intervention of another century offer historians a chance to transcend the understanding of men in their own time.

This book has tried to follow the story of railroad development from the beginning—as it might have been seen by those whose lives were changed—while retaining that unique advantage of historical perspective. The narrative places people and events in an overview of the developing railroad network itself. The ambiguity of the metaphor—the "bonds" of enterprise—arises precisely from this blending of contemporary and historical vision. My intention was to reach beyond our knowledge of the story's end to discover the dynamic exchanges that produced such stunning results. Nineteenth-century people engaged their world ignorant of the final outcome of their efforts; their enthusiasm and frustrations were unique in many ways because theirs was the first transportation revolution. No American after 1900 was ignorant of speed and power, and few could doubt that man would fly. Consequently, the enormity of changes in the century before is lost to later readers. The first task of historians is to rediscover the uncertainty surrounding things in the making and then to connect history with the present. It is the purpose of the epilogue to link one century to the next.

THE ENTREPRENEUR

John Murray Forbes was an entrepreneur and a thoroughly nineteenth-century man. The terms defined each other, and it was fitting that his life did not extend beyond the 1800s. Although in time his pace was inexorably slowed, he maintained his interest and counsel in the CB&Q until age utterly prevented it. Looking back on his career in 1889, Forbes remembered retiring "at 24" and then taking the "easy (*as I was told*) place of President of the Michigan Central a few years later" as a punishment for his "sins & follies!" Forbes recalled how John W. Brooks had "built & *made*" the Michigan Central "when he was about 25" and much farther off "from his Directors than England would be *to day* measuring by time and trouble to reach him." Forbes always saved his fondest praise for youth, and he claimed to have been "going down hill for too many years not to know that all the good work is done by vigorous young and middle-aged men."[1] Nevertheless, Forbes had stayed in harness almost five decades after the Michigan Central purchase.

The experience of fifty years as a merchant, a railroad man, and a general entrepreneur had satisfied Forbes that change itself was all a man could count on in the railway age. He was often struck by the recurrent bouts of foolishness that plagued investors and legislators in turn. Panics in 1837, 1857, and 1873 had all followed wild speculations, and each had spawned an angry public reaction bent on curbing the influence of the "evil men" who caused such distress. But the people's temper always cooled, and the lure of progress through enterprise brought a new round of investment and growth. By the early 1890s what worried John Murray Forbes more than hostile regulation was the long-overdue panic that he knew must follow frantic railroad expansion, speculation, and the steady inflation of the currency.[2]

The crash came in 1893—later than Forbes expected but no less severe. With an eerie repetition of dates and events, the depression of 1893-96 recalled the Granger era just twenty years before. Financial panic sparked rapidly falling prices and high unemployment. Farm income suffered immediately, giving urgency to a new farmers' movement that was organizing in the South and West. More radical than the Grangers, the Farmers' Alliance developed a plan for cooperative enterprise that truly rivaled the structures of contemporary finance capitalism. But the politics of self-interest once more divided the farmers. The Alliance gave birth to the People's party; and like the Antimonopolists before them, the Populists were ultimately stranded in a partisan campaign that simplified complex issues into slogans about gold and silver coinage. John Murray Forbes was an old "goldbug" and a lifelong student of the currency. In 1896, as the Populists fused with the Democrats behind William Jennings Bryan and the free silver standard, Forbes took great delight in penning sermons to his friends about the evils of silver and the madness of Bryanism. It was his last presidential campaign, and to his fading view the election of William McKinley was the vindication of a century of progress.[3]

The century of progress was also the age of the entrepreneur, and John Murray Forbes had played the role of the public businessman to perfection. Finally, in 1891, someone suggested that his own reminiscences might make "a valuable contribution to history, showing what an average citizen can do toward benefiting his neighbors without taking office." Forbes thought there was a "grain of truth" to the notion, but "what a mass of chaff must be first winnowed out" of the details of decades. More important, change was all around, and the "atoms in the great wheel of life" were soon forgotten. In an age when "science and politics, and perhaps metaphysical research" were bringing out "new truths, if not new principles, in all directions," Forbes thought it was "absurd to expect any great good" from the "lessons of any common man's life." The accomplishments of individuals in modern America were, like the "work done by each coral insect," embedded in structures that overwhelmed them. Common sense discouraged him from "hoping to leave anything that will live longer than the product of the typewriter, which challenges no criticism, asks no verdict from the public press, and leaves behind a few dried leaves or twigs, like a two-year-old bird's nest, for a short-lived reminiscence to one's very near and very dear friends."[4]

By his eightieth year Forbes was visibly failing. He continued to chair the board of directors of the CB&Q, but he did not always "take much active interest" in the business before him. On occasion he would enter into complex discussions of expansions, mergers, and competitive strategy, and his insights were sometimes crucial. At other times, however, he seemed to be asleep. Through it all he continued to write letters endlessly. His careless hand grew feeble and shaky, but his wit and humor survived. Toward the end Forbes suffered periods of bitter depression from which he could find no relief. "He would not rouse to do anything," recorded his daughter, "and would sit on the piazza, the tears rolling down his cheeks, and calling himself a fool, and yet quite unable to stop it." His daughter busied him with revising his *Reminiscences* at these times, and he managed to conceal his weakness from friends like Charles Perkins. When the men came around Forbes composed himself with instinctive concentration on business.[5]

On October 12, 1898, just after returning to Milton from a last summer on his beloved Naushon Island, John Murray Forbes died. The directors of the Burlington railroad recorded their sorrow and attributed to his "far-seeing sagacity, his courage and energy," a large measure of the success of their enterprise. "Among the first to see the possibilities" of railroad development, they continued, Forbes had lived to "share in its realization." He left his fellow directors "at the age of eighty-five, after a long and useful life."[6] The eulogy was fitting. Forbes's years had spanned the century that was coming to a close. His life had encompassed the American railway age.

THE RAILROAD

After 1900 the railroads ceased to be the leading features of American business; they took their place alongside manufacturing and commercial enterprises of equal size and complexity. Transportation in the new century was but one giant among many large industries, and competing forms of transport together with fast-growing demands from all sectors would prevent the railroads from dominating markets the way they had in the Gilded Age. The logic of systems continued to bring about consolidations, as individual railroads and pioneer systems reached for greater efficiency, stability, and security of traffic. With almost none of the celebration and fanfare that accompanied construction of the first railroads, the American rail network was greatly expanded and almost entirely rebuilt in the first two decades of the new century. Such an enormous achievement was taken in stride by the new generation: The railway age was past.

As the nineteenth century drew to a close, Charles Perkins paused to survey the Chicago, Burlington & Quincy Railroad. It had been almost twenty years since he took the reins, and the patchwork of new lines and affiliated properties he had accumulated were in need of integration. Financial and structural streamlining began on March 15, 1899, when the CB&Q formally purchased the Chicago, Burlington & Northern and its multitude of smaller proprietary lines. The resulting system reached all the major cities of the Midwest and knit together broad sections of five states in a thick network of railroad lines.[7]

Perkins's railroad was strong and efficient in 1900. The company was paying smaller dividends and working harder for its profits than in earlier times, but it had survived the disastrous depression of 1893–96 and recovered its vigor as quickly as any firm. The CB&Q was an interior system without connection to a final terminal on any coast, and as the next round of consolidations took shape it was clear that the Burlington must reach the Pacific either on its own tracks or as part of a new, larger system. Both E. H. Harriman of the Central Pacific–Union Pacific and James J. Hill of the Great Northern and Northern Pacific had an interest in buying the Burlington, and Perkins confidently offered his road to the first man who paid a whopping $200 cash for every last share.

For James J. Hill the CB&Q was well worth the price. Hill was a master of railroading who had built the only transcontinental line to the Pacific coast without government subsidies. Since the recovery in the late 1890s, he and Harriman had emerged as the only two railroad magnates in the northwestern region, and they had struggled for years over control of the region's traffic. Hill needed a Chicago outlet and a foothold in Harriman's territory. The Burlington offered both, and the fact that Harriman badly wanted it insured that Hill would finally have it. It remained for Perkins to get his price.[8]

America's railroads had forever outgrown the talents and fortunes of individual entrepreneurs and small personal syndicates like the old Forbes Group. Enormous sums were required at each reorganization, and the great bankers like J. P. Morgan for Hill and Jacob Schiff for Harriman—backed up by investment firms unlike anything seen in Forbes's day—played as crucial a role as the railroad men. Beginning in January 1901 both sides bid for the Burlington shares. Widely distributed and closely held as an investment property, CB&Q shares were not easily purchased without the advice and consent of the Boston managers that Burlington owners had come to trust. Still, brisk trading drove the price up toward $150 per share, and at such a premium even the most conservative investors were bound to bend. Sensing that the end of independence was near, Perkins resigned as president in February and devoted his entire energy to negotiating the sale of this proud old line.

Through February and March Perkins resolutely stuck to his $200 cash price while the market pressure on the stock increased. At one point Malcolm Forbes, who now occupied his father's seat on the board, feared that the bargain was lost to Wall Street. Perkins never wavered. Both Harriman and Hill cringed at the prospect of paying $200 cash for all the shares. Hill finally offered 4 percent bonds with a cash alternative to a limit of $50 million. Word of the offer was made public April 20, 1901, and the deal was completed one month later. Perkins called on his stockholders to sell, and an astonishing 97 percent of the shares came in. Despite biting suggestions that he had sold out, Perkins was properly satisfied: "It is a great trade all around," he wrote to his wife, "and future generations will say so."[9]

James J. Hill created the Northern Securities Company as a holding company for the CB&Q and his other properties. Corporate integration of the three really began in 1904, after the U.S. Supreme Court declared Northern Securities an illegal trust and ordered it disbanded. Hill brought even tighter system and control to the old Burlington Route than it had known even under Charles Perkins.

The physical plant itself was brought into top shape, old or inadequate facilities were replaced or improved, and freight trains were loaded up to their capacity for every run. In 1904 the Burlington signed its first agreement with a national railroad brotherhood, marking a new era in labor relations. An active agricultural development and outreach program further marked the Hill methods that had worked so well in the Northwest. Where the existing system was inefficient or vulnerable Hill bought or built his own routes, and the sheer expansion between 1901 and 1915 was stunning. By the latter date the Burlington had acquired new or better access to Colorado Springs, Leadville, Grand Junction, and Pueblo, Colorado; Dallas, Fort Worth, Houston, and Galveston, Texas; Billings, Montana; Cheyenne, Wyoming; St. Louis; Kansas City; and Paducah, Kentucky. No longer governed by the developmental logic of western geography, Hill's empire reflected markets for lumber and cotton, foodstuffs and coal on a grand scale befitting a new century. The Burlington itself grew 1,373 miles in these years, reaching 9,366 miles total—and this was but part of the larger system.[10]

Hill's Burlington was one of the strongest companies among American railroads before World War I. Because of the solid business it commanded, and with the efficiencies Hill realized in management, revenues supported the huge inputs of capital and a steadily rising dividend. Funded debt rose 37 percent by 1915, but revenue ton-miles rose between two and three times as fast and falling interest rates drove down the actual cost of money by 4 percent. Integration into the Hill system had provided the capital necessary to rebuild the CB&Q and keep it in the forefront of carriers in the early 1900s. Many other roads were not so fortunate. The mushrooming demands for transportation after 1900 sent railroads into the capital markets for sums that were not readily ventured in an industry whose revenues were closely watched by regulatory agencies. It is the irony of the new age that, while the railroads reached for perfection in the modern transport network, the political framework that governed them became ever more punitive in regulation.[11]

THE PUBLIC INTEREST

William Larrabee's crusade in Iowa in 1888 was hardly the last of the angry efforts by popular interests to curtail the power of railroads. Tough laws like Larrabee's were reiterated in Minnesota and

Nebraska and other points in the West as the wounding of local enterprise spread into newer country. The federal courts proved to be the railroads' surest refuge into the 1890s; the Iowa joint-rate law of 1890 and Nebraska's rate-fixing Newberry Law of 1893 were each struck down by judicial review. Nevertheless railroad men like Charles Perkins, for all their raging against the "populists," were coming to realize that politics and government would never leave an open field for corporate enterprise. "When Adam Smith wrote his book," wrote a resigned Perkins in 1891, "the masses did not rule—now they do; and we are governed, in this country at least, not by the highest but by the average intelligence."[12]

This inevitable role for popular government was the heart of the regulation question. When William Larrabee left Iowa politics in 1890, he retired to his country home to write a definitive treatise on *The Railroad Question.* Larrabee focused his attention almost exclusively on power. In an early chapter on monopoly he found his target: "From time immemorial efforts have been made by designing men to control either commerce or its avenues, the highways on the land and on the sea, by a power which law, custom, ingenuity, artifice or some other agency had placed in their hands."[13] No one doubted the prevalence of such oppressions in former times and under European forms of government, but Larrabee feared that Americans naively believed that their system of government prevented monopoly. Their very faith left them defenseless! Larrabee recited example after example of railroad companies exercising monopolistic powers with impunity, and he assured his readers that only those who received special favors were unaware of the power in this "iron hand." Finally, the railway company was portrayed as "a closely organized body of shrewd, active men" against which unorganized citizens were powerless. Three hundred pages of detailed charges and remedies followed, but every turn of the argument flowed from the assumption that railroad corporations, like medieval bandits, inevitably sought to tyrannize the shipping public.[14]

If Governor Larrabee's argument fell short of comprehending the actual problems of the railroad network, it was an excellent expression of popular sentiment. It is not surprising, given these assumptions, that legislators and reformers rejected pooling and self-regulation by the railroads as absurd. Arguments that exploitation by shippers was the real cause of discrimination, even when true, could not gain credibility with the public. Restraints of cutthroat competition earned no popular sanction in the Gilded Age unless they carried with them a sense of victory over the perpetrators of railroad injustices. Calls for legal minimum rates, however sophisticated, were laughable. Larrabee's warning, not to let the appearance of popular government lull men out of their vigilance, struck a responsive chord in individuals whose local institutions had been snubbed one way or another by a railroad official. Corporation lobbyists were unavoidably recognized as corrupters of republican government. The fact that railroad managers were often arrogant, that their agents were arbitrary and their lobbyists corrupting, brought this moral interpretation fully to life.

Even at the federal level, where corporations had sought protection from irresponsible localism, the vigor of regulatory injunctions continued to grow. After 1887, the Interstate Commerce Commission quickly found the limits of its effectiveness. Like any party at law, the commission could not address inequities in the rate structure as a whole or satisfy more than the individual whose complaint was before it. Further legislation was likely as long as the public complained of injury and abuse, and the popularity of reform was increasing dramatically by 1900. The Elkins Act of 1903 prohibited railroads from abandoning in any case their published schedule of rates. In 1906, the Hepburn Act finally granted the Interstate Commerce Commission the power to fix reasonable maximum rates with the force of law. The Mann-Elkins Act of 1910 forbade long- and short-haul discriminations *under any circumstances;* and like the Iowa law of 1888, it placed the burden of proof for any rate on the railroad company itself. Theoretically, the designs of evil men had just about been proscribed at either the state or federal level by 1910. Unfortunately the causes of distress in the railroad market lay elsewhere, and this regulatory approach missed its mark.[15]

The generation that erected the framework of government regulation in the late nineteenth and early twentieth centuries failed to understand all that was behind the hardships they suffered and the benefits they sought. Most reformers did not intend to destroy corporate enterprise as a part of some vengeful attack on progress. On the contrary, the reformers' political arm in 1912 boasted the label Progressive Party. Like the Grangers and Alliance before them, many so-called Progressives were victimized by opportunistic politicians among their ranks, but their movement was not totally cynical. What reformers sought in every case was to reestablish popular authority wherever an individual's right to strive and gain seemed threatened by corporate power. At times their anger led them to punish enterprise excessively, but their attacks on industry no more than matched the abuses they had suffered in the past. Unfortunately, by the time the regulatory structure was in place in the United States, the time for guiding the development of railroads was past. The transformation of the marketplace was largely complete, and the objectives of localism were simply out of place.

In 1813, when John Murray Forbes was born, the fastest vehicle on land was a coach-and-four, and the age of steam on water had barely dawned. In 1903, just five years after his death, the Wright brothers abandoned both land and water and took to the air at Kitty Hawk. The scale of the accomplishment and the forward-looking bias of the leading actors tend to blind us to the distance that was crossed. The "progress" of the nineteenth century liberated men from the mean, small, narrow boundaries of eighteenth-century life, and it armed them with almost limitless ambitions. Even radical agrarians of the Gilded Age found much in their present day to be preserved. Forbes himself condemned history in deference to youth and the future; and Americans at century's end, for all their quarreling, were pretty pleased with their achievement.

There were actually two transformations going on at once in the American railway age. The conquest of space and time involved a moving target; the frontier of settlement moved steadily ahead of the transportation and communication systems that must sustain civilization. Acceleration of movement was matched by intensification of production through industrialization. Progress moved along two vectors, producing a stereoscopic vision of the marvelous future. In fields almost unbounded by scarcity, enterprise ran free in the United States. Throughout the century foreign observers could find no more universal feature of Americans than their "busy-ness."

The lives of John Murray Forbes and the whole cast of characters who shared his world explain American "busy-ness"in the nineteenth century. Restless energies set free by abundant resources and liberal institutions brought into being, by 1900, a world more vast, more complex, and more richly endowed with material and cultural advantages than could be imagined a century before. That same liberty and restlessness insured that the changes would not come smoothly: The course of progress was not uncontested and the fruits of the effort were not altogether fairly shared. Then, as complexity advanced, the space for liberty in American life inexorably narrowed. Institutions of business and government were erected to constrain this outpouring of energies, and where the new systems became most delicately entangled they finally neutralized the power of the maverick entrepreneur. Men like John Murray Forbes, who created the American railroad systems, could not themselves be comfortably governed by them. For this reason theirs is a nineteenth-century story. It is unlikely that another generation will ever totally enjoy the social confidence, the personal power, and the economic freedom that marked the American railway age.

Notes

CHAPTER ONE NOTES

1. Robert Bennet Forbes, *Personal Reminiscences*, 2d ed., rev. (Boston: Little, Brown, 1882), pp. 3-24.

2. Mary Caroline Crawford, *Famous Families of Massachusetts*, 2 vols. (Boston: Little, Brown, 1930), 1: 295-96; Robert Bennet Forbes, *Personal Reminiscences*, pp. 1-2; *Letters and Recollections of John Murray Forbes*, 2 vols., ed. Sarah Forbes Hughes (Boston: Houghton Mifflin, 1899), 1: 3-4; *Reminiscences of John Murray Forbes*, 3 vols., ed. Sarah Forbes Hughes (Boston: Geo. H. Ellis, 1902), 1: 6; *Letters of John Murray Forbes*, suppl., 3 vols., ed. Sarah Forbes Hughes (Boston: Geo. H. Ellis, 1905), 1: 24; Carl Seaburg and Stanley Paterson, *Merchant Prince of Boston: Colonel Thomas Handasyd Perkins, 1764-1854* (Cambridge, Mass.: Harvard University Press, 1971), pp. 270-72.

3. Seaburg and Paterson, *Merchant Prince*, pp. 285, 295-96; Crawford, *Famous Families*, 1: 296; *Letters and Recollections of J.M.F.*, 1: 40-43.

4. See M. A. DeWolfe Howe, *Life and Letters of George Bancroft*, 2 vols., (New York: Charles Scribner's Sons, 1908), 1: 162-74.

5. *Letters and Recollections of J.M.F.*, 1: 42-51; *Letters of J.M.F.*, suppl., 1: 14-15; *Reminiscences of J.M.F.*, 1: 13.

6. See *Letters and Recollections of J.M.F.*, 1: 45-46.

7. *Reminiscences of J.M.F.*, 1: 71-72, 119-20; *Letters and Recollections of J.M.F.*, 1: 49-50.

8. *Reminiscences of J.M.F.*, 1: 119-24.

9. See John King Fairbank, *Trade and Diplomacy on the China Coast*, rev. ed. (Stanford, Calif.: Stanford University Press, 1969), chaps. 2 and 3; and Michael Greenberg, *British Trade and the Opening of China, 1800-1842* (Cambridge: Cambridge University Press, 1951), chaps. 1 and 3.

10. Fairbank, *Trade and Diplomacy*, pp. 33, 50-51.

11. Ibid., pp. 51-53. Greenberg denies that the Cohong ever worked well enough to set prices or truly monopolize the trade (see *British Trade*, p. 52).

12. See Greenberg, *British Trade*, pp. 3-15.

13. Ibid., pp. 18-38, 161-65; see also Jacques M. Downs, "American Merchants and the China Opium Trade, 1800-1840," *Business History Review* 42 (1968): 434. American bills were of minor importance before the late 1820s, but after that time they fueled the opium business and inextricably tied all parties to the drug traffic. In Downs's words, by the 1830s "opium was balancing East-West trade through the American commerce in London bills."

14. The formation and growth of the Perkins firm receives full treatment in Seaburg and Paterson, *Merchant Prince*, pp. 155-60, 263-67, but their handling of the opium business is superseded by Jacques Downs, "American Merchants," pp. 422-29. The Lintin system was initially a British innovation and became, after 1823, a "model of efficiency, security and profit" for British and American smugglers alike (428). Opium ships called at "outside anchorages" at Lintin

Island, dropped their drug cargo, and proceeded upriver to Whampoa. Chinese smugglers bought opium chits from Western merchants at the Canton factories, paying in silver. The chits were presented at Lintin and the drug was delivered.

15. Downs, "American Merchants," pp. 429-30; Greenberg, *British Trade,* pp. 29-30; see also Crawford, *Famous Families,* 1: 295; and Seaburg and Paterson, *Merchant Prince,* pp. 263-317.

16. For a good discussion of the evolution of the agency house at Canton, see Greenberg, *British Trade,* especially chap. 6. See also Downs, "American Merchants," and Henrietta Larsen, "A China Trader Turns Investor," *Harvard Business Review* 12 (1934): 345-58.

17. Downs, "American Merchants," pp. 430-35; Larsen, "A China Trader," pp. 350-51.

18. Larsen, "A China Trader," pp. 350-51; *Letters and Recollections of J.M.F.,* 1: 60-61.

19. *Letters and Recollections of J.M.F.,* 1: 63.

20. Ibid., 1: 69; see also 63-70; and *Reminiscences of J.M.F.,* 1: 14-21.

21. Howqua to JMF, [Feb., 1834]; Howqua to Robert Bennet Forbes, April 14, 1834; JMF to Captain Bancroft (of the *Logan*), Aug. 15, 1834; in Forbes Family Papers, Baker Library, Harvard University, Cambridge Mass. (hereafter cited as Forbes-Baker). See also *Reminiscences of J.M.F.,* 1: 190-91.

22. JMF to Sarah Hathaway Forbes, Feb. 20, 1835; in Forbes-Baker; *Reminiscences of J.M.F.,* 1: 192.

23. *Reminiscences of J.M.F.,* 1: 147, 214, 236-37. JMF to Thomas Handasyd Perkins, Jan. 1, 1835; JMF to Sarah Hathaway Forbes, April 20, 1836 and journal letter April 30-May 17, 1836; in Forbes-Baker.

24. *Letters of J.M.F.,* suppl., 1: 29; *Reminiscences of J.M.F.,* 1: 194-95, 215. JMF to Sarah Hathaway Forbes, journal letter April 30-May 17, 1836; JMF to Samuel Cabot, April 27, 1835; in Forbes-Baker. Forbes likened the commission merchant to a tavern keeper, always trying to stay "on the right side of his customers!!!"

25. Howqua to JMF, [Feb., 1834]; Russell & Co. for Howqua to John Cushing, Feb. 18, 1834; JMF to Cushing, Oct. 29, 1834; JMF to Joseph Ballestier, April 21, 1836; in Forbes-Baker.

26. See Downs, "American Merchants," pp. 437-39; *Letters and Recollections of J.M.F.,* 1: 62-72.

27. *Letters and Recollections of J.M.F.,* 1: 63-64.

28. JMF to Joshua Bates, Oct. 28, 1834 and Nov. 25, 1835, in Forbes-Baker.

29. JMF to Robert Bennet Forbes, July "3 say 4th," 1835, in Forbes-Baker (emphasis original).

30. *Letters and Recollections of J.M.F.,* 1: 160; Fairbank, *Trade and Diplomacy,* pp. 168-72.

31. See Russell & Co. to Parish & Co., Jan. 20, 1834; Howqua to John P. Cushing, Oct. 29, 1834; see Letterbook "F-5" generally for December, 1833-February, 1834, for countless examples of the routine reliance on personal judgment and faithful service; in Forbes-Baker.

32. See JMF to Bates, Oct. 28, 1834 and Nov. 25, 1835, in Forbes-Baker. See also JMF to Joseph Ballestier, Jan. 26, 1836; and JMF to John P. Cushing, Jan. 3, 1835; in Forbes-Baker.

33. JMF to John P. Cushing, Jan. 3, 1835, in Forbes-Baker.

34. JMF to William Sturgis, Aug. 17, 1835, Oct. 26, 1835, Aug. 21, 1836; JMF to Samuel Cabot, Aug. 21, 1835, Aug. 28, 1836; in Forbes-Baker.

35. JMF to William Sturgis, Sept. 5, 1834, in Forbes-Baker.

36. *Letters of J.M.F.,* suppl., 1: 22–23. JMF to Robert Bennet Forbes, Jan. 27, Mar. 12, April 4, Sept. 28, and Oct. 28, 1836; JMF to John P. Cushing, Mar. 13, 1836; JMF to Samuel Cabot, Mar. 21, 1836; in Forbes–Baker.

37. JMF to Samuel Cabot, Mar. 13, 1836, in Forbes–Baker.

38. JMF to Joshua Bates, Nov. 20, 1836, in Forbes–Baker.

39. JMF to Sarah Hathaway Forbes, July 11–12, 1835, in Forbes–Baker; *Reminiscences of J.M.F,* 1: 52, 141. Fairbank explains the Confucian code of right conduct as a belief that virtue *is* power and that the "virtuous ruler gained prestige and influence over his people merely by exhibiting his virtue." (*Trade and Diplomacy,* pp. 26–27.)

40. *Reminiscences of J.M.F.,* 1: 52. JMF to Russell & Co., April 21, May 3, and July 25, 1837; JMF to A. A. Low, May 18, 1837; JMF to W. C. Hunter, May 18, 1837; in Forbes–Baker.

41. JMF to Russell & Co., April 5, 1837, in Forbes–Baker.

42. Russell & Co. to JMF, July 3, Oct. 20, and Nov. 19, 1838, July 12, 1839, in Forbes–Baker.

43. See generally letters from Russell & Co. to JMF, May 5, 1838, through July, 1839 (case 1, folders 12 and 13), in Forbes–Baker. On Forbes's strategy for controlling Russell & Co., see JMF to Robert Bennet Forbes, Mar. 8 and April 5, 1839; JMF to A. A. Low, April 5, 1839; JMF to Joseph Cabot, [c. June 9, 1839], and several following in Letterbook 8; in Forbes–Baker. Forbes's control of Russell & Co. was not yet really secure. Bennet was not entirely welcomed on his own terms, and John had to press through Howqua to get his cousin Paul S. Forbes employed there in 1842. Bennet retired at the end of the term in 1846, at which time Paul took his share. By 1849 John was looking toward control "for some time to come," and recommended sending out partners who would do the work but "*not rule* the roost." The dynasty was finally secured in 1857, when John got legal possession of the Russell & Co. name from old Samuel Russell for the consideration of a fresh supply of tea as long as the old man lived. See Robert Bennet Forbes to Paul S. Forbes, April 10, 1838; JMF to Howqua, Dec. 31, 1842; in Forbes–Baker; JMF to Paul S. Forbes, June 5, 1849 and April 7, 1857, in John Murray Forbes Letters, Typescript, in Forbes–Baker (hereafter cited as J.M.F. Typescript). See also the articles of partnership for Russell & Co. for each term, in Forbes–Baker.

44. JMF to Robert Bennet Forbes, Jan. 19, 1840, in Forbes–Baker. See also JMF to "Gov." Swain, April 7, 1839; JMF to Robert Bennet Forbes, Dec. 20, 1839 and Jan. 19, 1840; in Forbes–Baker; and Duncan Yaggy, "John Forbes: Entrepreneur" (Ph.D. diss., Brandeis University, 1974), p. 181 and note 44.

45. JMF to Robert Bennet Forbes, Sept. 26, 1836, in Forbes–Baker. Yaggy's thesis outlines many of Forbes's investments in the first few years after his return from China (see especially chapter 3). See also JMF to Paul S. Forbes, June 21 and Nov. 14, 1844, Oct. 31, Nov. 30, and Dec. 31, 1846, in J.M.F. Typescript; Robert Bennet Forbes to Paul S. Forbes, Sept. 25 and Oct. 31, 1846; in Forbes–Baker. John Murray Forbes's own estimate of the amount of Howqua's capital entrusted to him at this time—about one-half million—is recorded in *Reminiscences of J.M.F.,* 1: 273. The exact details and scope of Forbes's investments after 1838 can be reconstructed from the Ledgers, Journals, and Trial Balances which are still housed at J. M. Forbes & Co., Boston.

46. *Reminiscences of J.M.F.,* 1: 255.

47. JMF to Paul S. Forbes, Nov. 29, 1847, and Dec. 21, 1851, in JMF Typescript, Forbes–Baker; Robert Bennet Forbes, *Personal Reminiscences,* pp. 138–39. Bennet estimated his losses in Farrandsville Coal & Iron at $100,000,

which he claimed drove him back to China in 1840. On subsequent investments see JMF to Paul S. Forbes, Nov. 29, 1847, and Dec. 21, 1859, in J.M.F. Typescript, Forbes-Baker; and Yaggy, "John Forbes," pp. 219-30.

48. See Robert Bennet Forbes, *Personal Reminiscences,* pp. 208-16, on steamboat ventures with John.

49. JMF to Robert Bennet Forbes, Jan. 9, 1836, in *Letters and Recollections of J.M.F.,* 1: 81; JMF to Mary A. Forbes, Dec. 30, 1842, in Forbes-Baker. JMF to Paul S. Forbes, Nov. 30, 1845, in J.M.F. Typescript; JMF to Paul S. Forbes, [August], 1845, and Sept. 1, 1845; in Forbes-Baker. See also Arthur M. Johnson and Barry E. Supple, *Boston Capitalists and Western Railroads* (Cambridge, Mass.: Harvard University Press, 1967), pp. 37-39, 48-49.

50. JMF to Paul S. Forbes, April 3, 1846, in Forbes-Baker.

51. JMF to Paul S. Forbes, Oct. 31 and Nov. 30, 1846, in J.M.F. Typescript; JMF to Paul S. Forbes, Jan. 31, 1839, July 3, Nov. 11, and Dec. 11, 1842; JMF to Robert Watson, Aug. 7, 1839, Feb. 17, 1840; JMF to Mary A. Forbes, Aug. 30, 1842; JMF to W. G. Eliot, Aug. 11, 1842; Robert Bennet Forbes to Paul S. Forbes, Sept. 25 and Oct. 31, 1846, Feb. 22, 1848; Paul S. Forbes to Robert Bennet Forbes, June 10, 1839, Oct. 14, 1838; JMF to Howqua, Dec. 31, 1842; in Forbes-Baker.

52. JMF to Robert Bennet Forbes, [torn, 1843]; JMF to Paul S. Forbes, Mar. 26, 1837; see also JMF to Robert Bennet Forbes, Jan. 30 and Feb. 16, 1839, Jan. 3, 1844; in Forbes-Baker.

53. JMF to Paul S. Forbes, Aug. 31, 1846, in J.M.F. Typescript, Forbes-Baker; Robert Bennet Forbes to Paul S. Forbes, Oct. 29, 1848, quoted in Yaggy, "John Forbes: Entrepreneur," p. 243; see also Yaggy, pp. 129, 202. Any dip into the Forbes correspondence for the 1840s is likely to turn up a "retirement," a protestation of laziness, and a comment about late hours and missed meals.

54. JMF to Paul S. Forbes, Oct. 31, 1847, May 10, 1848, in J.M.F. Typescript, Forbes-Baker.

CHAPTER TWO NOTES

1. In the vast literature on early railroads and transportation improvements, the starting point is still George Rogers Taylor, *The Transportation Revolution, 1815-1860* (New York: Holt, Rinehart, and Winston, 1951). Edward C. Kirkland, *Men, Cities and Transportation,* 2 vols. (Cambridge, Mass.: Harvard University Press, 1948); Ulrich B. Phillips, *A History of Transportation in the Eastern Cotton Belt to 1860* (New York: Columbia University Press, 1908); Robert G. Albion, *The Rise of New York Port* (New York: Charles Scribner's Sons, 1939); Louis C. Hunter, *Steamboats on the Western Rivers* (Cambridge, Mass.: Harvard University Press, 1949); and Alan R. Pred, *Urban Growth and the Circulation of Information: The United States System of Cities, 1790-1840* (Cambridge, Mass.: Harvard University Press, 1973) all have made special contributions to the interpretation given here.

2. See Kirkland, *Men, Cities and Transportation,* 1; Julius Rubin, *Canal or Railroad? Imitation and Innovation in the Response to the Erie Canal in Philadelphia, Baltimore and Boston* (Philadelphia: American Philosophical Society, 1961); Edward Hungerford, *The Story of the Baltimore & Ohio Railroad,* 2 vols. (New York: G. Putnam & Sons, 1928); and Stephen Salsbury, *The State, The Investor, and the*

Railroad: The Boston & Albany, 1825-1867 (Cambridge, Mass.: Harvard University Press, 1967).

3. Older works, such as Henry Varnum Poor, *History of Railroads and Canals of the United States of America* (New York: J. H. Schultz, 1860) and Charles Francis Adams, Jr., *Railroads: Their Origin and Problems* (New York: G. P. Putnam & Co., 1878), were more sensitive to the complexities of early technological development than are more recent studies. For the British situation at this time, see H. J. Dyos and D. H. Aldcroft, *British Transport* (Leicester: University Press, 1969); W. T. Jackman, *The Development of Transportation in Modern England*, 4 vols. (Cambridge: University Press, 1916); and Harold Pollins, *Britain's Railways: An Industrial History* (Newton Abbot: David and Charles, 1972).

4. Massachusetts Board of Internal Improvements, *Senate No. 4: Report of the Board . . . for a Railway from Boston to Providence; with a Memoir of the Survey* (Boston: Dutton & Wentworth, 1828).

5. Massachusetts Board of Internal Improvements, *Senate No. 5: Report of the Board . . . for a Railway from Boston to Albany* (Boston: Dutton & Wentworth, 1828), pp. 23-24 and passim; *Report of the Board . . . on the Practicability and Expediency of a Rail-Road from Boston to the Hudson River, and from Boston to Providence* (Boston: Press of the Boston Daily Advertiser, 1829), p. 26 and passim.

6. *American Rail Road Journal*, Jan. 21, 1832; H. S. Tanner, *A Description of the Canals and Railroads of the United States . . .* (New York: T. R. Tanner and J. Disturnell, 1840).

7. See Salsbury, *The State, The Investor, and the Railroad*, pp. 80-81; Kirkland, *Men, Cities and Transportation*, 1: 41. The *American Rail Road Journal* reported charter provisions each time a new company was formed; its numbers provide a chronicle of structural evolution. On the adoption of monopoly operations, see Massachusetts Senate, *Report of the Committee on Railways & Canals . . . Relative to the Public Use of Rail-Roads* (Boston: Dutton & Wentworth, 1838); "The Massachusetts Rail Road Continued to Narragansett Bay," signed "New England" (pamphlet, n.p., [c. 1836]); *Evidence Showing the Manner in Which Locomotive Engines Are Used Upon Rail-Roads . . .* (Boston: Centinel & Gazette Press, 1838); and *American Rail Road Journal*, Feb. 11, 1832.

8. *Evidence Showing the Manner in Which Locomotive Engines Are Used Upon Rail-Roads*, pp. 13, 16. See also *American Rail Road Journal*, Jan. 21 and Jan. 28, 1832, on the variety of technical systems and gauges; and Feb. 11, 1832, on the system of operations on the Baltimore & Ohio Railroad.

9. Baltimore & Ohio Railroad, *Annual Report, 1831*, quoted in *American Rail Road Journal*, Jan. 7, 1832. See Salsbury, *The State, The Investor, and the Railroad*, pp. 299-300, on management problems on Massachusetts railroads.

10. *American Rail Road Journal*, Jan. 14, 1832; *The Merchant's Magazine* **3** (1840): 287, 275-93; H. S. Tanner, *Canals and Railroads of the United States*, pp. 11-12.

11. Tanner, *Canals and Railroads of the United States*, p. 18; *The Merchant's Magazine* **9** (1843): 145-48.

12. *Ohio State Journal & Gazette*, Jan. 11, 1832, quoted in *American Rail Road Journal*, Feb. 11, 1832.

13. Robert J. Parks, *Democracy's Railroads: Public Enterprise in Jacksonian Michigan* (Port Washington, N.Y.: Kennikat Press, 1972), pp. 43-50, 68, 78. For a treatment of similar materials for Illinois, see John H. Krenkel, *Illinois Internal Improvements, 1818-1848* (Cedar Rapids, Ia.: Torch Press, 1958); for Ohio, see Harry N. Scheiber, *Ohio Canal Era: A Case Study of Government and the Economy, 1820-1861* (Athens, Ohio: Ohio University Press, 1969); and for Pennsylvania,

see Louis Hartz, *Economic Policy and Democratic Thought* (Cambridge, Mass.: Harvard University Press, 1948).

14. Quoted in Parks, *Democracy's Railroads*, p. 96; see generally pp. 95-156.

15. Quoted in Parks, *Democracy's Railroads*, pp. 101-2; see also pp. 172-73.

16. Johnson and Supple, *Boston Capitalists*, pp. 90-92; Thomas C. Cochran, *Railroad Leaders, 1845-1890: The Business Mind in Action* (Cambridge, Mass.: Harvard University Press, 1953), pp. 266-67; Marian V. Sears, "A Michigan Bureaucrat Promotes the State's Economic Growth: George F. Porter Sells Michigan's Central Railroad to Eastern Capitalists, 1846," *Explorations in Entrepreneurial History*, 2d ser., no. 3 (1966), pp. 200-219; Duncan Yaggy, "John Forbes," p. 229.

17. James F. Joy, "Railroad History of Michigan," *Michigan Pioneer and Historical Collections* 22 (1894): 292-304; Cochran, *Railroad Leaders*, p. 364; Sears, "A Michigan Bureaucrat," pp. 200-210. Forbes's own reminiscence is faulty, and accounts built upon it place Forbes at the center of these early negotiations. Yaggy's and Sears's evidence suggests that Forbes hung back, possibly until the charter was drafted and he was named president of the company. See *Reminiscences of J.M.F.*, 1: 272-75.

18. Quoted in Johnson and Supple, *Boston Capitalists*, p. 90; *Messages of the Governors of Michigan*, ed. George N. Fuller (Lansing: Michigan Historical Commission, 1926), 2: 44-48; see also Sears, "A Michigan Bureaucrat," pp. 202-5.

19. The final charter for the Michigan Central is printed in John W. Brooks, *Report upon the Merits of the Michigan Central Railroad, as an Investment for Eastern Capitalists* (Detroit: Charles Willcox, 1846), pp. 30-78; Parks, *Democracy's Railroads*, pp. 104-5, further discusses the provisions of the sale.

20. See Johnson and Supple, *Boston Capitalists*, chap. 5; Salsbury, *The State, The Investor, and the Railroad*, introduction and chap. 1; Duncan Yaggy, "John Forbes," pp. 201-8, 229-34; and Marian Sears, "A Michigan Bureaucrat," pp. 202-5.

21. *Reminiscences of J.M.F.*, 1: 273; JMF to Paul S. Forbes, [1845], in Forbes-Baker. See also Forbes's letters to Paul S. Forbes in J.M.F Typescript, Forbes-Baker, for 1845-1847.

22. *The Merchant's Magazine* 12 (1845): 158, 323-24. Before this time *The Merchant's Magazine* had carefully avoided editorial endorsements of railroad projects. After 1845, there was an unmistakable shift in Hunt's position.

23. John W. Brooks, *Merits of the Michigan Central*, pp. 1-11.

24. Ibid., pp. 12-28.

25. JMF to Paul S. Forbes, Aug. 31 and Sept. 30, 1846, in J.M.F. Typescript, Forbes-Baker; Sears, "A Michigan Bureaucrat," pp. 207-8; Johnson and Supple, *Boston Capitalists*, p. 94.

26. Sears, "A Michigan Bureaucrat," pp. 206-10; Irene D. Neu, *Erastus Corning: Merchant and Financier, 1794-1872* (Ithaca: Cornell University Press, 1960), pp. 74-77.

27. JMF to Josiah Grinnell, Sept. 1, 1846, in Cochran, *Railroad Leaders*, p. 360; John W. Brooks to Erastus Corning, Dec. 25, 1846, in Johnson and Supple, *Boston Capitalists*, p. 97; Erastus Corning to John W. Brooks, Jan. 12, 1847, in Cochran, *Railroad Leaders*, p. 303; JMF to John W. Brooks, April 27 and Sept. 10, 1847, in Cochran, *Railroad Leaders*, pp. 326, 99.

28. JMF to Paul S. Forbes, June 30, 1847, in J.M.F. Typescript, Forbes-Baker; JMF to Sarah Forbes, June 11, 1847, in Henry Greenleaf Pearson, *An American Railroad Builder: John Murray Forbes* (Boston: Houghton Mifflin, 1911), p. 33.

29. Michigan Central Railroad, *Annual Report, 1848*, pp. 3–4, 22–23; JMF to D. D. Williamson, Sept. 30, 1846, in Cochran, *Railroad Leaders*, p. 326.

30. See above note 5.

31. Charles Hirschfield, *The Great Railroad Conspiracy: The Social History of a Railroad War* (Michigan State College Press, 1953), p. 5. Hirschfield's account is extremely detailed and well documented. See also *Reminiscences of J.M.F.*, 1: 280–83.

32. Forbes later interpreted the Michigan war as a "Granger" uprising (*Reminiscences of J.M.F.*, 1: 282).

33. JMF to Paul S. Forbes, Sept. 5, Oct. 3, Nov. 28, and Dec. 27, 1848, in J.M.F. Typescript, Forbes–Baker.

34. JMF to Paul S. Forbes, Jan. 23, Feb. 21, and Oct. 22, 1849, in J.M.F Typescript, Forbes–Baker; see also Pearson, *An American Railroad Builder*, pp. 40–45; and Johnson and Supple, *Boston Capitalists*, pp. 51–53, 98–103.

35. Michigan Central Railroad, *Annual Report, 1850*, p. 23; see also pp. 3–6, 18–23; and Michigan Central Railroad, *Annual Report, 1849*, pp. 3–8.

36. Michigan Central Railroad, *Annual Report, 1851*, p. 5.

37. Michigan Central Railroad, *Annual Report, 1850*, pp. 7, 16.

38. See Brooks, *Merits of the Michigan Central*, pp. 8–12; Pearson, *An American Railroad Builder*, pp. 42–43; Michigan Central Railroad, *Annual Report, 1850*, pp. 16–17; and Yaggy, "John Forbes," p. 276.

39. See Johnson and Supple, *Boston Capitalists*, pp. 111–115.

40. See Richard C. Overton, *Burlington West: A Colonization History of the Burlington Railroad* (Cambridge, Mass.: Harvard University Press, 1941), pp. 25–31.

41. Michigan Central Railroad, *Annual Report, 1854*, p. 5. Compare Forbes's official statements in the Michigan Central *Reports* for 1851 and 1852 with JMF to Robert Schuyler, May 31, 1851, in Illinois Central Railroad Archives, Newberry Library, Chicago (hereafter cited as IC–Newberry).

42. Michigan Central Railroad, *Annual Report, 1852*, pp. 4–8.

43. JMF to John W. Brooks, Aug. 11, 1855, in Cochran, *Railroad Leaders*, p. 329; Pearson, *An American Railroad Builder*, p. 98; *Reminiscences of J.M.F.*, 1: 291. The term "general entrepreneur" has been given a specific meaning by Johnson and Supple, who use Forbes to illustrate this type of investor (see *Boston Capitalists*, pp. 56–57).

44. JMF to Paul S. Forbes, Jan. 28, 1856, Nov. 28, 1854, and Jan. 13, 1857, in J.M.F. Typescript, Forbes–Baker; JMF to Erastus Corning, Feb. 2, 1855, in Cochran, *Railroad Leaders*, p. 329; see also *Reminiscences of J.M.F.*, 2: 9, 45–48, and J.M.F. Typescript, Forbes–Baker, Nov., 1854 through Feb., 1857, for excellent details on the midcentury system of capital formation.

45. See John W. Brooks to JMF, April 1, 1851, in Cochran, *Railroad Leaders*, p. 268; and Johnson and Supple, *Boston Capitalists*, p. 159.

46. JMF to Russell Sturgis, [Sept.], 1851, quoted in Pearson, *An American Railroad Builder*, p. 45; see also James F. Joy to JMF, Aug. 23, 1851, in Box 1J7.1, IC–Newberry; John W. Brooks to Erastus Corning, Sept. 17, 1851, in Cochran, *Railroad Leaders*, p. 268; and Overton, *Burlington West*, pp. 31–33.

47. For the detailed narrative of the Illinois roads see Richard C. Overton, *Burlington Route: A History of the Burlington Lines* (New York: Alfred A. Knopf, 1965), pp. 3–52; and Overton, *Burlington West*, pp. 33–44. In about 1880 Chauncy Colton prepared a long manuscript account that is reprinted in Overton, *Burlington West*, pp. 506–15. See also Earnest Elmo Calkins, "Genesis of a Railroad," *Transactions of the Illinois State Historical Society* **42** (1935): 43–56; and

the Chauncy S. Colton Letters, transcribed into Charles E. Perkins, Memoranda, V, 360-400, in Box 3P4.91, Burlington Archives, Newberry Library, Chicago (hereafter cited as CB&Q-Newberry).
48. William McMurtry to Chauncy S. Colton, June 10, 1852; Silas Willard to Chauncy S. Colton, July 5, July 14, and July 17, 1852; James F. Joy to Chauncy S. Colton, July 27, 1852; in Box 3P4.91, CB&Q-Newberry.
49. Chauncy S. Colton to Nehemiah Bushnell, Aug. 3, 1852, in Box 3P4.91, CB&Q-Newberry; *Records (copy) of the Central Military Tract Railroad,* pp. 53-85, in Box f8C2.3, CB&Q-Newberry.
50. See *Records (copy) of the CMT,* pp. 80-82, 90-91, 105-106, 109-110, 115-117, and 121-125, in Box f8C2.3, CB&Q-Newberry; also John W. Brooks to W. W. Duffield, July 21, 1853, in Box 8M1.1, CB&Q-Newberry.
51. JMF to William P. Burrall, Feb. 3, 1854, in Box 1F3.1, IC-Newberry. John W. Brooks to JMF, Nov. 27, 1852; James F. Joy to Nehemiah Bushnell, Nov. 19, 1852; John W. Brooks to Nehemiah Bushnell, Dec. 6, 1852; in Box 8M1.1, CB&Q-Newberry.
52. John W. Brooks to J. F. Dunn, Dec. 22, 1852; John W. Brooks to John C. Green and D. D. Williamson, May 23, 1853; in Box 8M1.1, CB&Q-Newberry; James F. Joy to Chauncy Colton, Aug. 3, 1854, in Box 3P4.91, CB&Q-Newberry; JMF to Erastus Corning, Oct. 19, 1853, quoted in Overton, *Burlington Route,* p. 40. The detailed process of consolidation can be followed in John W. Brooks's letters, March 1854 through June 1856, in Box 8C2.1, CB&Q-Newberry.
53. JMF to Paul S. Forbes, Mar. 10, 1857, in J.M.F. Typescript, Forbes-Baker.

Chapter Three Notes

1. Leland L. Sage, *A History of Iowa* (Ames, Ia.: Iowa State University Press, 1974), is a good modern history of the state, but it lacks detail in many areas. The following narrative draws from various specialized studies, especially articles published in the *Iowa Journal of History* (cited as *I.J.H.*) and its predecessor, the *Iowa Journal of History and Politics* (cited as *I.J.H.P.*). Cyrenus Cole, *Iowa Through the Years* (Iowa City: State Historical Society of Iowa, 1940), is a lively but often inaccurate account; Benjamin F. Gue, *History of Iowa,* 4 vols. (New York: Century History Co, 1903), is the best of the commercial histories. See also, Cardinal Goodwin, "The American Occupation of Iowa, 1833-1860," *I.J.H.P.* 17 (1919): 83-102; William J. Peterson, "Population Advance to the Upper Mississippi Valley, 1830-1860," *I.J.H.P.* 32 (1934): 312-53; Morton Rosenberg, *Iowa on the Eve of the Civil War: A Decade of Frontier Politics* (Norman, Okla.: University of Oklahoma Press, 1972), chap. 1; and "Territorial Conventions of 1837," *I.J.H.P.* 9 (1911): 385-407 (reprinted proceedings of local conventions).
2. James W. Grimes to Sarah C. Grimes, Dec. 29, 1836, quoted in William Salter, *The Life of James W. Grimes* (New York: D. Appleton & Co., 1876), p. 15; *Wisconsin Territorial Gazette and Burlington Advertiser,* Sept. 7, 1837, reprinted in *I.J.H.P.* 10 (1912): 255-60; Dubuque *Visitor,* Nov. 9, 1836, quoted in Roscoe L. Lokken, *Iowa Public Land Disposal* (Iowa City: State Historical Society of Iowa, 1942), p. 133. See also Allan G. Bogue, "Iowa Claim Clubs: Symbol and Substance," *Mississippi Valley Historical Review* 45 (1958): 231-53.
3. James M. Morgan to an editor in Chillicothe, Ohio, Jan., 1839, quoted

in John Plumbe, Jr., *Sketches of Iowa and Wisconsin* (1839; reprinted Iowa City: State Historical Society of Iowa, 1948), pp. 47, 97; John B. Newhall, *A Glimpse of Iowa in 1846 Or, The Emigrants' Guide* . . ., 2d ed. (1846; reprinted Iowa City: State Historical Society of Iowa, 1957), pp. 23–51. See also Isaac Galland, *Galland's Iowa Emigrant* (1840; reprinted Iowa City: State Historical Society of Iowa, 1950). Promotional tracts like these condensed and clarified expressions of pioneer cultural values, but they did not invent them.

4. Benjamin F. Shambaugh, ed., *Documentary Material Relating to the History of Iowa*, 3 vols. (Iowa City: State Historical Society of Iowa, 1895) 1: 137, 142–43, 148–49, 176–84, 213. A good analysis of parties and issues surrounding the Iowa constitutions can be found in Erling A. Erickson, *Banking in Frontier Iowa, 1836–1865* (Ames: Iowa State University Press, 1971), pp. 30–45 and appendix. See also *Fragments of the Debates of the Iowa Constitutional Conventions of 1844 and 1846* . . ., ed. Benjamin F. Shambaugh (Iowa City: State Historical Society of Iowa, 1900), pp. 48ff.; and Louis Pelzer, "History and Principles of the Democratic Party in the Territory of Iowa," *I.J.H.P.* 6 (1908): 3–54 (the quotation is on page 51).

5. See Benjamin F. Shambaugh, ed., *Messages and Proclamations of the Governors of Iowa*, 7 vols. (Iowa City: State Historical Society of Iowa, 1903), 1: 6–8, 256–57, 267, 270, 388–89, 407. See also Jacob A. Swisher, "The Des Moines River Improvement Project," *I.J.H.P.* 35 (1937): 142–80; and Leonard F. Ralston, "Iowa Railroads and the Des Moines River Improvement Land Grant of 1846," *I.J.H.* 56 (1958): 97–128.

6. Burlington *Hawk-Eye*, Jan. 15, 1846, quoted in George A. Boeck, "A Decade of Transportation Fever in Burlington, Iowa, 1845–1855," *I.J.H.* 56 (1958): 132.

7. Burlington *Hawk-Eye*, June 27, 1848. As early as March, 1848, negotiations were under way to connect Burlington with St. Louis by telegraph; see the *Hawk-Eye* for Mar. 16 and Mar. 23, 1848.

8. Burlington *Hawk-Eye*, June 27 and Dec. 14, 1848.

9. Boeck, "Transportation Fever," pp. 140–43.

10. Salter, *Grimes*, pp. 1–18; Boeck, "Transportation Fever," p. 143.

11. Minutes of Directors Meetings, Jan. 15 and Jan. 17, 1852, *Records (copy) of the Burlington & Missouri River Rail Road Co.*, in CB&Q–Newberry (hereafter cited as *B&MR Records*). See also Boeck, "Transportation Fever," p. 152; and Overton, *Burlington West*, pp. 52–55.

12. Burlington *Daily Telegraph*, Jan. 5 and Feb. 2, 1852, quoted in Overton, *Burlington West*, pp. 52, 57; Minutes of Directors Meeting, Feb. 2, 1852, *B&MR Records*, CB&Q–Newberry; G. D. R. Boyd, "Sketches of History and Incidents Connected with the Settlement of Wapello County," *Annals of Iowa*, 1st ser., no. 6 (1868), p. 186.

13. John W. Brooks to JMF, Nov. 22, 1852; Brooks to J. C. Green, Nov. 22, 1852; Brooks to Erastus Fairbank, Nov. 22, 1852; Brooks to James W. Grimes, Dec. 7, 1852; in Box 8M1.1, CB&Q–Newberry.

14. Minutes of Directors Meeting, Mar. 9, 1833, *B&MR Records*, CB&Q–Newberry; see Overton, *Burlington West*, pp. 59–62, especially quotation from Burlington *Weekly Telegraph*, Mar. 12, 1853, on p. 62. Similar responses can be found in the Fairfield (Ia.) *Ledger*, Mar. 24, 1853.

15. Fairfield *Ledger*, Mar. 24, July 14, July 21, and Aug. 4, 1853; Boeck, "Transportation Fever," p. 149; James W. Grimes to Chauncy S. Colton, May 29, 1853, in Box 3P4.91, CB&Q–Newberry; Minutes of Directors Meeting, June 1, 1853, *B&MR Records*, CB&Q–Newberry; Burlington *Weekly Telegraph*, April 30, 1853, quoted in Overton, *Burlington West*, p. 64.

16. Robert Bennet Forbes to Rose Forbes, June 10 and 11, 1853, in General Material, 1 (first of seven notebooks of typescripts), CB&Q-Newberry. (These copies were prepared by Mrs. Edith Perkins Cunningham with the help of Richard C. Overton. Materials cover Forbes and Perkins family members. They are now housed in the CB&Q Archives but have no Newberry Library call number. Hereafter cited as General Material.) See also Minutes of Directors Meetings, June 30 and July 2, 1853, *B&MR Records,* CB&Q-Newberry.

17. Minutes of Directors Meeting, Oct. 26, 1853; Stockholders Meeting, Nov. 25, 1853; *B&MR Records,* CB&Q-Newberry.

18. Boyd, "Wapello County," p. 187; Overton, *Burlington West,* p. 64. Minutes of Directors Meetings, Mar. 8, Mar. 22, and Mar. 30, 1854; Minutes of Annual Meeting, Mar. 29, 1854; *B&MR Records,* CB&Q-Newberry; Mount Pleasant *Iowa Weekly Observer,* April 13 and April 20, 1854.

19. Minutes of Directors Meetings, May 3, May 4, June 30, July 5, and Aug. 8, 1854, *B&MR Records,* CB&Q-Newberry.

20. Minutes of Annual Meeting, Mar. 28, 1855; Minutes of Directors Meetings, Nov. 7, 1855, and April 2, 1856; *B&MR Records,* CB&Q-Newberry. A. W. Saunders of Mount Pleasant, Iowa, was named president. He resigned two months later and J. C. Hall of Burlington took the office. Joy resigned November 7 and was replaced by another Burlington man, E. D. Rand, leaving the entire board in Iowa hands. However, James F. Joy's letter to John W. Brooks, Mar. 16, 1855, in Cochran, *Railroad Leaders,* p. 116, reaffirms the close interest of the Forbes group in this period.

21. See *B&MR Records,* Aug. 3, 1855–June 28, 1856, CB&Q-Newberry; also Overton, *Burlington West,* pp. 70–72.

22. See "Articles of Incorporation," Jan. 15, 1852, *B&MR Records,* CB&Q-Newberry.

23. See Shambaugh, *Messages,* 1: 462–79, for Governor Hemstead's views. See also Rosenberg, *Iowa,* pp. 37–53, 76–90, for political disintegration.

24. See Rosenberg, *Iowa,* pp. 91–109.

25. James W. Grimes, "Address to the People of Iowa," campaign pamphlet dated Apr. 8, 1854, reprinted in Salter, *Grimes,* pp. 34–50; Greeley quoted in Rosenberg, *Iowa,* p. 106.

26. James W. Grimes, "Address to Iowa General Assembly," Dec. 9, 1854, reprinted in Salter, *Grimes,* p. 56; see also Shambaugh, *Messages,* 2: 5.

27. David Sparks, "Iowa Republicans and the Railroads, 1856–1860," *I.J.H.* 53 (1955): 275–82. Sparks is perhaps too hard on the Republicans, blaming them for a style of politics that typified the age. See Overton, *Burlington West,* pp. 73–97, for a full account of land grant passage.

28. *Laws of Iowa* (extra session), 1856, chap. 1, p. 5. See Overton, *Burlington West,* pp. 81, 84–85.

29. See Overton, *Burlington West,* pp. 89–95. See Box 759.2, CB&Q-Newberry, for correspondence between Bernhart Henn, special land agent for the Iowa roads, and the federal land department.

30. JMF to Charles Sumner, Feb. 14, 1853, *Letters of J.M.F.,* suppl., 1: 82–83; see also JMF to Eben Farnsworth, Jan. 24, 1853, in same, pp. 79–81; Pearson, *American Railroad Builder,* pp. 84–88.

31. JMF to Paul S. Forbes, Mar. 17, 1857, in J.M.F. Typescript, Forbes–Baker; Circular to Michigan Central and CB&Q stockholders, Mar. 21, 1857, tipped into vol. 6 of Box 5D4.1, CB&Q-Newberry; Minutes of Annual Meeting, Mar. 25, 1857, in *B&MR Records,* CB&Q-Newberry. See also Burlington *Daily Hawk-Eye,* Mar. 26, 1857.

32. JMF to Erastus Corning, May [probably March] 11, 1857, quoted in

Pearson, *American Railroad Builder,* p. 68; JMF to James F. Joy, Mar. 19, 1857, in *Letters of J.M.F.,* suppl., 1: 191–93.

33. Minutes of Directors Meetings, May 18 and June 9, 1857, in *B&MR Records,* CB&Q-Newberry; John N. Denison to Oliver Cock, June 4, 1857, in Box 5D4.1, CB&Q-Newberry. Regular meetings of the directors began in Boston on July 7, 1857.

34. See Treasurer John N. Denison's letters from late May through June, 1857, in Box 5D4.1, CB&Q-Newberry. Denison to James F. Joy, June 9, 1857, lists shareholders and number of shares to date. See also JMF to Paul S. Forbes, Mar. 17, 1857, in *J.M.F.* Typescript, Forbes-Baker. Edward L. Baker to W. H. Starr, June 8, 1857; Baker to Hans Thielson, June 19, 1857; and Baker to James F. Joy, June 23, 1857; in Box 5D4.1, CB&Q-Newberry.

35. See Taylor, *Transportation Revolution,* chap. 15.

36. Michigan Central Railroad, *Annual Report, 1857,* p. 10, shows floating debts of $1,450,823, which apparently rose even higher by the autumn. In his letters Forbes referred to a $2 million debt. See *Reminiscences of J.M.F.,* 2: 36–37.

37. JMF to Paul S. Forbes, Oct. 16, 1857, in *J.M.F.* Typescript, Forbes-Baker.

38. JMF to Paul S. Forbes, Nov. 8, 1857, in J.M.F. Typescript, Forbes-Baker.

39. JMF to Paul S. Forbes, Dec. 7 and Dec. 22, 1857, in J.M.F. Typescript, Forbes-Baker; Overton, *Burlington Route,* p. 47.

40. JMF to William H. Swift, June 17, 1858, in J.M.F. Typescript, Forbes-Baker. See also Pearson, *American Railroad Builder,* pp. 89–92; and Overton, *Burlington Route,* pp. 53–56, on the Hannibal & St. Joseph story.

41. JMF to Paul S. Forbes, July 19, 1857, in J.M.F. Typescript, Forbes-Baker. The Hannibal loan was carried and the road was opened the following year, but not without an armed confrontation with John Duff, the contractor, who refused to give up operations (see Overton, *Burlington Route,* pp. 54–55).

42. See Overton, *Burlington Route,* p. 47; and Michigan Central Railroad, *Annual Report, 1858,* pp. 11–14 and *Annual Report, 1859,* pp. 11–12, 16. The second and third Hannibal loans, 1858 and 1860, were secured by sinking funds as well (see JMF to Paul S. Forbes, Feb. 3, 1860, with circulars enclosed, in J.M.F. Typescript, Forbes-Baker).

43. *Reminiscences of J.M.F.,* 2: 45; Pearson, *American Railroad Builder,* p. 86; JMF to Paul S. Forbes, June 27, 1858 and Feb. 3, 1860, in J.M.F. Typescript, Forbes-Baker; see also, *Letters and Recollections of J.M.F.,* 1: 176–83.

44. Quoted from a Keokuk, Iowa, newspaper, in Rosenberg, *Iowa,* p. 163.

45. Edward L. Baker to W. H. Starr, Aug. 24, 1857, in Box 5D4.1, CB&Q-Newberry.

46. John N. Denison to Ephrium Kilpatrick, Aug. 29 and Sept. 7, 1857; Denison to John G. Read, Sept. 30, 1857; Edward L. Baker to Read, Oct. 2 and Oct. 8, 1857; in Box 5D4.1, CB&Q-Newberry.

47. Edward L. Baker to John G. Read, Sept. 25 (quoting Forbes), Sept. 28, Oct. 5, Oct. 14, and Oct. 30, 1857, in Box 5D4.1, CB&Q-Newberry.

48. John N. Denison to John G. Read, Sept. 22, 1857; Edward L. Baker to Read, Oct. 15, 1857; Baker to Oliver Cock, Oct. 15, 1857; Baker to J.V.L. Pruyn, Oct. 21, 1857; John N. Denison to H. H. Hunnewell, Nov. 19, 1857; in Box 5D4.1, CB&Q-Newberry.

49. Edward L. Baker to James F. Joy, Dec. 1, 1857; John N. Denison to William F. Coolbaugh, Dec. 11, 1857; Edward L. Baker to Hans Thielson, Dec. 2, 1857; in Box 5D4.1, CB&Q-Newberry. Forbes wrote to Joy on Jan. 1,

1858, saying Thayer, Corning, and Brooks were all paid up and, once Joy came clear, they could "pitch into any delinquents in earnest. . . ." (quoted in Cochran, *Railroad Leaders*, p. 331).

50. John N. Denison to W. H. Starr, Jan. 21 and Jan. 28, 1858; Denison to Edward L. Baker, Jan. 28, 1858; Denison to John G. Read, Feb. 19 and Mar. 11, 1858; Denison to James F. Joy, Feb. 19, 1858; Edward L. Baker to Julius Movius, Mar. 9, 1858; in Box 5D4.1 CB&Q-Newberry; Minutes of Directors Meeting, Mar. 3, 1858, in *B&MR Records*, CB&Q-Newberry.

51. See Edward L. Baker to the County Judge of Mills Co., Iowa, April 8, 1858; Baker to E. C. Bosbyshell, et al., April 8, 1858; Baker to the Mayor and City Council of Burlington, April 10, 1858; Baker to Hans Thielson, April 10, 1858, and Baker to the Wapello County Judge, April 12, 1858; in Box 5D4.1 CB&Q-Newberry. See also Burlington *Daily Hawk-Eye*, April 27, 1858.

52. Burlington *Daily Hawk-Eye*, May 10, 1858; see aso *Daily Hawk-Eye*, May 11, 1858, for letters signed "Citizen" on same theme; Overton, *Burlington West*, p. 101; JMF to Paul S. Forbes, May 3 and May 17, 1857, in J.M.F. Typescript, Forbes-Baker. John N. Denison to Erastus Corning, Jan. 14, 1858, carried an announcement of the formation of Iowa Land Assn. with a stock list and other particulars (quoted in Cochran, *Railroad Leaders*, p. 305).

53. Edward L. Baker to John G. Read, telegram May 7, 1858 and letter May 12, 1858; Baker to J. R. Horton, May 25, 1858; Baker to Judge Flint, May 26, 1858; in Box 5D4.1, CB&Q-Newberry. See Baker's May letters generally.

54. Edward L. Baker to James F. Joy, Aug. 3, 1858; Baker to John G. Read, Oct. 22 and Dec. 31, 1858; in Box 5D4.1, CB&Q-Newberry.

55. Edward L. Baker to John G. Read, Jan. 12, 1859, in Box 5D4.1, CB&Q-Newberry; Burlington *Weekly Hawk-Eye*, Feb. 1, 1859; Fairfield *Ledger*, Feb. 8, 1859. The *Hawk-Eye's* attack was stimulated by a mildly worded editorial in the *Ledger*, Jan. 27, 1859, which expressed sympathy for the railroad's troubles but denied the validity of their claim to further bonds or interests from Jefferson County.

56. Burlington *Weekly Hawk-Eye*, Mar. 1, 1859.

57. Edward L. Baker to Jason B. Packard, Feb. 19, 1859; Baker to John Ellis, Mar. 29, 1859; in Box 5D4.1, CB&Q-Newberry.

58. Edward L. Baker to A. H. Hamilton, Mar. 23, 1859, in Box 5D4.1, CB&Q-Newberry. See the Fairfield *Ledger*, Jan. 13, 1859; Burlington *Weekly Hawk-Eye*, Feb. 1, 1859; and John N. Denison's letters, Feb. 25-Mar. 23, 1859; in Box 5D4.1, CB&Q-Newberry. For final agreement with Ottumwa see Minutes of Directors Meetings, June 29 and July 17, 1859, in *B&MR Records*, CB&Q-Newberry.

59. Edward L. Baker to John G. Read, Feb. 9, 1859; John N. Denison to Erastus Corning, June 20, 1859; in Box 5D4.1, CB&Q-Newberry.

60. Edward L. Baker to William F. Coolbaugh, Aug. 1, 1859, enclosing petitions from John H. Gear, et al., and a draft of Baker's reply, with a request to publish it all in the local press, in Box 5D4.1, CB&Q-Newberry.

61. See John G. Foote to Charles Dunham, Editor, in the Burlington *Weekly Hawk-Eye*, Aug. 13, 1859; John N. Denison to William F. Coolbaugh, Aug. 16, 1859, enclosing a draft of a reply to Foote; Edward L. Baker to Coolbaugh, Aug. 19, 1859; John N. Denison to Coolbaugh, Sept. 3, 1859; in Box 5D4.1, CB&Q-Newberry. See also Burlington *Weekly Hawk-Eye*, Aug. 20 and Aug. 27, 1859.

62. JMF to James W. Grimes, Nov. 11, 1859, in Cochran, *Railroad Leaders*, p. 332.

63. See Earl S. Beard, "Local Aid to Railroads in Iowa," *I.J.H.* 50 (1952): 1–34.
64. JMF to Paul S. Forbes, Sept. 6 and Sept. 21, 1858, in J.M.F. Typescript, Forbes-Baker.
65. Burlington *Daily Hawk-Eye*, Nov. 24, 1858.
66. Shambaugh, *Messages*, 2: 125, 174. See Leonard Ralston, "Governor Ralph P. Lowe and State Aid to Railroads: Iowa Politics in 1859," *I.J.H.* 58 (1960): 207–18.
67. George B. Sargent, "Lecture on the West. Delivered by Special Request, at Tremont Temple, Boston, Mass., February 24, 1858," in *I.J.H.P.* 45 (1947): 172; see pp. 133–74.

CHAPTER FOUR NOTES

1. Baltimore & Ohio Railroad, *Annual Report, 1831,* quoted in *American Rail Road Journal,* Jan. 7, 1832 (see chapter 2, note 9).
2. See David M. Potter, *The Impending Crisis* (New York: Harper & Row, 1976); Eric Foner, *Free Soil, Free Labor, Free Men* (New York: Oxford University Press, 1970); and Don E. Fehrenbacher, *Prelude to Greatness: Lincoln in the 1850s* (Stanford, Calif.: Stanford University Press, 1962).
3. The campaign slogan, "Free Soil, Free Labor, Free Men," has been justly adopted as the title of Foner's excellent study of the prewar Republican ideology. John Murray Forbes's personal views take their meaning from the framework of ideas that Foner articulates in that work. See also Rosenberg, *Iowa,* passim; Frank I. Herriott, "Iowa and the First Nomination of Abraham Lincoln," *Annals of Iowa,* 3d ser., no. 8 (1907-1908), pp. 81–115, 186–220, 444–66, and no. 9 (1909-1910), pp. 45–64, 186–228. For a more recent look at the ideological climate of the prewar decades, see George Forgie, *Patricide in the House Divided* (New York: W. W. Norton, 1979).
4. JMF to George Upton, Oct. 15, 1856, in *Letters of J.M.F.,* suppl. 1: 174–75; see also *Reminiscences of J.M.F.,* 2: 59.
5. JMF to William Appleton, April 1, 1852, in *Letters of J.M.F.,* suppl., 1: 63–64; JMF to Mary and Sarah Forbes, Mar. 11, 1856, in *Reminiscences of J.M.F.,* 2: 16–18.
6. JMF to W. S. Thayer, April 7, 1854, in *Letters of J.M.F.,* suppl., 1: 126–28; JMF to Amos Lawrence, Mar. 21, 1855, in Cochran, *Railroad Leaders,* p. 208; JMF to Charles H. Fisher, Sept. 19, 1856, in *Letters of J.M.F.,* suppl., 1: 167–69; JMF to J. Hamilton Cowper, Sept. 18, 1856, in *Letters of J.M.F.,* suppl., 1: 165–67; JMF to George Upton, Oct. 15, 1856, in *Letters of J.M.F.,* suppl., 1: 173–75. See also *Reminiscences of J.M.F.,* 2: 55, 76–88.
7. See James Connor, "The Antislavery Movement in Iowa," *Annals of Iowa,* 3d ser., no. 40 (1970), pp. 343–76, 450–79. Iowa's position was repeated throughout the upper Midwest in this period, as evidenced in Leon F. Litwack, *North of Slavery: The Negro in the Free States, 1790-1860* (Chicago: University of Chicago Press, 1961). See also Eugene H. Berwanger, *The Frontier Against Slavery* (Urbana: University of Illinois Press, 1967).
8. Connor, "Antislavery Movement," pp. 371–75.
9. James W. Grimes, "Address to the People of Iowa," 1854, reprinted in Salter, *Grimes,* pp. 39–50.
10. Quoted in Salter, *Grimes,* pp. 61, 112.

11. JMF to J. Hamilton Cowper, Sept. 18, 1856, in *Letters of J.M.F.*, suppl.,
1: 165–67; Cowper to JMF, Nov. 6, 1856; JMF to Cowper, Dec. 4, 1856; in
Letters and Recollections of J.M.F., 1: 148–58.

12. J. Hamilton Cowper to JMF, Nov. 6, 1856; JMF to Cowper, Dec. 4,
1856; in *Letters and Recollections of J.M.F.*, 1: 148–58.

13. See Connor, "Antislavery Movement," pp. 454–57; Rosenberg, *Iowa*,
pp. 129–30.

14. Quoted in Rosenberg, *Iowa*, p. 165.

15. The key figures in Iowa's antislavery underground are identified in
Connor, "Antislavery Movement," pp. 464–67. For a broader investigation of
the sources of antislavery agitation see Gilbert Hobbs Barnes, *The Anti-Slavery
Impulse, 1830–1844* (1933; reprinted New York: Harcourt, Brace & World,
1964); for John Brown see Stephen B. Oates, *To Purge This Land With Blood* (New
York: Harper & Row, 1970). Forbes's telling of Brown's story was recorded in
JMF to Nassau W. Senior, Dec. 26, 1859, in *Reminiscences of J.M.F.*, 2: 56–58.

16. Connor, "Antislavery Movement," pp. 467–68; Shambaugh, *Messages*,
2: 229–51; Dan Elbert Clark, *Samuel Jordan Kirkwood* (Iowa City: State Historical
Society of Iowa, 1917), pp. 179–84. Details of Iowa's political involvement in the
Chicago convention can be found in Herriott, "First Nomination," and in Her-
riott, "Republican Presidential Preliminaries in Iowa, 1859–1860," *Annals of
Iowa*, 3d ser., no. 9 (1909–1910), pp. 241–83; Herriott, "The Republican State
Convention, January 18, 1860," *Annals of Iowa*, 3d ser., no. 9 (1909–1910), pp.
401–46.

17. JMF to J. Hamilton Cowper, Dec. 4, 1856, in *Letters and Recollections of
J.M.F.*, 1: 157. The formation of the Republican ideology is brilliantly described
in Foner, *Free Soil*.

18. See David Brion Davis, *The Slave Power Conspiracy and the Paranoid Style*
(Baton Rouge: Louisiana State University, 1969). For a fascinating contempo-
rary argument see George Fitzhugh, *Cannibals All!* (1857; reprinted Cambridge,
Mass.: Belknap Press, 1960).

19. Salter, *Grimes*, pp. 112–13.

20. JMF to Frederick W. Brune, Jan. 28, 1861, in *Letters of J.M.F.* suppl.,
1: 239–46.

21. JMF to George Upton, Feb. 10 and Feb. 13, 1861, in *Letters of J.M.F.*
suppl., 1: 250–54; see also *Letters and Recollections of J.M.F.*, 1: 188–97.

22. JMF to John A. Andrew, Feb. 2, 1861, in *Letters of J.M.F.*, suppl.,
1: 246–47; see also *Letters and Recollections of J.M.F.*, 1: 205–11; Henry Greenleaf
Pearson, *The Life of John A. Andrew, Governor of Massachusetts 1861–1865* (Boston:
Houghton Mifflin, 1904), 1: 165–81; JMF to William Schouler, Aug. 10, 1867,
in *Letters of J.M.F.*, suppl., 3: 98–101.

23. JMF to John A. Andrew, April 23, 1861, in *Letters and Recollections of
J.M.F.*, 1: 213; JMF to Andrew, May 2, 1861, in *Letters of J.M.F.*, suppl., 1: 261;
see also Pearson, *Andrew*, 1: 215–21.

24. JMF to John Tucker, May 14, 1861, in *Letters of J.M.F.*, suppl.
1: 266–67.

25. JMF to Charles Sumner, Mar. 18, 1861; JMF to the President of the
United States, April 22, 1861; JMF to George S. Boutwell, April 26, 1861; JMF
to Gideon Welles, May 4, 1861; in *Letters of J.M.F.*, suppl., 1: 254–64. Plans for
a steam sloop for the navy are explained in a copy of a letter from JMF to an
unknown recipient, April 29, 1861, in Forbes-Baker.

26. See JMF to G. V. Fox, June 12, 1861, in *Letters of J.M.F.*, suppl.,
1: 273–75. Forbes later had second thoughts about opening the cotton ports, but
he was always willing to try (see JMF to N. M. Beckwith, Dec. 31, 1861, in

Letters of J.M.F., suppl., 1: 296). Forbes's "diplomatic" correspondence began with his letter to Nassau W. Senior, May 27, 1861, and continued throughout the war (ibid., 269ff.).
 27. JMF to Nassau W. Senior, May 27 and 28, 1861, in *Letters of J.M.F.,* suppl., 1: 269-72; JMF to Senior, Sept. 30, 1861, in *Letters and Recollections of J.M.F.,* 1: 250; JMF to Samuel Gridley Howe, Aug. 21, 1861, in *Letters and Recollections of J.M.F.,* 1: 239 (see generally pp. 238-50).
 28. Nassau W. Senior to JMF, Nov. 20, 1861; JMF to Senior, Dec. 10, 1861; in *Letters and Recollections of J.M.F.,* 1: 251-56. Forbes's interpretation of the war, as put forth to Senior in 1861, only hardened in the years to come. By autumn, 1864, he had concluded that the Southern slave system was "anti-republican, anti-peace, anti-material progress, anti-civilization. . . ." This was his clearest indictment ever (see JMF to William Evans, Oct. 18, 1864, in *Letters of J.M.F.,* suppl., 2: 298-99).
 29. JMF to Charles B. Sedgwick, Aug. 5, 1861 and Jan. 17, 1862, in *Letters of J.M.F.,* suppl., 1: 286-87, 300-302; JMF to Sedgwick, Mar. 11, 1864, in *Letters of J.M.F.,* suppl., 2: 231; see also JMF to Paul S. Forbes, Aug. 12, 1863, in J.M.F. Typescript, Forbes-Baker; *Letters of J.M.F.,* suppl., 2: 226-33.
 30. JMF to William Pitt Fessenden, Jan. 13, 1862, in *Letters and Recollections of J.M.F.,* 1: 277-78; JMF to Fessenden, Jan. 21 and Feb. 19, 1862, in *Letters of J.M.F.,* suppl., 1: 302-4, 308-9.
 31. JMF to Joshua Bates, Dec. 11, 1862, in *Letters of J.M.F.,* suppl., 2: 28-29; JMF to William Pitt Fessenden, Jan. 29, 1863, in *Reminiscences of J.M.F.,* 2: 215-17; JMF to Salmon P. Chase, June 29,1864, in *Letters of J.M.F.,* suppl., 2: 270. See generally Forbes's letters to Chase, Sedgwick, and Fessenden in *Letters of J.M.F.,* suppl., 2, for a continuing discussion of details of public finance.
 32. JMF to William Pitt Fessenden, Feb. 19, 1862; JMF to John Tucker, Jan. 2, 1862; JMF to Andrew, [May], 1861; in *Letters of J.M.F.,* suppl., 1: 309, 297, 268; JMF to William Cullen Bryant, Aug. 24, 1861, in *Letters and Recollections of J.M.F.,* 1: 241-42; JMF to Bryant, Aug. 25, 1861, in *Letters of J.M.F.,* suppl., 1: 290; JMF to Bryant, Nov. 10, 1862, in *Letters of J.M.F.,* suppl., 2: 21; JMF to W. H. Aspinwall, Jan. 5, 1863, in *Reminiscences of J.M.F.,* 2: 207; JMF to L. M. Sargent, Feb. 24, 1863; JMF to James W. Grimes, June 24, 1864; in *Letters of J.M.F.,* suppl., 2: 90, 267. Sometimes Forbes's irritation overran his private communications network, spilling into the public press over the signature "Audax."
 33. JMF to Henry Wilson, Feb. 11, 1863; JMF to Charles B. Sedgwick, Dec. 7, 1862; in *Letters of J.M.F.,* suppl., 2: 67, 26; Charles E. Perkins to JMF, Nov. 13, 1863, in Perkins letters, Letterbook A, CB&Q-Newberry (hereafter cited as C-05); JMF to Joshua Bates, Dec. 19, 1862, in *Letters of J.M.F.,* suppl., 2: 34-35; see also *Reminiscences of J.M.F.,* 2: 197-98; *Letters and Recollections of J.M.F.,* 1: 333-34, 2: 7.
 34. JMF to Sarah Hathaway Forbes, Mar. 4, 1862, in *Letters and Recollections of J.M.F.,* 1: 295-96; JMF to the editor of the Boston *Advertiser,* May 23, 1862, quoted in Willie Lee Rose, *Rehearsal for Reconstruction: The Port Royal Experiment,* paper ed. (New York: Vintage Books, 1964), p. 141; JMF to George Ashburner, June 16, 1862, in *Letters of J.M.F.,* suppl., 1: 326; JMF to Charles Sumner, Jan. 17, 1863; JMF to Rufus Saxton, Jan. 16, 1863; quoted in Rose, *Rehearsal,* pp. 213-14. Rose's book is an excellent study of the Port Royal experiment in its several dimensions.
 35. See Rose, *Rehearsal,* pp. 223-29, 297-319. Rose unfairly includes Forbes as a typical Boston investor as a result of his support for large enterprise.

For a more complete picture of his subtle position see his letters from Nov. 9, 1863, through April 11, 1864, in *Letters of J.M.F.*, suppl., 2: 171–256.

36. JMF to Charles B. Sedgwick, June 7, 1862, in *Letters and Recollections of J.M.F.*, 1: 317; JMF to Edwin M. Stanton, June 20, 1862, in *Letters of J.M.F.*, suppl., 1: 328; *Reminiscences of J.M.F.*, 2: 188.

37. JMF to Robert W. Hooper, Dec. 3, 1862; JMF to David Hunter, Dec. 18, 1862; in *Letters of J.M.F.*, suppl., 2: 25, 30–31; JMF to Charles Sumner, Dec. 27, 1862, in *Letters and Recollections of J.M.F.*, 1: 351; see also *Letters of J.M.F.*, suppl., 2: 82–90. Rose, *Rehearsal*, pp. 248–60, tells the story of the Massachusetts 54th at Battery Wagner.

38. JMF to E. B. Ward, Sept. 19, 1863; JMF to William Evans, Oct. 18, 1864, in *Letters of J.M.F.*, suppl., 2: 145–46, 298–99. Compared with the intellectual turmoil experienced by many of the North's best social thinkers, Forbes survived the Civil War with few scars after his initial position had been established. During the years of war Forbes concentrated on a few key principles and gradually rotated his view of these "conservative" ideas to keep abreast of changes. See George M. Frederickson, *The Inner Civil War: Northern Intellectuals and the Crisis of the Union* (New York: Harper & Row, 1965).

39. JMF to William Curtis Noyes, Aug. 12, 1862, in *Letters and Recollections of J.M.F.*, 1: 327; JMF to Noyes, Feb. 11 and Feb. 18, 1863, in *Letters of J.M.F.*, suppl., 2: 69, 79; JMF to Edward Everet Hale, Feb. 23, 1863; JMF to John A. Stevens, Jr., Mar. 2, 1863; JMF to Frederick Law Olmstead, Mar. 4, 1863, in *Letters of J.M.F.*, suppl., 2: 88–95. Forbes had recognized since before Lincoln's election that the language of "Democracy" was an important advantage to the southern party (see *Reminiscences of J.M.F.*, 2: 69).

40. *Diary of Gideon Welles*, 3 vols., ed. Howard K. Beale (New York: W. W. Norton, 1960), 2: 4. JMF to George W. Curtis, May 2, 1864; JMF to Joseph S. Ropes, Aug. 4, 1864; in *Letters of J.M.F.*, suppl., 2: 248–51, 283–85; JMF to Peter Cooper, Oct. 25, 1864, in *Reminiscences of J.M.F.*, 2: 300–2.

41. Quoted in Clark, *Kirkwood*, p. 226.

42. See George H. Miller, *Railroads and the Granger Laws* (Madison: University of Wisconsin Press, 1971), p. 1; Frank L. Klement, *The Copperheads of the Middle West* (Chicago: University of Chicago Press, 1960), pp. 3–11; Overton, *Burlington Route*, pp. 75–76; and James W. Grimes to Samuel J. Kirkwood, Jan. 28, 1861, in Salter, *Grimes*, p. 136. The *Report of the Iowa State Agricultural Society* for 1862 found the state's farmers subject to the "tender mercies of relentless gamblers in Rail Road stocks" (p. 126).

43. William B. Ogden, president of the Chicago & North Western, quoted in Overton, *Burlington Route*, p. 74; see generally pp. 64–74.

44. John N. Denison to John G. Read, Feb. 11, 1861, in Box 5D4.1, CB&Q–Newberry. The executive committee of the B&MR finally issued special income bonds maturing in four years at 8 percent, in order to cover interest on existing bonded debt. See Minutes of Directors Meeting, June 7, 1862, in *B&MR Records*, CB&Q–Newberry.

45. Burlington *Daily Hawk-Eye*, Nov. 7, 1861. See also John N. Denison's letters from May through June, 1861, in Box 5D4.1, CB&Q–Newberry.

46. John N. Denison to Henry Coffin, Jan. 31, 1862, in Box 5D4.1, CB&Q–Newberry; Charles E. Perkins to JMF, Nov. 16, 1861, in Charles E. Perkins Letters, Transcripts, Set C, CB&Q–Newberry (hereafter cited as C.E.P. Transcripts. Richard C. Overton prepared typescripts of hundreds of Perkins letters and memoranda—including stray Forbes letters. Because of the deterioration of fragile letterbooks, these copies have become the only recoverable sources

of some Perkins and Forbes material. Where originals could not be read or located, these copies have been cited).

47. John N. Denison to John G. Foote, Feb. 11, 1862; Edward L. Baker to Foote, Feb. 12, 1862; in Box 5D4.1, CB&Q-Newberry.

48. John N. Denison to Fitz Henry Warren, Feb. 11, 1862; Denison to William F. Coolbaugh, Feb. 15, 1862; in Box 5D4.1, CB&Q-Newberry.

49. John N. Denison to Charles E. Perkins, Nov. 19, 1862, in Box 5D4.1, CB&Q-Newberry.

50. Quoted in Earle D. Ross, "Northern Sectionalism in the Civil War Era," *I.J.H.P.* **30** (1932): 473–74; see also pp. 455–512; Ross, *Iowa Agriculture* (Iowa City: State Historical Society of Iowa, 1951), pp. 51–54; Frank L. Klement, "Middle Western Copperheadism and the Genesis of the Granger Movement," *Mississippi Valley Historical Review* **38** (1951–1953): 679–94; Wyatt W. Belcher, *The Economic Rivalry Between St. Louis and Chicago* (New York: Columbia University Press, 1947), pp. 140–49.

51. John N. Denison to John N. A. Griswold, Oct. 26, 1863; Denison to Charles E. Perkins, Oct. 28, 1863; in Box 5D4.1, CB&Q-Newberry; see also Overton, *Burlington West,* pp. 166–69.

52. John N. Denison to James F. Joy, Jan. 22, 1864, in Box 5D4.1, CB&Q-Newberry; Charles E. Perkins to JMF, Mar. 9, 1864, in C-05, Letterbook C, CB&Q-Newberry.

53. Charles E. Perkins to JMF, Mar. 8, 1864, in C.E.P. Transcripts, Set C, CB&Q-Newberry. See Minutes of Directors Meeting, April 28, 1864, in *B&MR Records,* CB&Q-Newberry, for agreement with the CB&Q; see also Perkins's letters to Forbes, June, 1864, in C-05, Letterbook C, CB&Q-Newberry.

54. Charles E. Perkins to JMF, May 1, 1864, in C-05, Letterbook C, CB&Q-Newberry; Perkins to JMF, Oct. 11, 1864, in C.E.P. Transcripts, Set C, CB&Q-Newberry.

55. See Edward M. Baker to JMF, Mar. 30, 1864, in Box 5D4.1, CB&Q-Newberry; Charles E. Perkins to JMF, July 30 and Aug. 12, 1864, in C.E.P. Transcripts, Set C, CB&Q-Newberry; Overton, *Burlington West,* pp. 169–70.

56. Charles E. Perkins to JMF, Feb. 12 and Mar. 27, 1865, in General Material, 2, CB&Q-Newberry; Perkins to JMF, April 9, 1865, in C.E.P. Transcripts, Set C, CB&Q-Newberry; *Letters and Recollections of J.M.F.,* 2: 140–41.

CHAPTER FIVE NOTES

1. JMF to Quincy A. Gilmore, May 21, 1865; JMF to William Pitt Fessenden, April 13, 1868; in *Letters of J.M.F.,* suppl., 3: 17, 113.

2. James W. Grimes, Speech in the U.S. Senate, May 8, 1866, in Salter, *Grimes,* pp. 292–93.

3. JMF to William Pitt Fessenden, May 23, 1868, in *Letters and Recollections of J.M.F.,* 2: 165.

4. For economic issues see Robert P. Sharkey, *Money, Class, and Party* (Baltimore: Johns Hopkins Press, 1959); Irwin Unger, *The Greenback Era* (Princeton: Princeton University Press, 1964); and Walter T. K. Nugent, *Money and American Society 1865–1877* (New York: The Free Press, 1968); for politics see Richard Jensen, *The Winning of the Midwest* (Chicago: University of Chicago Press, 1971); and Paul Kleppner, *The Cross of Culture* (New York: The Free Press, 1970).

5. See chapter 3, note 12. For a careful analysis of this intellectual reversal in its economic and legal contexts see Morton J. Horowitz, *The Transformation of American Law, 1780-1860* (Cambridge, Mass.: Harvard University Press, 1977); and James Willard Hurst, *Law and the Conditions of Freedom* (Madison: University of Wisconsin Press, 1956).

6. John N. Denison to Henry Coffin, Jan. 31, 1862, in Box 5D4.1, CB&Q-Newberry. For the first appearance of such dislocations, see Lee Benson, *Merchants, Farmers, and Railroads: Railroad Regulation and New York Politics, 1850-1887* (Cambridge, Mass.: Harvard University Press, 1955).

7. See Belcher, *Rivalry*, pp. 23-24; Taylor, *Transportation Revolution*, p. 389; and John G. Clark, *The Grain Trade in the Old Northwest* (Urbana: University of Illinois Press, 1966), pp. 264-65, 269, 272.

8. See Clark, *Grain Trade*, pp. 270-78.

9. Miller, *Railroads*, p. 9 and chap. 1 generally; John F. Stover, *History of the Illinois Central Railroad* (New York: Macmillan, 1975), pp. 71-79; Belcher, *Rivalry*, pp. 102-3, 150, 171; Albert Fishlow, *American Railroads and the Transformation of the Ante-Bellum Economy* (Cambridge, Mass.: Harvard University Press, 1965), pp. 275-98. Miller points out that the *diversion* of established trade was not significant, but that almost all of the *new* commerce in the fast-growing valley was carried through Chicago.

10. According to Miller, *Railroads*, p. 12, the process of "refinement and rationalization almost always meant loss of local control." See Belcher, *Rivalry*, chaps. 8 and 9 for restrictions on the wartime river trade.

11. For a brilliant treatment of the rate-making process and its historical development see Miller, *Railroads*, pp. 16-41.

12. Ibid.

13. Quoted in Overton, *Burlington West*, p. 112. See also Charles E. Perkins to JMF, May 5, May 16, May 31, and July 1, 1859, in C.E.P. Transcripts, Set C, CB&Q-Newberry; Richard C. Overton, "Charles Elliott Perkins," *Business History Review* 31 (1957): 292-309.

14. Charles E. Perkins to JMF, Aug. 11, 1862, in C.E.P. Transcripts, Set C, CB&Q-Newberry; Perkins to JMF, Oct. 11, 1862, in C-O5, Letterbook A, CB&Q-Newberry.

15. See for example Charles E. Perkins to JMF, May 8, 1865, in C-O5, Letterbook D, CB&Q-Newberry, where Perkins tells of "redeeming" a "dead town" for the Land Association.

16. See John N. Denison to Charles E. Perkins, May 15, 1865, in General Material, 2, CB&Q-Newberry. Perkins to JMF, June 17, June 20, Aug. 27, and Nov. 10, 1865; Perkins to James F. Joy, Dec. 16 and Dec. 21, 1865; in C-O5, Letterbook D, CB&Q-Newberry. The contract for aid from the CB&Q was recorded on June 20, 1865, in *B&MR Records*, CB&Q-Newberry.

17. Minutes of Directors Meeting, April 27, 1866, in *B&MR Records*, CB&Q-Newberry. Charles E. Perkins to James F. Joy, Nov. 2, 1866; Perkins to JMF, Jan. 9, Feb. 8, and Mar. 18, 1867; in C-O5, Letterbook E, CB&Q-Newberry; CB&Q, *Annual Report, 1867*, pp. 53, 56-57.

18. Charles E. Perkins to L. D. Carpenter, Jan. 27, 1866, in C-O5, Letterbook D, CB&Q-Newberry; Perkins to John F. Tracy, Feb. 6, 1866, in C-O5, Letterbook E, CB&Q-Newberry; Perkins to JMF, Aug. 30 and Sept. 10, 1867, in C-O5, Letterbook F, CB&Q-Newberry.

19. Charles E. Perkins to JMF, Sept. 4, Sept. 11, and Sept. 15, 1867, in C-O5, Letterbook F, CB&Q-Newberry.

20. Charles E. Perkins to JMF, Jan. 17 and July 13, 1868; Perkins to

Henry Strong, Jan. 31, 1868; Perkins to John W. Brooks, Feb. 21, 1868; in C-O5, Letterbook F, CB&Q-Newberry.
21. See Charles E. Perkins to JMF, Feb. 24 through Aug. 24, 1868, in C-O5, Letterbook F, CB&Q-Newberry. See also Johnson and Supple, *Boston Capitalists*, p. 224.
22. Charles E. Perkins to JMF, Aug. 24, 1868, in C-O5, Letterbook F, CB&Q-Newberry.
23. See Charles E. Perkins to JMF, Aug. 9 and Nov. 2, 1868, in C-O5, Letterbook F, CB&Q-Newberry; Perkins to JMF, Jan. 31, 1869, in C.E.P. Transcripts, Set C, CB&Q-Newberry. See also Overton, *Burlington Route*, pp. 95-96; C.B.& Q., *Annual Report*, 1869, p. 13.
24. Julius Grodinsky, *The Iowa Pool: A Study in Railroad Competition, 1870-1884* (Chicago: University of Chicago Press, 1950), pp. 9-11 and chap. 1 generally. See also Julius Grodinsky, *Transcontinental Railway Strategy, 1869-1893* (Philadelphia: University of Pennsylvania Press, 1962), chap. 2; Daniel Hodas, *The Business Career of Moses Taylor* (New York: New York University Press, 1976), chap. 13. Statistics are from CB&Q *Annual Reports*, compiled for Richard C. Overton and quoted here with his permission.
25. John W. Brooks to Charles Brydges, May 28 and July 30, 1863, in Cochran, *Railroad Leaders*, p. 276; B&MR, *Annual Report, 1865*, pp. 4-5.
26. See CB&Q, *Annual Report, 1866* and *Annual Report, 1867*.
27. JMF to James F. Joy, Nov. 21, 1866, in Cochran, *Railroad Leaders*, p. 333. See Minutes of Directors Meeting, Dec. 13, 1866, in *B&MR Records*, CB&Q-Newberry; Johnson and Supple, *Boston Capitalists*, pp. 226-28.
28. Grimes quoted in John N. Denison to James F. Joy, Jan. 9, 1867, in Box 5D4.1, CB&Q-Newberry. See also Denison to Nathaniel Thayer, Dec. 31, 1866, for a lengthy review of the Bellevue problem and the Nebraska strategy.
29. John N. Denison to "Boston" [C.B.& Q. Office], Jan. 14, 1867; Denison to James W. Grimes, Jan. 30, 1867; in Box 5D4.1, CB&Q-Newberry.
30. CB&Q, *Annual Report*, 1867, p. 13.
31. JMF to John W. Brooks, July 5, 1867; John N. Denison to James F. Joy, Sept. 4 and Sept. 10, 1867; in Box 5D4.1, CB&Q-Newberry.
32. John N. Denison to James F. Joy, Sept. 4, 1867, in Box 5D4.1, CB&Q-Newberry; C.B.& Q. Circulars, Sept. 18, 1867 and Feb. 20, 1868, quoted in Johnson and Supple, *Boston Capitalists*, pp. 231-232; see also Minutes of Directors Meeting, Dec. 18, 1867, in *B&MR Records*, CB&Q-Newberry.
33. CB&Q, *Annual Report, 1869*, p. 20.
34. See Grodinsky, *Iowa Pool*, pp. 15-27; John W. Brooks to Charles E. Perkins, May 26, 1870, in Cochran, *Railroad Leaders*, p. 278.
35. C.B.& Q., *Annual Report, 1870*, pp. 11-15, 19-20; *Annual Report, 1871*, pp. 10-11; see Johnson and Supple, *Boston Capitalists*, pp. 233-37.
36. John N. Denison to James F. Joy, June 10, 1871, quoted in Grodinsky, *Iowa Pool*, pp. 12-13; Charles E. Perkins to JMF, Oct. 25, 1871, in C.E.P. Transcripts, Set C, CB&Q-Newberry.
37. The full story of the River Roads can be followed in Overton, *Burlington Route*, pp. 120-39. For an example of the branch-line contracts Joy preferred, see James F. Joy to John Newhall, Mar. 27, 1871, in Cochran, *Railroad Leaders*, p. 368.
38. Charles E. Perkins to JMF, Aug. 8, 1871, in C.E.P. Transcripts, Set C, CB&Q-Newberry.
39. See Overton, *Burlington Route*, pp. 130-32. CB&Q President James M. Walker's letters for 1871-72 comprise an excellent source for the details of Joy's

effort to salvage the River Roads undetected (see Box 3W3.1, CB&Q-Newberry).

40. Statistics are from CB&Q *Annual Reports*, compiled for Richard C. Overton and quoted here with his permission. Consolidation of the CB&Q and B&MR in 1872 resulted in eight months' adjustment in bookkeeping between the two companies, which makes a continuous series of earnings difficult to construct. Profit margins were shrinking, but the CB&Q remained strong compared to other Chicago roads. (Raw figures drawn from CB&Q *Annual Reports*.)

41. Copy of a letter, JMF to a stockholder [possibly Edward M. Cheney], [c. June 16, 1873], in Box 8C6.5, CB&Q-Newberry.

42. JMF to John C. Green, June 16 and June 24, 1873, in Box 8C6.5, CB&Q-Newberry; JMF to John W. Brooks, Oct. 29, 1873, in Box 3W3.5, CB&Q-Newberry.

43. JMF to Sidney Bartlett, Nov. 12, 1873, in *Reminiscences of J.M.F.*, 3: 128-33; see also pp. 98-100, 127. See also Overton, *Burlington Route*, pp. 133-35.

44. Quoted in Overton, *Burlington Route*, p. 135

45. Burlington *Weekly Hawk-Eye*, Jan. 13, Jan. 20, and Jan. 27, 1866; see Miller, *Railroads*, pp. 100-109.

46. *Proceedings of the Fourth Annual Meeting of the Iowa State Grange* (Des Moines: Iowa Homestead Steam Press, 1873).

47. *Fourth . . . Iowa State Grange, 1873*, p. 33; Burlington *Daily Hawk-Eye*, Oct. 9, 16, 17, and 24, 1872.

48. James M. Walker to E. D. Rand, et al., Dec. 31, 1873, in Box 3W3.1, CB&Q-Newberry; Minutes of Annual Stockholders Meeting, Feb. 25, 1874, in *B&MR Records*, CB&Q-Newberry; Burlington *Daily Hawk-Eye*, Jan. 8, 1874.

49. See farm price series quoted in Mildred Throne, "The Grange in Iowa, 1868-1875," *I.J.H.* **47** (1949): 291; see also Miller, *Railroads*, pp. 104-11.

50. See Oliver Hudson Kelly, *Origin and Progress of the Order of the Patrons of Husbandry . . .* (Philadelphia: J. A. Wagonseller, 1875); Solon J. Buck, *The Granger Movement* (Cambridge, Mass.: Harvard University Press, 1933); and D. Sven Nordin, *Rich Harvest: A History of the Grange, 1867-1900* (Jackson: University of Mississippi Press, 1974). The best single account on Iowa is Throne, "Grange."

51. Iowa State Agricultural Society, *Report, 1862* (Des Moines, 1863), pp. 126-27; James W. Grimes, Speech in the Senate, 1866, quoted in Fred B. Lewellen, "Political Ideas of James W. Grimes," *I.J.H.P.* **42** (1944): 350.

52. Iowa Agricultural, *Report, 1869*, p. 77; *Iowa Homestead*, Mar. 15, 1872.

53. Iowa Agricultural, *Report, 1872*, pp. 168-76. (Published after the Jan., 1873, meeting.)

54. Iowa Agricultural, *Report, 1872*, pp. 194-95; Mildred Throne, *Cyrus Clay Carpenter and Iowa Politics, 1854-1898* (Iowa City: State Historical Society of Iowa, 1974), p. 159.

55. Iowa Agricultural, *Report, 1872*, pp. 194-201.

56. Ibid., pp. 201-13.

57. Throne, *Carpenter*, p. 160; Jonathon Periam, *The Groundswell: A History of the Origins, Aims, and Progress of the Farmers' Movement* (Cincinnati: E. Hannaford & Co., 1874), p. 264; Des Moines *Iowa State Daily Register*, Jan. 28 and Jan. 31, 1873; *Fourth . . . Iowa State Grange, 1873*, pp. 23-24, 29.

58. Robert Harris to T. J. Carter, Mar. 24, 1873, quoted in Miller, *Railroads*, p. 22; see also Miller, chap. 4, on Illinois legislation.

59. JMF to a stockholder, [c. June 16, 1873], in Box 8C6.5, CB&Q-Newberry.

60. Charles E. Perkins to John W. Brooks, Mar. 2, 1873, in C.E.P. Transcripts, Set A, CB&Q-Newberry; *The Nation,* April 10, 1873, p. 249-50.

61. *The Nation,* June 12, 1873, pp. 397-98; June 19, 1873, p. 407; July 17, 1873, pp. 36-37; July 31, 1873, pp. 68-69.

62. Charles E. Perkins to JMF, Sept. 9, 1873, in General Material, 2, CB&Q-Newberry; *The Nation,* Oct. 2, 1873, p. 220. See the Des Moines *Iowa State Daily Register,* Sept. 27, 1873, for reprinted editorial clips from around the country.

63. Edward Winslow Martin, *History of the Grange Movement or, The Farmer's War Against Monopolies* . . . (Philadelphia: National Publishing Co., 1873), p. 509; "A Letter to Farmers from Jones Co.," *Iowa Homestead,* Dec. 12, 1873; *Fourth* . . . *Iowa State Grange,* 1873, p. 28.

64. Quoted in Nordin, *Rich Harvest,* p. 182. Mildred Throne, "The Anti-Monopoly Party in Iowa, 1873-1874," *I.J.H.* **52** (1954): 289-326, narrates the rise and fall of this political party. The Des Moines Anti-Monopoly platform is reprinted in Martin, *Grange Movement,* p. 513; see also Des Moines *Iowa State Daily Register,* Aug. 24, 1873, for James S. Clarkson's commentary.

65. Charles E. Perkins to J.N.A. Griswold, Mar. 7, 1874, in C-O1, P4.1, CB&Q-Newberry; see James M. Walker to John N. Denison, Feb. 28, 1874, in Box 3W3.1 CB&Q-Newberry. Throne, *Carpenter,* pp. 177-83; Miller, *Railroads,* pp. 114-16; and the Des Moines and Burlington newspapers for Jan. through Mar., 1874, provide additional detail on the legislative process.

66. Des Moines *Iowa State Daily Register,* May 8, 1874, quoted in Throne, *Carpenter,* p. 181.

67. See Miller, *Railroads,* pp. 29, 161-71.

68. See Horowitz, *American Law,* p. 255; Hurst, *Law and the Conditions,* chap. 3.

69. See for example the "Declaration of Purposes," drawn up at the National Grange Meeting, St. Louis, Feb. 11, 1874, reprinted in Martin, *Grange Movement,* pp. 535-39.

70. *Fifth* . . . *Iowa State Grange, 1874,* pp. 34-35.

CHAPTER SIX NOTES

1. See James M. Walker's letters for 1874 in Box 3W3.1, CB&Q-Newberry.

2. JMF memoranda [c. Sept., 1874], [c. Dec. 1874] and [c. Jan. 1875], in Box ¹8C6.4, CB&Q-Newberry. For additional narrative see Overton, *Burlington Route,* pp. 132-39 and Cochran, *Railroad Leaders,* pp. 111-15. The memo of January, 1875, contained Forbes's notes for his presentation to the bondholders. The "guilty" directors were asked to meet by noon, Feb. 2, and when they failed, Forbes went ahead with his ultimatum (see JMF to Sidney Bartlett, Feb. 1, 1875, in Box 8C6.4, CB&Q-Newberry).

3. JMF to John W. Brooks, Feb. 13, 1875; Brooks to JMF, Feb. 15, 1875; in *Reminiscences of J.M.F.,* **3**: 134-37; Brooks to James F. Joy, Mar. 11, 1875, in Cochran, *Railroad Leaders,* p. 282.

4. James F. Joy to Sidney Bartlett, Feb. 22, 1875, in Box J7.1, IC-Newberry; JMF to John C. Green, Feb. 16, 1875, in Box 8C6.5, CB&Q-Newberry. See also James F. Joy to Nathaniel Thayer, Sept. 10, 1875, quoted in Cochran, *Railroad Leaders,* p. 113.

5. *Reminiscences of J.M.F.,* **3**: 138-39; JMF to James F. Joy, May, 1875, in

Letters of J.M.F., suppl., 3: 124–26. A reasonably good account of the takeover can be found in *Reminiscences of J.M.F.,* 3: 139–43.

6. JMF testifying before Congress, Jan. 20, 1874, quoted in *Reminiscences of J.M.F.,* 3: 101–11; Charles E. Perkins to Hans Thielsen, June 10, 1875, in C-O1, P4.1, CB&Q-Newberry.

7. JMF to Charles E. Perkins, June 4, 1875, in Forbes–Perkins Letters, CB&Q-Newberry (three unnumbered boxes of letters between these two men beginning Sept., 1871, hereafter cited as Forbes–Perkins Letters, CB&Q-Newberry).

8. JMF to John N. Denison, July 18, 1875, in Cochran, *Railroad Leaders,* p. 130. JMF to James M. Walker, Oct. 17, 1875; JMF to John W. Brooks, Nov. 12, 1875; in Cochran, *Railroad Leaders,* p. 335; JMF to Charles E. Perkins, Dec. 26, 1875, in Forbes–Perkins Letters, CB&Q-Newberry.

9. JMF to James M. Walker, Mar. 14, 1874, in Box 3W3.5, CB&Q-Newberry. Forbes was active in the national Republican committee from 1876 until his break with the bosses in 1884. Unwilling to join the Liberal Republicans, he remained loosely independent ever after. (See *Reminiscences of J.M.F.,* 3: 159–79.)

10. James M. Walker to Charles E. Perkins, May 16, 1874, in Box 3W3.1, CB&Q-Newberry; Walker to John N. Denison, June 11, 1874, in Cochran, *Railroad Leaders,* p. 489; Burlington *Daily Hawk-Eye,* July 11, 1874; James M. Walker to J. D. Wright, Oct. 7, 1874, in Box 3W3.1, CB&Q-Newberry. The application for an injunction, Jan. 5, 1875, is in Box 33-1870-4.1, CB&Q-Newberry. For an account of the legal questions see George H. Miller, "Chicago, Burlington and Quincy Railroad Company v. Iowa," *I.J.H.* 54 (1956): 289–312.

11. Charles E. Perkins to JMF, May 15, 1875, in C.E.P. Transcripts, Set C, CB&Q-Newberry; see also Miller, "C.B.&Q. v. Iowa," pp. 304–5. Perkins had gained control of the Burlington *Hawk-Eye* through loans totaling $5,000 of Forbes's money (Perkins to JMF, Jan. 11, 1875, in C.E.P. Transcripts, Set C, CB&Q-Newberry).

12. James M. Walker to J.N.A. Griswold, May 19, 1875, in Box 3W3.1, CB&Q-Newberry.

13. Charles E. Perkins to JMF, June 26, 1875, in C.E.P. Transcripts, Set C, CB&Q-Newberry; Perkins memorandum (draft of an essay), [c. June, 1875], in C-O1, P4.1, CB&Q-Newberry.

14. C. E. Sherman to "Editor," *The Nation,* June 30, 1875, transcribed in Perkins's hand, in Box 3P4.2, CB&Q-Newberry. Charles E. Perkins to Robert Harris, Aug. 6, 1875; Harris to Perkins, Aug. 9, 1875; in Box 3P4.2, CB&Q-Newberry.

15. Charles Francis Adams, Jr., "The Granger Movement," *North American Review* 120 (1875): 399; see generally 394–424.

16. Charles E. Perkins to E. L. Godkin, Nov. 6, 1875, in General Material, 3: CB&Q-Newberry; JMF to W. P. Garrison, Mar. 18, 1870, in *Letters of J.M.F.,* suppl., 3:115.

17. Mildred Throne, "Repeal of the Iowa Granger Law, 1878," *I.J.H.* 51 (1953): 107, 110.

18. Charles E. Perkins memorandum (draft of an article), [c. Feb., 1876], in Box 33-1880-4.65, CB&Q-Newberry. This box contains a number of additional documents that trace Perkins's thoughts and activities regarding repeal of the Iowa law. The public misrepresentation of the Burlington's rate structure was exposed late in the campaign for repeal, but by then petitions begging for relief had done their harm.

19. Charles E. Perkins to Robert Harris, Mar. 25, 1876, in Box

33-1880-4.65, CB&Q-Newberry; see Throne, "Repeal," pp. 110-16 for details of legislative actions.

20. See Overton, *Burlington Route,* p. 147.

21. Robert Harris to JMF, May 31, 1876, in Box 3H4.2, CB&Q-Newberry. See also Cochran, *Railroad Leaders,* pp. 347-63.

22. See Charles E. Perkins to JMF, July 16, 1876, in C.E.P. Transcripts, Set C; JMF to Perkins, July 23, 1876, in Forbes-Perkins Letters; Perkins to JMF, July 29, 1876, in C.E.P. Transcripts, Set A; CB&Q-Newberry.

23. JMF to Charles E. Perkins, Feb. 3, 1877, in Forbes-Perkins Letters, CB&Q-Newberry.

24. JMF to Charles E. Perkins, April 15, 1877, in Forbes-Perkins Letters, CB&Q-Newberry. See Overton, *Burlington Route,* pp. 156-57, for details of Gould's offer and Perkins's rejection of the "Quintuple Contract." See also Grodinsky, *Strategy,* pp. 79-82, for an interpretation more sympathetic to Gould.

25. Charles E. Perkins to JMF, Aug. 2, 1877, quoted in Overton, *Burlington Route,* p. 159; Robert Harris to JMF, July 31, 1877, in Box 3H4.2, CB&Q-Newberry.

26. JMF to [Charles E. Perkins], [c. Dec., 1877], in Forbes-Perkins Letters, CB&Q-Newberry.

27. Ibid.

28. Robert Harris to John R. Leslie, Nov. 24, 1877, in Box 3H4.2, CB&Q-Newberry.

29. Boxes 33-1870-4.2, 4.33 and 4.41, CB&Q-Newberry, contain miscellaneous documents relating the repeal of the Granger Law and the establishment of the Iowa Railroad Commission, including a draft of Walker's proposal for such a bill (in 4.33).

30. Memorial of the Citizens of Clinton, Iowa, [c. Feb., 1878], in Box 33-1870-4.3, CB&Q-Newberry.

31. Ibid. See also Des Moines *Iowa State Daily Register,* Mar. 7 and 12, 1878; Burlington *Daily Hawk-Eye,* Mar. 8, 9, and 10, 1878; Throne, "Repeal," pp. 117-30. Throne places a good deal of emphasis on the interference by railroad lobbyists in the legislative process; however, it is not necessary to prove "corruption" to explain the general support for repeal.

32. Charles E. Perkins to Thomas J. Potter (telegram), Mar. 12, 1878, in Box 33-1870-4.41, CB&Q-Newberry. Robert Harris to W. C. Sipple, Mar. 28, 1878; Harris to J. W. McDill, to Peter A. Dey and to Cyrus C. Carpenter, Mar. 28, 1878; in Box 3H4.2, CB&Q-Newberry.

33. *Statistical History of the United States From Colonial Times to the Present,* U.S. Bureau of the Census (New York: Basic Books, 1976), Series K 17-81, pp. 459-63. See also Allan G. Bogue, *From Prairie to Cornbelt* (Chicago: University of Chicago Press, 1963), pp. 283-87; Donald L. Winter, *Farmers Without Farms: Agricultural Tenancy in Nineteenth-Century Iowa* (Westport, Conn.: Greenwood Press, 1978), p. 20.

34. Winter, *Farmers Without Farms,* pp. 23-25. See Winter generally for detailed calculations of farm costs and returns for tenants and owner-operators. See also Robert E. Ankli, "Farm-Making Costs in the 1850s," and Judith L.V. Klein, "Farm-Making Costs in the 1850s: A Comment," in *Farming in the Midwest, 1840-1900* (Washington, D.C.: Agricultural History Society, 1974), pp. 51-74; Bogue, *Prairie to Cornbelt,* p. 286.

35. See Bogue, *Prairie to Cornbelt,* p. 285, for a good index of Iowa farm prices. Robert Higgs, "Railroad Rates and the Populist Uprising," *Agricultural History* 44 (July, 1970): 291-97, reestablishes after a generation the credibility of the farmers' complaints against the railroads by comparing real declines in

freights with prices. Mark Aldrich, "A Note on Railroad Rates and the Populist Uprising," *Agricultural History* 54 (July, 1980): 424-32, criticizes Higgs's method and adjusts his findings to show improvement for the farmers to 1880, then rising transportation costs.

36. JMF to Charles E. Perkins, Feb. 5 and 17, 1878, in Forbes-Perkins Letters, CB&Q-Newberry.

37. JMF to Charles E. Perkins, Mar. 17 and June 9, 1878, in Forbes-Perkins Letters, CB&Q-Newberry. See also Overton, *Burlington Route,* pp. 160-62.

38. JMF to [J. H.] Simpson, May 29, 1878; JMF to N. M. Beckwith, June 2, 1878; in Box 3F3.1, CB&Q-Newberry; JMF to Charles E. Perkins, May 29, 1878, in Cochran, *Railroad Leaders,* p. 134. See also Overton, *Burlington Route,* pp. 174-75.

39. Charles E. Perkins to JMF, June 3, 1878, in C-O1, P4.6, vol. 4, CB&Q-Newberry. Compare Overton, *Burlington Route,* pp. 166-75, with Grodinsky, *Strategy,* chap. 5, on Perkins and Gould.

40. JMF to F. B. Sanborn, June 10, 1878, in Box 3F3.1, CB&Q-Newberry.

41. JMF to Charles E. Perkins, Jan. 5, 10, and 12, 1879, in Forbes-Perkins Letters, CB&Q-Newberry. Perkins to JMF, May 30, 1879; Perkins to Peter Geddes, Nov. 24, 1879; quoted in Overton, *Burlington Route,* pp. 168-69; Perkins to JMF, Nov. 28, 1879, in C-O1, P4.6, vol. 4, CB&Q-Newberry.

42. JMF to Charles E. Perkins, May 15, 1879, in Forbes-Perkins Letters, CB&Q-Newberry. JMF to Perkins, July 12, 1879; JMF to Peter Geddes, Sept. 30, 1879; in Box 3F3.1, CB&Q-Newberry.

43. JMF to Charles E. Perkins, Jan. 12, 1880, in Forbes-Perkins Letters, CB&Q-Newberry; [JMF] to Lucius Tuckerman, Feb. 14, 1880, in Box 3F3.1, CB&Q-Newberry.

44. JMF to Charles E. Perkins, May 14, 1880; JMF to Frederick L. Ames, Sept. 8, 1880; in Box 3F3.1, CB&Q-Newberry.

45. JMF to Charles E. Perkins, Nov. 21, 1880, in C.E.P. Transcripts, Set C, CB&Q-Newberry. See also Forbes's letters for November, 1880, in Box 3F3.1 and Forbes-Perkins Letters, CB&Q-Newberry for evidence of Forbes's anguish over watering CB&Q stock.

46. JMF to William H. Vanderbilt, quoted in Julius Grodinsky, *Jay Gould: His Business Career* (Philadelphia: University of Pennsylvania, 1957), p. 247; see also Overton, *Burlington Route,* pp. 172-73.

47. Statistics are from CB&Q *Annual Reports,* compiled for Richard C. Overton, and quoted here with his permission.

CHAPTER SEVEN NOTES

1. See Alfred D. Chandler, Jr., *The Visible Hand: The Managerial Revolution in American Business* (Cambridge, Mass.: Belknap Press, 1977); Glen Porter, *The Rise of Big Business, 1860-1910* (New York: Thomas Y. Crowell, 1973); Samuel P. Hays, *The Response to Industrialism, 1885-1914* (Chicago: University of Chicago Press, 1957); and Robert H. Wiebe, *The Search for Order, 1877-1912* (New York: Hill and Wang, 1967).

2. Hurst, *Law and the Conditions of Freedom,* details this trend in government-business relations. See also James A. Ward, "Image and Reality: The Railway-Corporate State Metaphor," *Business History Review* 55 (1981): 491-516.

3. See Benson, *Merchants, Farmers;* and Miller, *Railroads,* on the localism behind regulation and federal agitation.

4. The universality of railroad reform after 1880 can be seen in the dozens of monographic studies of reform in the Gilded Age and Progressive Era. Local ramifications of the transportation revolution occupied reformers long after national legislation had been passed.

5. Edward C. Kirkland, *Charles Francis Adams, Jr., 1835-1915: The Patrician at Bay* (Cambridge, Mass.: Harvard University Press, 1965), p. 114.

6. Charles E. Perkins to Frederick Billings, Nov. 10, 1884, in Cochran, *Railroad Leaders,* p. 437. Perkins deserves a full-length biography, but none exists. Richard C. Overton alone has read a significant portion of Perkins's voluminous writings; his "Charles Elliott Perkins," *Business History Review* 31 (1957): 292-309, introduces Perkins's character, and *Perkins/Budd* (Westport, Conn.: Greenwood Press, 1982) analyzes a good sample of his writings. Chandler, *The Railroads,* pp. 97-128, sets Perkins in context with his fellow railroad managers.

7. Charles E. Perkins to Thomas J. Potter, Dec. 22, 1884; Perkins to William W. Baldwin, Mar. 18, 1885; in Cochran, *Railroad Leaders,* pp. 185, 440; Overton, *Burlington Route,* p. 202.

8. Charles E. Perkins to JMF, May 29, 1879, in Box 3F3.2, CB&Q-Newberry; Perkins to James M. Walker, April 23, 1880, in C.E.P. Transcripts, Set A, CB&Q-Newberry. See also Cyrenus Cole, *A History of the People of Iowa* (Cedar Rapids, Ia.: The Torch Press, 1921), pp. 449-50.

9. Charles E. Perkins to JMF, June 29, 1879, in Cochran, *Railroad Leaders,* p. 432; see also Overton, *Burlington Route,* pp. 197-98.

10. JMF to Charles E. Perkins, Feb. 21 and June 9, 1884, in Box 3F3.1, CB&Q-Newberry; see Overton, *Burlington Route,* pp. 186-87.

11. JMF to Frederick Billings, Dec. 19, 1884, in Box 3F3.1 CB&Q-Newberry.

12. JMF to C. A. Whittier, July 20, 1885; JMF to Major [?], July 25, 1885; JMF to Peter Geddes, Sept. 1, 1885; in Box 3F3.1, CB&Q-Newberry. See also Overton, *Burlington Route,* pp. 188-90.

13. Charles E. Perkins to JMF, April 12, 1887, in Box C-O, F3.1, CB&Q-Newberry; JMF to Peter Geddes, Sept. 1, 1885, in Box 3F3.1, CB&Q-Newberry; JMF to Henry Lee Higginson, Oct. 16, 1887, in *Letters of J.M.F.,* (suppl.), 3: 204-5.

14. Albro Martin, "The Troubled Subject of Railroad Regulation in the Gilded Age, A Reappraisal," *Journal of American History* 61 (1974-1975): 339-71, brilliantly summarizes the whole problem and its bearing on the passage of the Interstate Commerce Act.

15. Higgs, "Railroad Rates," 293-96; Aldrich, "Note," pp. 428-32; Martin, "Troubled Subject," pp. 343-44. No single statement on rates in the period can escape attack from another point of view. These authorities disagree on details, timing, and emphasis. Suffice it to say that it would have been hard for contemporaries to argue against high or rising rates by the late 1870s.

16. See Grodinsky, *Iowa Pool,* for details. Paul W. MacAvoy, *The Economic Effects of Regulation: The Trunk-Line Railroad Cartels and the Interstate Commerce Commission* (Cambridge: Massachusetts Institute of Technology Press, 1965), chaps. 2-4, analyzes pooling and its effects on rates.

17. N. B. Ashby, *Riddle of the Sphinx* (Des Moines, 1890), quoted in Throne, "Grange," p. 311.

18. JMF to Charles E. Perkins, July 12, 1879, in C-O1, P4.6, vol. 4, CB&Q-Newberry.

19. Charles E. Perkins to JMF, Sept. 24, 1879, in Box 3F3.2, CB&Q-Newberry.

20. JMF to Charles E. Perkins, Mar. 25, 1881, in Box 3F3.1, CB&Q-Newberry; Perkins to JMF, June 11, 1885, in Cochran, *Railroad Leaders,* p. 441; Perkins memorandum, Dec. 20, 1883, quoted in Overton, *Burlington Route,* p. 182.

21. Charles E. Perkins to JMF, Dec. 19, 1882, in C.E.P. Transcripts, Set C, CB&Q-Newberry; Perkins to George S. Morison, Aug. 3, 1885, in Cochran, *Railroad Leaders,* p. 442.

22. Charles E. Perkins, *Letter to Hon. S. M. Cullom* (Cambridge, Mass.: University Press of John Wilson & Son, 1885), pp. 3-8. This is the pamphlet edition of the original letter, dated Sept. 21, 1885, at Burlington, Iowa.

23. Ibid., pp. 8, 21-22, 26-27.

24. JMF to Charles E. Perkins, Aug. 25, 1885, in Box 3F3.1, CB&Q-Newberry.

25. JMF to Charles E. Perkins, Sept. 12, 1885, in Forbes-Perkins Letters, CB&Q-Newberry; Perkins to Edith Forbes Perkins, April 7, 1886, in C-O1, P4.6, vol. 6, CB&Q-Newberry.

26. Charles E. Perkins to Edith Forbes Perkins, April 7, 1886, in C-O1, P4.6, vol. 6, CB&Q-Newberry.

27. See Benson, *Merchants, Farmers,* pp. 242-245; Gabriel Kolko, *Railroads and Regulation* (Princeton: Princeton University Press, 1965), pp. 42-63; Martin, "Troubled Subject," pp. 361-64.

28. Iowa Railroad Commissioners, *Report, 1886* (Des Moines, 1886), p. 33 (hereafter cited as Ia. R.R., *Report, 1886*). For a careful examination of the first Iowa commissioner law and its workings, see Frank H. Dixon, *State Railroad Control: With a History of Its Development in Iowa* (New York: T. Y. Crowell & Sons, 1896), chaps. 1 & 2.

29. J. W. McDill to Charles E. Perkins, Dec. 24, 1884, in Box 33-1880-4.65, CB&Q-Newberry.

30. McDill to Perkins, Feb. 2, 1886, in Box 33-1880-4.65, CB&Q-Newberry.

31. Ia. R.R. Commissioners to Charles E. Perkins, Mar. 18, 1886; Perkins to Ia. R.R. Commissioners, April 14, 1886; in Box 33-1880-4.65, CB&Q-Newberry.

32. Ia. R.R. *Report, 1887,* pp. 31-46.

33. See J. Brooke Workman, "Governor William Larrabee and Railroad Reform," *I.J.H.* **57** (1959): 231-34; Des Moines, *Iowa State Daily Register,* May 20, 1885.

34. William Larrabee to Ia. R.R. Commissioners, Dec. 6, 1886, in William Larrabee Papers, Iowa State Historical Department, Division of Historic Preservation, Montauk, Clermont, Iowa. (This collection of miscellaneous private papers was owned by the family when I used it but has since passed into the hands of the Iowa State Historical Department. Hereafter cited as Larrabee-Montauk.) See also "State of Iowa v. C.B.&Q." (filed Dec. 7, 1886, decided Feb. 10, 1887), in Box 33-1880-4.65, CB&Q-Newberry. William Larrabee to E. C. Morgan, Jan. 4, 1887; Larrabee to Ia. R.R. Commissioners, Mar. 7, 1887; in Larrabee-Montauk; see additional material in Box 33-1880-4.65, CB&Q-Newberry.

35. Ia. R.R., *Report, 1887,* p. 650; see pp. 634-70 for notes on the hearings, April 9, 1887.

36. "Governor William Larrabee v. C.B.&Q." (Rehearing, filed Mar. 7, 1887, decided May 7, 1887), in Box 33-1880-4.65, CB&Q-Newberry. See also

J. W. McDill to Charles E. Perkins, Feb. 15, 1887, in Box 33-1880-4.65, CB&Q-Newberry.

37. Thomas J. Potter to Charles E. Perkins, April 10, 1887, in Box 33-1880-4.65, CB&Q-Newberry.

38. William Larrabee to Charles E. Perkins, Aug. 9, 1887; Perkins to Larrabee, Aug. 16 and Oct. 31, 1887; Larrabee to Perkins, Nov. 18, 1887; Perkins to Larrabee, Dec. 2, 1887; Larrabee to Perkins, Dec. 19, 1887; in Box 3P4.13, CB&Q-Newberry. The entire correspondence from June through December, 1887, is in this box.

39. Joseph W. Blythe to Charles E. Perkins, July 25, 1887, in Box 3P4.5, ser. 1, no. 4, CB&Q-Newberry; see also Perkins to JMF, Sept. 1, 1887, in Box C-O, F3.1, CB&Q-Newberry.

40. Iowa, Twenty-Second General Assembly, *Journal of the Senate* (Des Moines, 1888), pp. 36-38 (hereafter cited as Iowa, *Senate, 1888*).

41. Ibid., p. 64. See JMF to Charles E. Perkins, Mar. 25, 1881, in Box 3F3.1, CB&Q-Newberry.

42. Des Moines *Iowa State Daily Register*, Jan. 13, 1888; see also James S. Clarkson to William Larrabee, Jan. 17, 1888, in Larrabee-Montauk.

43. Charles E. Perkins to Joseph W. Blythe, Dec. 17, 1887, in Cochran, *Railroad Leaders*, p. 446. See also Blythe's letters to Perkins, Jan. through March, 1888, in Box 3P4.5, ser. 1, no. 5, CB&Q-Newberry.

44. Joseph W. Blythe to Charles E. Perkins, Feb. 5, 8, and 29, 1888, in Box 3P4.5, ser. 1, no. 5, CB&Q-Newberry. Legislative details and final passage appear in Iowa, *Senate, 1888*, pp. 822-28; Iowa, Twenty-Second General Assembly, *Journal of the House of Representatives* (Des Moines, 1888), p. 826 (hereafter cited as Iowa, *House, 1888*).

45. *Laws of Iowa, 1888*, chaps. 28, 29. (Chapter 29 called for the election of railroad commissioners.) Ivan L. Pollock, *History of Economic Legislation in Iowa* (Iowa City: State Historical Society of Iowa, 1918), chap. 2, gives a brief survey of railroad and transportation legislation that helps establish the legal context of the 1888 Commissioner Law.

46. See Ia R.R., *Report, 1888*, pp. 31-41; Charles E. Perkins to JMF, June 19 and 22, 1888, in Box 33-1880-4.65, CB&Q-Newberry; Henry B. Stone to Perkins, June 8, 1888, in Box 3S7.1, CB&Q-Newberry. The complaint filed with U. S. Circuit Court, Southern District of Iowa, on June 27, 1888, is in Box 33-1880-4.65.

47. See Box 33-1880-4.65, CB&Q-Newberry, for documents relating to legal proceedings. Judge Brewer's decision of July 28, 1888, was clipped from the Des Moines Iowa State Daily Register of that date. See also renewed investigations in Ia. R.R., *Report, 1888*, pp. 805ff. For compromise, see James C. Peasley to Charles E. Perkins, Oct. 19, 1888, in Box 33-1880-4.5, CB&Q-Newberry; and Perkins to Jacob Rich, Oct. 30, 1888, in C.E.P. Transcripts, Set A, CB&Q-Newberry.

48. Charles E. Perkins to JMF, Oct. 19, 1888, in Box C-O, F3.1, CB&Q-Newberry. Perkins memorandum, Dec. 25, 1889; Edward C. Perkins to Charles E. Perkins, Jan. 23, 1889; Wirt Dexter to Charles E. Perkins, Jan. 2, 1889; in Box 33-1880-4.65, CB&Q-Newberry. Brewer's final decision of Feb. 2, 1889, was clipped from the Des Moines *Iowa State Daily Register* of that date. On Feb. 4, 1889, Perkins notified the Iowa Railroad Commissioners that the Burlington would comply (Ia. R.R., *Report, 1889*, p. 29).

49. Overton, *Burlington Route*, pp. 212-14; Donald L. McMurray, *The Great Burlington Strike of 1888* (Cambridge, Mass.: Harvard University Press, 1956).

50. JMF to Peter Geddes, Feb. 8, 1889, in Box 3F3.1, CB&Q-Newberry;

JMF to [deleted by editor], [c. Jan., 1889], in C-O1, P4.6, vol. 8, CB&Q-Newberry.
    51. *The Nation*, Apr. 10, 1873.

EPILOGUE NOTES

    1. JMF to Peter Geddes, Mar. 31, 1889, in Box 3F3.1, CB&Q-Newberry.
    2. See JMF memoranda, Nov. 23 and Dec. 6, 1886 (draft and revision), in Box 3F3.1, CB&Q-Newberry. JMF to George F. Edmunds, May 13, 1890; JMF to Charles E. Perkins, May 6, 1893, in *Letters of J.M.F.* (suppl.), 3: 226-27, 277.
    3. See *Letters of J.M.F.* (suppl.), 3: 280ff. See also Lawrence Goodwyn, *Democratic Promise: The Populist Moment in America* (New York: Oxford University Press, 1976), on the Farmers' Alliance and the People's Party.
    4. *Letters of J.M.F.* (suppl.), 3: 258-262.
    5. Mrs. Hastings Hughes to Charles E. Perkins, Nov. 25, 1898, in General Material, 6, CB&Q-Newberry.
    6. Resolution of the Board of Directors of the CB&Q, Oct. 18, 1898, in C-O1, P4.6, vol. 12, CB&Q-Newberry.
    7. The following account of the Burlington's development after Forbes's death is primarily based upon Overton, *Burlington Route*, pp. 244-92.
    8. See Albro Martin, *James J. Hill and the Opening of the Northwest* (New York: Oxford University Press, 1976), pp. 487-91.
    9. Quoted in Overton, *Burlington Route*, p. 260; see Martin, *Hill*, p. 490.
    10. Overton, *Burlington Route*, p. 268.
    11. See Albro Martin, *Enterprise Denied: Origins of the Decline of American Railroads, 1897-1917* (New York: Columbia University Press, 1971).
    12. Charles E. Perkins to T.M. Marquette, Jan. 3, 1891, in R.C.O. no. 9, CB&Q-Newberry.
    13. William Larrabee, *The Railroad Question* (Chicago: Schulte Publishing Company, 1893), p. 90.
    14. Ibid., pp. 91-123.
    15. Kolko, *Railroads and Regulation*, chaps. 5-9, treats this development as steady progress, but compare the argument with Martin, *Enterprise Denied*.

A Note on Sources

A BIBLIOGRAPHIC ESSAY exhausting the scholarly materials that bear on the life and times of John Murray Forbes is beyond the scope of the present note; however, some account is due of the core resources and of those interpretive studies which marked the boundaries of my subject. The notes to each chapter and the bibliography contain complete listings of sources and references used in the text. This essay is intended to introduce and evaluate the central body of material.

The only published biography of John Murray Forbes is Henry Greenleaf Pearson, *An American Railroad Builder* (1911), a brief, old-style biographical sketch. Duncan Yaggy's dissertation, "John Forbes: Entrepreneur" (1974), is strong on Forbes's early career, but it uses primarily Boston area sources and disregards Forbes's postwar activities in the Midwest. Arthur M. Johnson and Barry E. Supple, *Boston Capitalists and Western Railroads* (1967), and Thomas C. Cochran, *Railroad Leaders* (1953), offer useful sketches of Forbes in context with other investors and railroad executives, but neither work develops Forbes's larger character. It is surprising, in the face of so little biographical literature, to find eight volumes of published letters and reminiscences of John Murray Forbes. Edited for the use of family and friends by Forbes's daughter, Sarah Forbes Hughes, the *Letters and Recollections* (2 vols., 1899), were quickly followed by *Reminiscences* (3 vols., 1902), and *Letters (Supplementary)* (3 vols., 1905). A collection of favorite poems, songs and quotations printed in Forbes's lifetime, *An Old Scrapbook* (1884, rev. 1891), completes the published legacy, although Robert Bennet Forbes, *Personal Reminiscences* (2d ed., rev., 1882), is an indispensable complementary resource.

This wealth of published primary material represents but a sampling of the letters and manuscripts once available in Forbes's papers. Much of the original collection has disappeared. A reasonably complete set of letters from Forbes's China years constitutes the bulk of the John Murray Forbes Papers at the Baker Library, Harvard

Graduate School of Business Administration. One large volume of typed copies of letters to Paul S. Forbes, 1843-1867, edited by William G. Forbes, completes the holdings at Baker Library. Another large collection of family papers (mostly other family members) is housed at the Museum of the American China Trade in Milton, Mass. All of these family papers were collected for microfilming in 1969 by the Massachusetts Historical Society, Boston. John Murray Forbes's business accounts and ledgers are extant in the custody of David C. Forbes, managing partner of J. M. Forbes & Co., Boston, but they are not open to public examination. Hundreds of Forbes's letters for later years are included in the Burlington Archives at the Newberry Library, Chicago, but they represent a narrow selection of his correspondence.

The Burlington Archives at the Newberry Library is one of the most remarkable collections of business manuscripts available in America. In 1943 CB&Q President Ralph Budd deposited whole rooms full of office records, executive correspondence, operating accounts, personnel records, ledgers, and the like in the Newberry Library for use by serious historical researchers. These materials related to every line ever owned, leased, or absorbed by the Burlington from its origins through the administration of Charles E. Perkins. Elizabeth Coleman Jackson and Carolyn Curtis catalogued the materials and compiled a *Guide to the Burlington Archives in the Newberry Library, 1851-1901* (1949), without which this massive collection would be useless. More recently Richard C. Overton, long-time student of the Burlington, has added a large body of Perkins materials left in his care by Mrs. Edith Perkins Cunningham (Cunningham-Overton Collection). The opportunities for scholarship in many fields of labor, business, economic, legal, and cultural history, represented by this single resource, have been little exploited in thirty years.

Richard C. Overton, *Burlington Route* (1965), is a model of business history and is the starting point for any study of the Burlington lines. Comprehensive as this volume is, there is a much longer manuscript version in the Burlington Archives that provides more detail. *Burlington West: A Colonization History of the Burlington Railroad* (1941) focuses more narrowly on the land grant roads in Iowa and Nebraska. Overton's most recent work, *Perkins/Budd* (1982), includes an annotated selection of Perkins's best letters and memoranda.

Since Donald L. McMurry's study of the *Great Burlington Strike of 1888* (1956), the CB&Q has attracted some attention from labor and social historians. Paul V. Black, "Experiment in Bureaucratic Centralization," *Business History Review* (1977), examines blacklisting and employee relations under Perkins, while Shelton Stromquist's forthcoming book (Univ. of Ill., 1984) looks at life in the Burlington's Iowa division towns. Except for selections in Johnson and Supple, *Boston Capitalists*, and Cochran, *Railroad Leaders*, there is little additional material on the Burlington railroad.

The state of Iowa boasts a good shelf of historical studies, largely because of three generations of publishing by the State Historical Society of Iowa. Benjamin F. Shambaugh, one of the Society's founders, began this publishing tradition with *Documentary Materials Relating to the History of Iowa* (3 vols., 1895-1897), *Fragments of the Debates of the Iowa Constitutional Conventions of 1844 and 1846* (1900), *Messages and Proclamations of the Governors* (7 vols., 1903 ff.), and his own study, *The Constitutions of Iowa* (1934). The Society has sponsored an economic history series, including Ivan Pollock, *History of Economic Legislation* (1918), and John E. Brindley, *History of Road Legislation* (1912), and a biography series including Dan Elbert Clark, *Samuel Jordan Kirkwood* (1917), Leland Sage, *William Boyd Allison* (1956), and Mildred Throne, *Cyrus Clay Carpenter* (1974). Monographs such as Earle D. Ross, *Iowa Agriculture* (1951), Roscoe Lokken, *Iowa Public Land Disposal* (1942), Erling A. Erickson, *Banking in Frontier Iowa* (1971), and Morton Rosenberg, *Iowa on the Eve of the Civil War* (1972), highlight important aspects of Iowa history. For over four decades the *Iowa Journal of History* published good scholarly articles while the *Annals of Iowa*, 3rd ser., collected source materials and interpretive essays. Summing up this literature is Leland Sage, *A History of Iowa* (1974), which offers an excellent critical introduction to the state.

Primary materials for Iowa history are also abundant. Although few of the Iowa manuscript collections bore directly on this study, newspapers and printed primary sources proved invaluable. Early files of the Burlington *Hawk-Eye*, the Fairfield *Ledger*, the Des Moines *Iowa State Register*, and the dozens of other papers around the state form a solid base of public information for studies of Iowa culture. Legislative documents detailed the activities of local lawmakers and reported the findings of investigative boards of all sorts. Public associations like the Iowa State Agricultural Society published statistical materials together with proceedings of their meetings and conventions; private bodies like the Grange did the same. State history, in this case, is blessed with a wide range of sources.

Primary research materials, of course, do not alone support a work of scholarship. A number of published histories—some recent, some well worn—provided critical insights and supportive materials for my interpretation of Forbes and the Burlington Route. My debts to these scholars are acknowledged in the footnotes. The bibliography that follows lists the works cited in the text and notes.

Bibliography

MANUSCRIPT COLLECTIONS

Chicago, Burlington & Quincy Railroad Archives, Newberry Library, Chicago.
Forbes Family Papers, Baker Library, Graduate School of Business Administration, Harvard University.
Illinois Central Railroad Archives, Newberry Library, Chicago.
William Larrabee Papers, Iowa State Historical Department, Division of Historic Preservation, Montauk, Clermont, Iowa.

PUBLISHED PRIMARY SOURCES

Brooks, John W. *Report upon the Merits of the Michigan Central Railroad, as an Investment for Eastern Capitalists.* Detroit: Charles Willcox, 1846.
Burlington & Missouri River Rail Road. *Annual Reports,* 1857–1872.
Chicago, Burlington & Quincy Railroad. *Annual Reports,* 1856–1901.
Evidence Showing the Manner in Which Locomotive Engines Are Used Upon Rail-Roads . . . . Boston: Centinel and Gazette Press, 1838.
Forbes, John Murray. *Letters and Recollections of John Murray Forbes,* 2 vols., Sarah F. Hughes, ed. Boston: Houghton, Mifflin & Co., 1899.
———. *Reminiscences of John Murray Forbes,* 3 vols., Sarah F. Hughes, ed. Boston: Geo. H. Ellis, 1902.
———. *Letters of John Murray Forbes (Supplementary),* 3 vols., Sarah F. Hughes, ed. Boston: Geo. H. Ellis, 1905.
Forbes, Robert Bennet. *Personal Reminiscences,* rev. ed. Boston, 1878.
Fuller, George N., ed. *Messages of the Governors of Michigan,* 4 vols. Lansing: Michigan Historical Commission, 1926.
Galland, Isaac. *Galland's Iowa Emigrant.* Orig. 1840; rpt. Iowa City: State Historical Society of Iowa, 1950.
Iowa. Twenty-Second General Assembly, *Journal of the House of Representatives.* Des Moines, 1888.
———. *Journal of the Senate.* Des Moines, 1888.
Iowa State Agricultural Society. *Reports.* Des Moines, 1862–1880.
Iowa State Grange. *Proceedings of the . . . Annual Meeting.* Des Moines, 1870–1875.
Iowa Railroad Commissioners. *Reports.* Des Moines, 1878–1892.

242   BONDS OF ENTERPRISE

Massachusetts. Senate, *Report of the Committee on Railways & Canals . . . Relative to the Public Use of Rail-Roads.* Boston: Dutton & Wentworth, 1838.

Massachusetts Board of Internal Improvements. *Report of the Board . . . on the Practicability and Expediency of a Rail-Road from Boston to the Hudson River, and from Boston to Providence.* Boston: Daily Advertiser, 1829.

———. Senate No. 5, *Report of the Board . . . for a Railway from Boston to Albany.* Boston: Dutton & Wentworth, 1828.

———. Senate No. 4, *Report of the Board . . . for a Railway from Boston to Providence; with a Memoir of the Survey.* Boston: Dutton & Wentworth, 1828.

The Massachusetts Rail Road Continued to Narragansett Bay. Pamphlet, n.p., n.d. [c. 1836]. [Copy found in Rider Collection, John Hay Library, Brown University.]

Michigan Central Railroad. *Annual Reports,* 1846–1859.

Newhall, John B. *A Glimpse of Iowa in 1846,* 2d ed. Orig. 1846; rpt. Iowa City: State Historical Society of Iowa, 1957.

Perkins, Charles E. *Letter to Hon. S. M. Cullom.* Cambridge, Mass.: University Press of John Wilson & Son, 1885.

Plumbe, John, Jr. *Sketches of Iowa and Wisconsin.* Orig. 1839; rpt. Iowa City: State Historical Society of Iowa, 1948.

Sargent, George B., "Speech Before the Boston Board of Trade," and "Lecture on the West . . . ," *Iowa Journal of History and Politics,* 45 (1947), 133–174.

Shambaugh, Benjamin F., ed. *Documentary Material Relating to the History of Iowa,* 3 vols. Iowa City: State Historical Society of Iowa, 1895–1897.

———. *Fragments of the Debates of the Iowa Constitutional Conventions of 1844 and 1846 . . . .* Iowa City: State Historical Society of Iowa, 1900.

———. *Messages and Proclamations of the Governors of Iowa,* 7 vols. Iowa City: State Historical Society, 1903 ff.

"Territorial Conventions of 1837," *Iowa Journal of History and Politics,* 9 (1911), 385–407.

U. S. Congress. Senate, Select Committee on Interstate Commerce, *Report,* 49th Cong., 1st sess. Washington, 1886.

———. *Testimony,* 49th Cong., 1st sess. Washington, 1886.

Welles, Gideon. *Diary of Gideon Welles,* 3 vols., Howard K. Beale, ed. New York: Norton, 1960.

NEWSPAPERS AND PERIODICALS

American Rail Road Journal (New York).
Burlington *Hawk-Eye.*
Des Moines *Iowa State Register.*
Fairfield *Ledger.*
The Merchant's Magazine (New York).
The Iowa Homestead (Des Moines).

Mount Pleasant *Iowa Weekly Observer.*
The Nation (New York).

BOOKS AND ARTICLES

Adams, Charles Francis, Jr. *Railroads: Their Origins and Problems.* New York: G. P. Putnam & Co., 1878.
――――. "The Granger Movement," *North American Review.* 120 (1875), 394-424.
Albion, Robert G. *The Rise of New York Port.* New York: Charles Scribner's Sons, 1939.
Appleby, Joyce. "The Social Origins of American Revolutionary Ideology," *Journal of American History,* 64 (1978), 935-958.
Barnes, Gilbert Hobbs. *The Anti-Slavery Impulse,* 1830-1844. Orig. 1933; rpt. New York: Harcourt, Brace & World, 1964.
Beard, Earl S. "Local Aid to Railroads in Iowa," *Iowa Journal of History,* 50 (1952), 1-34.
Belcher, Wyatt W. *The Economic Rivalry Between St. Louis and Chicago.* New York: Columbia University Press, 1947.
Benson, Lee. *Merchants, Farmers, and Railroads: Railroad Regulation and New York Politics, 1850-1887.* Cambridge, Mass.: Harvard University Press, 1955.
Berwanger, Eugene H. *The Frontier Against Slavery.* Urbana: University of Illinois Press, 1967.
Boeck, George A. "A Decade of Transportation Fever in Burlington, Iowa, 1845-1855," *Iowa Journal of History,* 56 (1958), 129-155.
Bogue, Allan G. "Iowa Claim Clubs: Symbol and Substance," *Mississippi Valley Historical Review,* 45 (1957-1958), 231-253.
Boyd, G.D.R. "Sketches of History and Incidents Connected with the Settlement of Wapello County," *Annals of Iowa,* 1st ser., 6 (1868), 186-187.
Brindley, John E. *History of Road Legislation in Iowa.* Iowa City: State Historical Society of Iowa, 1912.
Buck, Solon J. *The Granger Movement.* Cambridge, Mass.: Harvard University Press, 1933.
Calkins, Earnest Elmo. "Genesis of a Railroad," *Transactions of the Illinois State Historical Society,* 42 (1935), 43-56.
Chandler, Alfred D., Jr., ed. *The Railroads: The Nation's First Big Business.* New York: Harcourt, Brace & World, 1965.
――――. *The Visible Hand: The Managerial Revolution in American Business.* Cambridge, Mass.: Belknap Press, 1977.
Clark, Dan Elbert. *Samuel Jordan Kirkwood.* Iowa City: State Historical Society of Iowa, 1917.
Clark, John G. *The Grain Trade in the Old Northwest.* Urbana: University of Illinois Press, 1966.
Cochran, Thomas C. *Railroad Leaders, 1845-1890: The Business Mind In Action.* Cambridge, Mass.: Harvard University Press, 1953.

Cole, Cyrenus. *A History of the People of Iowa*. Cedar Rapids, Iowa: Torch Press, 1921.

———. *Iowa Through the Years*. Iowa City: State Historical Society of Iowa, 1940.

Colton, Kenneth E. "The Stagecoach Comes to Iowa," *Annals of Iowa*, 3rd ser., 35 (1960), 161–186.

Connor, James. "The Antislavery Movement in Iowa," *Annals of Iowa*, 3rd ser., 40 (1970), 343–376, 450–479.

Crawford, Mary Caroline. *Famous Families of Massachusetts*, 2 vols. Boston: Little, Brown & Co., 1930.

Davis, David Brion. *The Slave Power Conspiracy and the Paranoid Style*. Baton Rouge: Louisiana State University, 1969.

Dixon, Frank H. *State Railroad Control: With a History of Its Development in Iowa*. New York: T. Y. Crowell & Sons, 1896.

Downs, Jacques M. "American Merchants and the China Opium Trade, 1800–1840," *Business History Review*, 42 (1968), 418–442.

Dyos, H. J. and D. H. Aldcroft. *British Transport*. Leicester: University Press, 1969.

Erickson, Erling A. *Banking in Frontier Iowa, 1836–1865*. Ames: Iowa State University Press, 1971.

Fairbank, John King. *Trade and Diplomacy on the China Coast*, rev. ed. Stanford: Stanford University Press, 1969.

Fehrenbacher, Don E. *Prelude to Greatness: Lincoln in the 1850s*. Stanford: Stanford University Press, 1962.

Fine, Sidney. *Laissez-Faire and the General-Welfare State*. Ann Arbor: University of Michigan, 1956.

Fishlow, Albert. *American Railroads and the Transformation of the Ante-Bellum Economy*. Cambridge, Mass.: Harvard University Press, 1965.

Fitzhugh, George. *Cannibals All!* Orig. 1857; rpt. Cambridge, Mass.: Belknap Press, 1960.

Foner, Eric. *Free Soil, Free Labor, Free Men*. New York: Oxford University Press, 1970.

Forgie, George. *Patricide in the House Divided*. New York: Norton, 1979.

Frederickson, George M. *The Inner Civil War: Northern Intellectuals and the Crisis of the Union*. New York: Harper & Row, 1965.

Goodrich, Carter. *Government Promotion of American Canals and Railroads, 1800–1890*. New York: Columbia University Press, 1960.

Goodwin, Cardinal. "The American Occupation of Iowa, 1833–1860," *Iowa Journal of History and Politics*, 17 (1919), 83–102.

Goodwyn, Lawrence. *Democratic Promise: The Populist Moment in America*. New York: Oxford University Press, 1976.

Greenberg, Michael. *British Trade and the Opening of China, 1800–1842*. Cambridge: University Press, 1951.

Grodinsky, Julius. *Jay Gould: His Business Career*. Philadelphia: University of Pennsylvania Press, 1957.

———. *Transcontinental Railroad Strategy, 1869–1893*. Philadelphia: University of Pennsylvania Press, 1962.

————. *The Iowa Pool: A Study in Railroad Competition, 1870–1884.* Chicago: University of Chicago Press, 1950.

Gue, Benjamin F. *History of Iowa,* 4 vols. New York: Century History Co., 1903.

Hartz, Louis. *Economic Policy and Democratic Thought.* Cambridge, Mass.: Harvard University Press, 1948.

Hays, Samuel P. *The Response to Industrialism, 1885–1914.* Chicago: University of Chicago Press, 1957.

Herriott, Frank I. "Iowa and the Nomination of Abraham Lincoln," *Annals of Iowa,* 3rd ser., 8 (1907–1908), 81–115, 186–220, 444–466; 9 (1909–1910), 45–64, 186–228.

————. "Republican Presidential Preliminaries in Iowa, 1859–1860," *Annals of Iowa,* 3rd ser., 9 (1909–1910), 241–283.

————. "The Republican State Convention, January 18, 1860," *Annals of Iowa,* 3rd ser., 9 (1909–1910), 401–446.

Hidy, Ralph. *The House of Baring in American Trade and Finance, 1763–1861.* Cambridge, Mass.: Harvard University Press, 1949.

Hirschfield, Charles. *The Great Railroad Conspiracy: The Social History of a Railroad War.* Michigan State College Press, 1953.

Hobsbawm, Eric J. *The Age of Capital.* New York: Charles Scribner's Sons, 1975.

Hodas, Daniel. *The Business Career of Moses Taylor.* New York: New York University Press, 1976.

Horowitz, Morton J. *The Transformation of American Law, 1780–1860.* Cambridge, Mass.: Harvard University Press, 1977.

Howe, M.A. DeWolfe. *Life and Letters of George Bancroft,* 2 vols. New York: Charles Scribner's Sons, 1908.

Hungerford, Edward. *The Story of the Baltimore & Ohio Railroad,* 2 vols. New York: G. Putnam & Sons, 1938.

Hunter, Louis C. *Steamboats on the Western Rivers.* Cambridge, Mass.: Harvard University Press, 1949.

Hurst, James Willard. *Law and the Conditions of Freedom in the Nineteenth-Century United States.* Madison: University of Wisconsin Press, 1956.

Jackman, W. T. *The Development of Transportation in Modern England,* 4 vols. Cambridge: University Press, 1916.

Jensen, Richard. *The Winning of the Midwest.* Chicago: University of Chicago Press, 1971.

Johnson, Arthur M., and Barry E. Supple. *Boston Capitalists and Western Railroads.* Cambridge, Mass.: Harvard University Press, 1967.

Joy, James F. "Railroad History of Michigan," *Michigan Pioneer and Historical Collections,* 22 (1894), 292–304.

Kelly, Oliver Hudson. *Origins and Progress of the Order of the Patrons of Husbandry. . . .* Philadelphia: J.A. Wagonseller, 1875.

Kirkland, Edward C. *Men, Cities, and Transportation,* 2 vols. Cambridge, Mass.: Harvard University Press, 1948.

————. *Dream and Thought in the Business Community,* 1860–1900. Ithaca: Cornell University Press, 1956.

———. *Industry Comes of Age*. New York: Holt, Rinehart & Winston, 1961.

———. *Charles Francis Adams, Jr., 1835-1915: The Patrician at Bay*. Cambridge, Mass.: Harvard University Press, 1965.

Klement, Frank L. *The Copperheads of the Middle West*. Chicago: University of Chicago Press, 1960.

———. "Middle Western Copperheadism and the Genesis of the Granger Movement," *Mississippi Valley Historical Review*, 38 (1951-1952), 679-694.

Kleppner, Paul. *The Cross of Culture*. New York: Free Press, 1970.

Kolko, Gabriel. *The Triumph of Conservatism*. Glencoe: Free Press of Glencoe, 1963.

———. *Railroads and Regulation, 1877-1916*. Princeton: Princeton University Press, 1965.

Krenkel, John H. *Illinois Internal Improvements, 1818-1848*. Cedar Rapids, Iowa: Torch Press, 1958.

Larson, Henrietta. "A China Trader Turns Investor," *Harvard Business Review*, 12 (1934), 345-358.

Litwack, Leon F. *North of Slavery: The Negro in the Free States, 1790-1860*. Chicago: University of Chicago Press, 1961.

Lewellen, Fred B. "Political Ideas of James W. Grimes," *Iowa Journal of History and Politics*, 42 (1944), 339-404.

Lokken, Roscoe. *Iowa Public Land Disposal*. Iowa City: State Historical Society of Iowa, 1942.

McClosky, Robert G. *American Conservatism in the Age of Enterprise, 1865-1910*. Cambridge, Mass.: Harvard University Press, 1951.

McCoy, Drew R. "Benjamin Franklin's Vision of a Republican Political Economy for America," *William and Mary Quarterly*, 3rd ser., 35 (1978), 605-628.

McMurry, Donald L. *The Great Burlington Strike of 1888*. Cambridge, Mass.: Harvard University Press, 1956.

Martin, Albro. *Enterprise Denied: Origins of the Decline of American Railroads, 1897-1917*. New York: Columbia University Press, 1971.

———. *James J. Hill and the Opening of the Northwest*. New York: Oxford University Press, 1978.

———. "The Troubled Subject of Railroad Regulation in the Gilded Age, A Reappraisal," *Journal of American History*, 61 (1974-1975), 339-371.

Martin, Edward Winslow. *History of the Grange Movement or, The Farmer's War Against Monopolies . . . .* Philadelphia: National Publishing Co., 1873.

Miller, George H. "Origins of the Iowa Granger Law," *Mississippi Valley Historical Review*, 40 (1953-1954), 657-680.

———. *Railroads and the Granger Laws*. Madison: University of Wisconsin Press, 1971.

———. "Chicago, Burlington and Quincy Railroad Company v. Iowa," *Iowa Journal of History*, 54 (1956), 289-312.

Neu, Irene D. *Erastus Corning: Merchant and Financier, 1794-1872.* Ithaca: Cornell University Press, 1960.

Nordin, D. Sven. *Rich Harvest: A History of the Grange, 1867-1900.* Jackson: University of Mississippi Press, 1974.

Nugent, Walter T.K. *Money and American Society, 1865-1877.* New York: Free Press, 1968.

Oates, Stephen B. *To Purge This Land With Blood: A Biography of John Brown.* New York: Harper & Row, 1970.

Overton, Richard C. *Burlington West: A Colonization History of the Burlington Railroad.* Cambridge, Mass.: Harvard University Press, 1941.

———. *Perkins/Budd: Railway Statesmen of the Burlington.* Westport, Ct.: Greenwood Press, 1982.

———. *Burlington Route: A History of the Burlington Lines.* New York: Alfred A. Knopf, 1965.

———. "Charles Elliott Perkins," *Business History Review,* 31 (1957), 292-309.

Parks, Robert J. *Democracy's Railroads: Public Enterprise in Jacksonian Michigan.* Port Washington, N.Y.: Kennikat Press, 1972.

Pearson, Henry Greenleaf. *An American Railroad Builder: John Murray Forbes.* Boston: Houghton, Mifflin & Co., 1911.

———. *The Life of John A. Andrew, Governor of Massachusetts 1861-1865,* 2 vols. Boston: Houghton, Mifflin & Co., 1904.

Pelzer, Louis. "The Whigs in the Iowa Territory," *Iowa Journal of History and Politics,* 5 (1907), 46-90.

———. "Origins of the Republican Party in Iowa," *Iowa Journal of History and Politics,* 4 (1906), 487-521.

———. "History and Principles of the Democratic Party in the Territory of Iowa," *Iowa Journal of History and Politics,* 6 (1908), 163-246.

Periam, Jonathon. *The Groundswell: A History of the Origins, Aims, and Progress of the Farmers' Movement.* Cincinnati: E. Hannaford & Co., 1874.

Peterson, William J. "Population Advance to the Upper Mississippi Valley, 1830-1860," *Iowa Journal of History and Politics,* 32 (1934), 312-353.

Phillips, Ulrich B. *A History of Transportation in the Eastern Cotton Belt to 1860.* New York: Columbia University Press, 1908.

Pollins, Harold. *Britain's Railways: An Industrial History.* Newton Abbot: David and Charles, 1972.

Pollock, Ivan L. *History of Economic Legislation in Iowa.* Iowa City: State Historical Society of Iowa, 1918.

Poor, Henry Varnum. *History of Railroads and Canals in the United States of America.* New York: J. H. Schultz, 1860.

Porter, Glen. *The Rise of Big Business 1860-1910.* New York: Thomas Y. Crowell, 1973.

Potter, David M. *The Impending Crisis, 1848-1861.* New York: Harper & Row, 1976.

Powers, Richard L. *Planting Corn Belt Culture: The Impress of the Upland Southerner and Yankee in the Old Northwest.* Indianapolis: Indiana Historical Society, 1953.

Pred, Alan R. *Urban Growth and the Circulation of Information: The United States System of Cities, 1790–1840.* Cambridge, Mass.: Harvard University Press, 1973.

Ralston, Leonard. "Iowa Railroads and the Des Moines River Improvement Land Grant of 1846," *Iowa Journal of History and Politics,* 56 (1958), 97–128.

———. "Governor Ralph P. Lowe and State Aid to Railroads: Iowa Politics in 1859," *Iowa Journal of History,* 58 (1960), 207–218.

Rose, Willie Lee. *Rehearsal for Reconstruction: The Port Royal Experiment.* Indianapolis: Bobbs-Merrill, 1964; pap. ed. New York: Vintage Books, 1964.

Rosenberg, Morton. *Iowa on the Eve of the Civil War: A Decade of Frontier Politics.* Norman: University of Oklahoma Press, 1972.

Ross, Earle D. *Iowa Agriculture.* Iowa City: State Historical Society of Iowa, 1951.

———. "Northern Sectionalism in the Civil War Era," *Iowa Journal of History and Politics,* 30 (1932), 455–512.

Rubin, Julius. *Canal or Railroad? Imitation and Innovation in the Response to the Erie Canal in Philadelphia, Baltimore and Boston.* Philadelphia: American Philosophical Society, 1961.

Sage, Leland. *A History of Iowa.* Ames: Iowa State University Press, 1974.

———. *William Boyd Allison.* Iowa City: State Historical Society of Iowa, 1956.

Salsbury, Stephen. *The State, the Investor, and the Railroad: The Boston & Albany, 1825–1867.* Cambridge, Mass.: Harvard University Press, 1967.

Salter, William. *The Life of James W. Grimes.* New York: D. Appleton & Co., 1876.

Seaburg, Carl and Stanley Paterson. *Merchant Prince of Boston: Colonel Thomas Handasyd Perkins, 1764–1854.* Cambridge, Mass.: Harvard University Press, 1971.

Sears, Marian V. "A Michigan Bureaucrat Promotes the State's Economic Growth: George F. Porter Sells Michigan's Central Railroad to Eastern Capitalists, 1846," *Explorations in Entrepreneurial History,* 2nd ser., 3 (1966), 200–219.

Semmel, Bernard. *The Rise of Free Trade Imperialism.* Cambridge: University Press, 1970.

Shambaugh, Benjamin F. *The Constitutions of Iowa.* Iowa City: State Historical Society of Iowa, 1934.

Sharkey, Robert P. *Money, Class, and Party.* Baltimore: Johns Hopkins Press, 1959.

Sheiber, Harry N. *Ohio Canal Era: A Case Study of Government and the Economy, 1820–1861.* Athens: Ohio University Press, 1969.

Sparks, David. "Iowa Republicans and the Railroads, 1856–1860," *Iowa Journal of History,* 53 (1955), 275–282.

Stover, John F. *History of the Illinois Central Railroad.* New York: Macmillan, 1975.

————. *Iron Road to the West: American Railroads in the 1850s.* New York: Columbia University Press, 1978.

Swisher, Jacob A. "The Des Moines River Improvement Project," *Iowa Journal of History and Politics,* 35 (1937), 142–180.

Tanner, H. S. *A Description of the Canals and Railroads of the United States.* . . . New York: T. R. Tanner & J. Disturnell, 1840.

Taylor, George Rogers. *The Transportation Revolution, 1815–1860.* New York: Holt, Rinehart and Winston, 1951.

Throne, Mildred. "The Grange in Iowa," *Iowa Journal of History,* 47 (1949), 289–324.

————. "Repeal of the Iowa Granger Law, 1878," *Iowa Journal of History,* 51 (1953), 97–130.

————. "The Anti-Monopoly Party in Iowa, 1873–1874," *Iowa Journal of History,* 52 (1956), 289–326.

————. *Cyrus Clay Carpenter and Iowa Politics, 1854–1898.* Iowa City: State Historical Society of Iowa, 1974.

Unger, Irwin. *The Greenback Era.* Princeton: Princeton University Press, 1964.

Van der Zee, Jacob. "The Roads and Highways of Territorial Iowa," *Iowa Journal of History and Politics,* 3 (1905), 175–225.

Wiebe, Robert. *The Search for Order, 1877–1920.* New York: Hill & Wang, 1969.

Workman, J. Brooke. "Governor William Larrabee and Railroad Reform," *Iowa Journal of History,* 57 (1959), 231–266.

Yaggy, Duncan. "John Forbes: Entrepreneur." Ph.D. dissertation, Brandeis, 1974.

Index

251